OFFENDER PROFILING SERIES: Vol. I

INTERVIEWING AND DECEPTION

OFFENDER PROFILING SERIES: Vol I

INTERVIEWING AND DECEPTION

Edited by

DAVID CANTER and LAURENCE ALISON
Centre for Investigative Psychology
University of Liverpool

Routledge
Taylor & Francis Group
LONDON AND NEW YORK

First published 1999 by Dartmouth and Ashgate Publishing

Reissued 2018 by Routledge
2 Park Square, Milton Park, Abingdon, Oxon, OX14 4RN
52 Vanderbilt Avenue, New York, NY 10017

Routledge is an imprint of the Taylor & Francis Group, an informa business

A Library of Congress record exists under LC control number: 98024989

ISBN 13: 978-1-138-36970-2 (hbk)
ISBN 13: 978-0-429-42851-7 (ebk)

Contents

Series Preface *vi*
Acknowledgements *xi*

1 Interviewing and Deception
David Canter and Laurence Alison 1

2 The Effectiveness of the Cognitive Interview
Mark R.Kebbell and Graham F. Wagstaff 23

3 Using Cognitive Interviewing to Construct Facial Composites
Christine E. Koehn, Ronald P. Fisher and Brian L. Cutler 41

4 British and American Interrogation Strategies
Lydia Sear and Tom Williamson 65

5 Statement Validation
Bryan Tully 83

6 Forensic Application of Linguistic Analysis
Malcolm Coulthard 105

7 The Decision to Die: The Psychology of the Suicide Note
Adam Gregory 127

8 Non Verbal Behaviour and Deception
Robert Edelmann 157

9 The Psychophysiology of Deception and the Orienting Response
Murray Kleiner 183

10 A Comparative Study of Polygraph Tests and Other Forensic Methods
Eitan Elaad 209

Series Preface

'Offender Profiling' has become part of public consciousness even though many people are not really sure what it is and the great majority of people have no idea at all of how it is done. This ignorance is just as prevalent in professional circles as amongst the lay public. Psychologists, psychiatrists, probation officers and social workers all have an interest in how their disciplines can contribute to police investigations, but few practitioners are aware of exactly what the possibilities for such contributions are. Others, such as police officers and lawyers, who seek advice from 'profilers' often also have only the vaguest ideas as to what 'profiling' consists of or what scientific principles it may be based on. The army of students who aspire to emulate the fictional activities of psychologists who solve crimes is yet another group who desperately need a systematic account of what 'offender profiling' is and what the real prospects for its development are.

The public fascination with the little understood activity of 'profiling' has meant that no fictional account of crime, whether it be heavy drama or black comedy, seems to be complete without at least one of the protagonists offering as a 'profile' their opinion on the characteristics of the perpetrator of the crime(s) around which the narrative is built. This popular interest combined with widespread ignorance has generated its own corpus of urban myths: such mythical 'profilers' produce uncannily accurate descriptions of unknown killers, solve cases that had baffled the police and seem to know before the criminal where he would strike next.

Sadly, like all myths not only do they only have a very loose connection with reality but they also distract attention away from a range of other significant and more intellectually challenging questions. These are the important questions that are inherent in the processes of criminal behaviour and its investigation. Such considerations include assessments of the quality and validity of the information on which police base their decisions and subsequent actions. This also involves assessing the possibilities for detecting deception. There also exist questions about the consistencies of a criminal's behaviour and what the crucial differences are between one offender and another.

Group processes of criminals raise other questions, which surprisingly are seldom touched upon by 'profilers' in fact or fiction. These ask about the form such groups take and the influence they have on the actions of the criminals, the role of leaders in crimes or the socio-cultural processes of which they are a part. There are also important issues about the implications and use of any answers that may emerge from scientific studies of crimes and their investigation

These and many other questions are raised by the mere possibility of psychology being of value to police investigations. To answer them it is essential to go beyond urban myth, fiction and the self-aggrandising autobiographies of self-professed 'experts'. A truly scientific stance is necessary that draws on a wide range of social and psychological disciplines

Many of these questions relate to others that are central to any psychological considerations of human actions, such as the nature of human memory, the processes of personality construction, group dynamics and interpersonal transactions. Therefore the systematic, scientific study of the issues relevant to 'offender profiling' are recognisably part of a burgeoning field of psychology and related disciplines. In an attempt to make this point and distinguish the steady accretion of knowledge in this area from the mythology, hyperbole and fiction of 'offender profiling' I labelled this field *Investigative Psychology*. This term seems to have taken root and is now evolving rapidly throughout the world.

Yet in the way that labels and terminology have a life of their own 'offender profiling' and its variants will just not lie down and die peacefully from a robust youth and dissolute old age. So we are stuck with it as a somewhat unhelpful shorthand and therefore the term has been kept for the title of this series in the hope that we may gradually re-define profiling as a systematic and scientific endeavour.

The books in this series provide a thorough introduction to and overview of the emerging field of Investigative Psychology. As such they provide a compendium of research and discussion that will place this important field firmly in the social sciences. Each volume takes a different focus on the field so that together they cover the full range of current activity that characterises this energetic area of research and practice.

David Canter
Series Editor

Acknowledgements

We are grateful to Julie Blackwell for the level of organisation, commitment and precision she has brought to pulling these volumes together, and to Steve Deprez and Julia Fossi for their help in compiling the volumes.

1 Interviewing and Deception

DAVID CANTER AND LAURENCE ALISON

Investigative or police decision making involves the identification of and choice between options from amongst a number of different possible lines of enquiry. We argue that this iterative process or feedback loop, the 'Investigative Cycle', involves three continuous processes: information collection, investigative inferences and the implementation of investigative actions. Within this cycle we identify a sequence of four stages of potential distortion in information processing: the collection, examination, evaluation and utilisation stages. These distortions include cognitive, presentational, social and pragmatic components. We argue that errors at any of these stages will profoundly effect the other two processes in the investigative cycle. The identification of these cycles, stages and types of distortion allow for the development of a more systematic approach to uncovering where potential weaknesses in an enquiry may evolve.

David Canter is Director of the Centre for Investigative Psychology at the University of Liverpool. He has published widely in Environmental and Investigative Psychology as well as many areas of Applied Social Psychology. His most recent books since his award winning *"Criminal Shadows"* have been *"Psychology in Action"* and with Laurence Alison *"Criminal Detection and the Psychology of Crime"*.

Laurence Alison is currently employed as a lecturer at the Centre for Investigative Psychology at the University of Liverpool. Dr Alison is developing models to explain the processes of manipulation, influence and deception that are features of criminal investigations. His research

Offender Profiling Series: I - ***Interviewing and Deception***
Edited by D. Canter and L. Alison. © 1999 Ashgate Publishing, Aldershot. pp 1-21

interests focus upon developing rhetorical perspectives in relation to the investigative process and has presented many lectures both nationally and internationally to a range of academics and police officers on the problems associated with offender profiling. He is currently working on false allegations of sexual assault and false memory. He is affiliated with The Psychologists at Law Group - a forensic service specialising in providing advice to the courts, legal professions, police service, charities and public bodies.

1 Interviewing and Deception

DAVID CANTER AND LAURENCE ALISON

The Investigative Process

Investigative Psychology draws upon a range of psychological principles to contribute to the conduct of criminal or civil investigations and uses behavioural science to assist the management, investigation and ensuing legal outcomes of criminal cases. The discipline has grown out of *offender profiling* in an attempt to introduce scientific rigour into what were essentially experience based procedures (Canter, 1995).

What fuels the investigative process is the information upon which sequences of decisions are made. A basic example would be matching fingerprints found at a crime scene with known suspects. From this straightforward use of the information drawn from the fingerprint a likely culprit can be identified prompting further actions such as arrest and questioning.

However, in many cases the investigative process is not so simple - detectives often have information that is rather more opaque. For example, they may suspect that the style of the burglary is typical of a number of people arrested in the past. Or they may infer from the disorder at a murder case that the offender was a burglar disturbed in the act. These inferences will either result in a decision to seek further information or to select from a possible range of actions including the arrest and charging of a potential suspect.

Investigative decision making therefore involves the identification and selection of options - options such as suspect selection or selection between specific lines of enquiry. The investigative team hope that such a selection process will lead to narrowing down search parameters. In order to generate and select from a range of options detectives and other investigators must draw upon an understanding of the actions of the offender(s) involved. In other words they must have some idea of typical ways in which offenders behave that will then enable them to make sense of the information obtained. Throughout this process a parallel concern is amassing the appropriate evidence to identify the perpetrator and prove their case in court.

Investigative psychology has systematically identified three psychological processes that may be of particular relevance to the process - assessing the accounts of the crime, making decisions upon this information and developing an understanding of the actual actions of the offenders themselves (Canter and Alison, 1997)

First, the collection and evaluation of information derived from accounts of the crime. Accounts may include photographs or other recordings derived from the crime scene; they may be records or other transactions such as bills paid or telephones calls made or they may be accounts from witnesses, informants or suspects. In the latter case the accounts are drawn from interviews or written reports. Moreover, once suspects are available there is often other information available about them - either directly from interviews, or indirectly through the accounts of others. In addition there may be information provided by experts (i.e. psychiatrists, psychologists) that has to be assessed and may influence subsequent investigative actions. The foundations of any police investigation therefore rest very squarely upon the shoulders of efficient and professional assessment and utilisation of a great variety and quantity of information.

Fictional and media accounts of the work done by detectives tend to exaggerate the second investigative psychology domain - i.e. decision making - as the dominant activity. However this usually takes up far less time than the collection and assessment stages. Though there is remarkably little study of exactly what decisions are made during an investigation, or how those decisions are made, decisions taken on the basis of the information available require some inferences to be made about the import of that information. Much of this import derives from views about, or an understanding of, criminal behaviour. For appropriate conclusions to be drawn from the accounts available of the crime is necessary to have, at the very least an implicit model of how various offenders act. An understanding of criminal behaviour is therefore the third domain.

A simple model of these three sets of tasks that gives rise to the field of *Investigative Psychology* is shown here. (Figure 1.1)

Figure 1.1 Investigation Cycle Giving Rise to Field of Investigative Psychology

Information - The collection phase: Interviewing suspects, witnesses, the collection of evidence

Inference - Inferential assessment based upon the information, previous cases etc.

Action - Investigative decisions taken based upon inferences

The present volume deals with the first area of *Investigative Psychology*, the examination of the accounts that are given in relation of offences which provide the information on which all aspects of the work of law enforcement agents, and the subsequent work of the courts are based. These accounts have to be collected, assessed and evaluated as effectively as possible if an investigation is to proceed with any chance of success. In the following chapters various aspects of the process of information retrieval and assessment are examined.

The Process of Information Retrieval and Its Assessment

The decision model of investigations demonstrates how crucial is the information that is collected a part of any criminal or civil enquiry. At many stages in the investigative cycle material of many kinds becomes available. It all has to be assessed for the information it offers. If the information derived from these accounts is to contribute to the investigation it must be systematically recorded and evaluated.

The process of recording and evaluation of information of relevance to criminal investigations and the legal process goes through a number of stages. At each of these stages there is the need for quality control - both in the way that the material is obtained and recorded and in the way that it is assessed. If professional standards are maintained throughout - from the collection stage, through to utilisation of the material, then there is increasing likelihood that any decisions based on the information will be valid and worthwhile. Yet there are many possibilities for distortion and the introduction of bias into this process, especially when relying on the verbal accounts given by the main participants in the crime, witnesses, victims and suspects.

The police investigator therefore has to carry out a task that has some parallels to a chemist trying to purify a compound in order to test its properties. There are many stages of filtration and titration that will remove impurities and at each of these stages there is the risk of introducing further impurities. But the analogy to a chemical process has to be treated with caution. The very impurities that need to be removed may themselves indicate important aspects of the crime, as when a suspect claims they have an alibi that is not substantiated. For even though this does not prove guilt it increases suspicion. Further there may be no definitive account of the offence ever available because everyone involved is trying to make sense of complex circumstances in which they were participants. Issues like motivation and consent, so crucial for the judicial process, for example, may always be matters of interpretation rather than clearly objective fact.

Success in collecting, assessing and evaluating the information needed for an investigation therefore requires a clear understanding of the theory behind the process, of the most appropriate means of collecting the materials and of the constraints and limits on those means. The investigator must secure strong evidence and ensure that the irrelevant, distorting information is removed. Reaching the 'best solution' (i.e. as close to the facts of the offence as possible), relies on a form of professionalism that requires a detailed understanding of the potential strengths and weaknesses of all aspects of collecting the information. Understanding of the most appropriate ways in which to assess and evaluate that information is also necessary.

The Processing of Investigative Information

In many areas of research involving responses from people the integrity of the initial information is taken for granted. Few opinion pollsters assume that the answers offered on the High Street are deliberately distorted. Historians examining early documents may expect the authors of those documents to be biased but will rarely consider how the trauma, for example, that the author might have faced during the events they describe, may have distorted his or her attention at the time. Psychologists do not seek, nor are they offered accounts of what goes on in their laboratories from the perspectives of different participants, deriving some consensus of the views offered on which to base the tests of their hypotheses. Yet all these approaches and issues form the day to day mix on which criminal investigations are based. As a consequence, it is of value to examine the various stages that information goes through, on a par with the purification of the chemist, in order to understand more fully the different aspects of information retrieval and assessment that are so crucial for solving crimes.

In essence, accounts of crimes are processed through four stages. A range of distortions may occur at any one (or all) of these stages. Different procedures may be necessary to enhance the detail and reduce distortions at any stage. A cumulative effect of 'impurities' introduced early in the process may also be expected. Assuming a crime had occurred, for instance when none had, as would be the case with a false allegation, could lead to many confusions and inappropriate actions.

A graphic representation of the sequence of stages is given (Figure 1.2).

Collect ➔ Examine ➔ Evaluate ➔ Utilise

Figure 1.2 Processing Investigative Information

The following chapters deal in various ways with each of these stages, but it is worth emphasising at present that as the information derived gets further away from the original source there is more influence of inference processes. With some training in collection, observing the crime scene or interviewing witnesses can be a relatively overt, neutral process. The examination of the information requires some consideration of how it was collected as well as some knowledge of the criminal processes to which it refers. Evaluation takes the inferences a stage further by comparing the actions revealed with known patterns and actions of offenders. At the end of the process the possibility for using the inferences as a guide for investigative actions has to be assessed in relation to other aspects of the investigation. Thus material that seems important in the early stage of the detection process may turn out to be of little utility when seen in the light of other information collected later.

This examination of the processing of accounts of crime helps to emphasise the ways in which inferences can become disassociated from the original, possibly hesitantly offered, material. For example the reconstruction of what an assailant may have looked like, or the possibility that a supposed murder victim had intended to commit suicide, or a description of abuse in childhood. may all take on an unchallenged existence by the time they are utilised to guide crucial decisions in an enquiry. Evidence cannot be constantly questioned in the throes of detection. Judgements have to be made about the information collected and the investigation moved on from there. This is all the more reason why each of the stages requires careful examination.

Possibilities of Distortion

There are many possibilities for distortion of the information at the different stages of an enquiry. Some aspects have been more fully examined by psychologists than others. but four aspects can be identified, which broadly map onto the four stages mentioned above.

Cognitive Distortions brought about through processes of attention or remembering Presentational Confusions in how the material is summarised Social Distortions that arise from interpersonal transactions Pragmatic Misuses of information

Figure 1.3 Possibilities for Distortion of Information in Police Investigations

At any stage a variety of distortions may occur - cognitive, presentational, social and pragmatic. The following chapters provide many examples of these possibilities. For instance a major aspect in the development of interview technique has been to reduce the distortions brought about by cognitive processes. By contrast research on the detection of deception has been more oriented to examining the ways in which the social transactions between people and the way information is presented can lead to biases and confusions. Some consideration of the use of expert testimony also highlights the ways in which material can be inappropriately used by investigators or the courts.

The People of the Drama: Explanatory Roles in the Investigation of Crime

Another aspect of investigative information that helps clarify the possibilities for distortion is the significance of the different relationships the people involved may have to the account they are giving or examining, their 'role in the drama'. As already emphasised the information can come from many different sources, what is left at the crime scene, or in various records, accounts given by witnesses, victims, informants or suspects, reports from experts and opinions from people involved in or associated with the investigative process. Perhaps the most significant variation this introduces is the form of contact the individual providing the account has to the account they are giving. This relationship brings with it many different contexts for the accounts that are given. Understanding the role and context of an account helps to alert us to the possibilities for distortion.

At each stage of the enquiry individuals (whether members of the enquiry team, witnesses, suspects or barristers) 'play' different roles. Each 'player' will have varying degrees of involvement with, and skill in conveying or eliciting an account of the offence and each individual will 'play' his/her role as a function of the context in which the event occurred and in which the account is given. For example, a witness to a fire that it later transpires is an arson attack has only incidental involvement and no expert knowledge when giving his/her version of events. The firesetter, in contrast has a person involvement and a degree of expertise peculiar to his/her own particular goals. These facets of 'involvement' and 'expertise' have been considered by Canter and Brown (1985) as highly influential on what features are highlighted in any given account:

> .....Just as the researcher will have special reasons for collecting his explanations, so will the person providing the explanations have a variety of purposes for giving them.....This is not to say that the individual is going, necessarily, to bias or distort his account for the different recorders. It is rather to point out that it is precisely because they are an aspect of interaction between individuals, that they will be expected to take on different content and structure for different purposes.
>
> p. 232

Harré (1979) for example discusses the importance of the elicitor of the account understanding the scenario or context of the account given. Therefore if account giving is seen as only being fully comprehensible when considered in context, the nature of the account is likely to vary from one context to another. It is not difficult to recognise in this process how an account given by a witness to a police officer may vary from the same account given by a police officer to the courts. The interdependent features of context and role and their unfolding impact on the enquiry are therefore the prime concerns at every stage of the assessment of account.

We can now consider in a little more detail the significance of process, role and context in relation to the stages of an enquiry.

Fixing the Nets: The Collection of Information

Police enquiries begin with the collection of information from a variety of sources. Pathology reports, feedback from the SOCOs (scene of crime officer) and very often a set of statements taken from witnesses all feature in the initial stages of any investigation. Typically, the information upon which further actions are taken is based upon witness material and not infrequently this is the only information available to the inquiry team. At the initial stages of the enquiry, the investigative 'net' may be terribly threadbare and so the investigator requires some intensive work to ensure that it is strong enough and secure enough to aid in catching and securing as much quality information as possible.

Despite the police service's lack of acknowledgement to its creators (Interviewer training 199 #) Fisher and Geiselman's (1992) Cognitive Interview (CI) has had wide ranging use in collecting this type of information. With no increases in error rates the cognitive interview has been shown to enhance information up to 35% more than for controls (Kohnken, Thurer and Zoberbier 1994). In chapter 2 Kebbell and Wagstaff consider in some detail the forensic effectiveness of this technique and illustrate how the process connects not only with the psychology of memory but also with social and communication issues. For example, they note that interruptions, inappropriate sequencing of questions and mode changing - whilst undoubtedly techniques that interfere with recall - are in fact social processes that disrupt communicative flow between police officer and eyewitness. Thus whilst the premises upon which the CI has been developed connect directly with encoding and retrieval processes, interference with these functions actually occurs through inappropriate social processes.

The connection between ability in terms of memory and communication in terms of social skills becomes evident in a consideration of the role of the account giver (witness) and the account taker (interviewer). The effectiveness of the interview relies on an appreciation of both roles. Whilst this may look like additional, unnecessary frippery or social nicety, this holds true at a very practical level. For example, as Kebbell and Wagstaff mention, the approach that a person takes to performing the role of an interviewer has direct implications for how the time constraints of an interview are handled. Better questioning does not necessarily imply more questioning (in fact it often means less) but rather a clearer appreciation of the roles involved.

In an attempt to single out the most constructive aspects of the CI, it is perhaps significant then that in light of our concentration upon role, context reinstatement and the social components of the CI are the two areas that Kebbell and Wagstaff and others before them (Memon and Stevenage, 1996) identify as the issues to concentrate upon. Reinstating the context places the witness back in the role that s/he played in the event and professional social standards are essentially a role that the investigating officer must play in order to maximise the amount of information elicited.

Following on from these ideas in Chapter 3, Koehn, Fisher and Cutler develop the same point in relation to the use of the CI in constructing facial composites. They note that because faces are holistically processed they are best recalled by reinstating the context within which they were seen. In contrast, attempting to reconstruct specific features occurs as featural processing in which each feature is recalled within the context of the rest of the face. This confirms Penrod's (1992) matching process in which the means of retrieval is effected by the way in which the individual is asked to generate the composite. Thus if an eyewitness is asked to consider the shape of the nose without any reference to the rest of the face that feature is likely to be recalled inaccurately. Similarly, if the individual is asked to concentrate on the face as a whole but not asked to consider where the individual was seen and what else was occurring at the time the retrieval process is not likely to bear fruit. Koehn et al therefore end with a number of recommendations, a central feature of which is, again, the consideration of the role that the witness played in the viewing of the event. The closer that the interviewer can get to re-establishing these contextual cues for the witness the more accurate their processing of the face is likely to be.

Complexities arise when it may not be in the individual's best interest to give a truthful account in an interview. Even more confusingly, an individual who was a witness yesterday, who may have been assumed to have been giving as truthful account as possible may, because of subsequent evidence, become a suspect today. Because of the change in circumstances the changed role may lead to the perception that everything said as a witness was false and everything now about to be said as a suspect is also likely to fall short of the truth. This role switching in the eyes of the investigator may however be counter-productive. Certainly, many of the features that Sear and Williamson discuss in chapter 4 indicate that many US police officers believe it is effective to obtain information from suspects that are essentially duplicitous, aimed at obtaining a confession.

Sear and Williamson suggest that British techniques are simply concerned with a search for the truth. However, it is unclear whether this is an optimistic or realistic perspective - particularly since the British police operate within an accusatorial framework. When an individual becomes a suspect it seems rather disingenuous to then suggest that the mind set of an investigating officer can adopt an inquisitorial framework at the interviewing stage. The mere fact that the individual is a suspect may strongly influence the interviewing strategy adopted and despite the politically correct claims that all police interviews are a search for the truth and objectivity can we honestly expect an officer not to be at least somewhat influenced by the role of the giver of the account? Especially since this role has been determined on the basis of what the investigator sees as a possible reason for suspicion.

Whilst we may be justified in criticising the deceptive and coercive techniques employed in the United States the Americans do at least have a clearer understanding of the communication process. Sear and Williamson point out that Leo (1992) advocates techniques that can exploit processes of justification and minimisation that an offender may employ to mitigate against full acceptance of responsibility for the crime. We may not agree with that method on ethical, legal or professional grounds but at least Leo shows an appreciation of the dynamics of persuasive communication - even though he appears to be ignorant of the very important fact that they may lead to false confessions.

Studies of British interrogation strategies have not been so zealous. Even the phrase 'police interrogation' is a taboo in the British model of interviewing, to be avoided and dutifully replaced by the softer 'investigative interview'. But avoidance of these very real issues ignores the wealth of social psychological processes that may be lead to a greater understanding of the explanatory roles of suspects under interrogations. It is exceptionally difficult to assess whether a confession is given voluntarily. Furthermore there are no criteria for establishing at what point an interview has become coercive. This state of confusion for all parties can only be a hindrance to the investigator. Moreover, the ever changing and evolving levels of skill required in training procedures may result in an unintelligible, impractical and over zealous set of impossible requirements. Given the attention the police now give to interviewing it does come as something of a surprise that there are no hard and fast rules to prevent coercion.

Research into dyad interaction has time and time again noted that conversation is a joint process. The myriad of social subtleties that occur across and within sets of interviews makes any assessment of just one of the party's statements impossible without reference to the other. Instead, the interaction is a social dynamic within which a number of communication processes play a part. Social scientists have for many years realised that it is unrealistic to regard an interview as a search for a single objective truth. Rather it is best viewed as the reconstruction from the viewpoint of a particular role. However, there is the further complexity that the role played in the interview itself will be different from that played in relation to the crime.

The central concern that derives from the study of the social processes at the heart of all interview has thus been to create as successful as possible an interaction between the researcher and the interviewee. Mishler (1986), refers to this process as an interactional accomplishment where meaning is jointly constructed as a function of the appreciation of each other's role. This may be labouring the common sense point that the interviewer and interviewee have to 'get along' but it is surprising how little attention is given to the social dynamics of police investigations.

The Statement of the Case: Examination and Evaluation of the Material

When the relevant information has been collected much of it is likely to be full of 'impurities' - distortions, biases and quite possibly untruths. The investigator therefore needs to examine this information and evaluate the material in terms of its relevance and veracity. As we have noted there has tended to be a focus upon the role of the individual in the sequence of action associated with the event. However, as Tully points out in chapter 5, Undeutsch's breakthrough in the 1950s was to concentrate solely on an assessment of the account of a crime rather than on the background (or profile) of the witness/suspect giving it. The Undeutsch hypothesis therefore appears to make no judgement about the explanatory role of the account giver. A closer examination though reveals that this is not the case.

Undeutsch's fundamental criteria (e.g. degree of detail, details of offender - victim relationships, contextual embedding) are all concerned with features that make for a convincing and coherent 'storyline'. Part of what convinces the listener is the role that the interviewee portrays themselves as playing within that account. For example, if the role player does not indicate the setting of the story (contextual embedding) this can be an indication that the individual is fabricating. Furthermore, as Tully points out developments in criteria based content analysis have centred around details outside of the statement itself with additional assessments being made on the psychological characteristics of the statement maker, characteristics of the interview, motivation and issues involved with investigative questions.

These additions beyond the sole consideration of the content material are employed to test the plausibility of various alternative hypotheses by examining various parts of the information. 'Statement Validity Analysis', as it is known, therefore concentrates on weaknesses throughout the investigation. The process focuses on the role of the statement maker within the context in which the statement was produced. In doing so the individual carrying out the assessment is looking for a coherent set of relationships between the details of the account and the context within which the events purportedly occurred. For example, children often accurately report details of sexual acts from a framework not yet equipped to report such violations - so ejaculation may be reported as "his snake spat at me".

Such assessments of role within context are very different to any simplistic, almost theatrical labelling of role that may be imposed upon the account giver. For example one may assume that an individual is a suspect on the basis of similar offences carried out by that individual in the past. However, examination of the coherence of the individual's alibi might be a reflection of an explanatory role that indicates that it is very unlikely he is the perpetrator. It is therefore important to distinguish between convenient labelling and understanding of explanatory viewpoints. This may be particularly significant when an individual is perceived (incorrectly) to be lying, when in fact his distortions of the facts are a function of his explanatory viewpoint. With the assessment of role the account can be assessed as not suspect but based on a different perspective than that expected.

The style in which an account is given we may be influenced by whom it is being given to. This frequently occurs in written texts and so may fall within the study for linguists. In chapter 6 Coulthard picks up these possibilities in reference to Grice's (1975) work on the imaginary reader:

> What Grice is concerned with ...... is the fact that all utterances are shaped for a specific addressee on the basis of the speaker's assumptions about shared knowledge and opinions.

Again, these are issues associated with the presumed (on the part of the addresser) role(s) of the addressee. For example Coulthard focuses on the Bentley statements in which he suggests that there is some suggestion that the police officer's notes on Bentley's statements deliberately distorted the facts - positioning Bentley in an active responsible role in Chris Craig's shooting of a police officer. His assertion is based on a corpora of occurrences of the work 'then' - a device used liberally in the statement to position Bentley in an active role in the list of events. Because 'then' occurs infrequently in such positioning in 'ordinary' language but, relatively, very frequently in police accounts, Coulthard suggests this is reason to question whether Bentley made any such confessions in his statement.

Whilst Coulthard highlights a number of interesting points regarding the forensic applications of linguistic analysis, there are a number of potential pitfalls from too heavy a reliance on such techniques. Features of context such as genre and modality can influence style of utterance enormously (Bahtia, 1993) Whilst it may be the case that certain words are rarely used by an individual in an everyday situation it is also likely to be the case that the parameters set upon statement making within an investigative context may stultify the language produced. This will probably influence the choice of words and their positioning. These contextual features are less frequently examined - especially within the forensic field.

Further, it is not even certain if individuals consistently differ from each other in the style of their speech or writing let alone why they might do so. Many of the underlying 'principles' of linguistic variation are therefore currently based upon assumption rather than substantive theory or empirical proof. But the possibilities for an investigative linguistics are clearly stated by Coulthard and he shows what a fruitful area for study this is.

As Gregory follows up in chapter 7 the linguistic analysis of suicide notes can be especially important. Most of the earlier studies of suicide notes were atheoretical, based on counting frequencies of various features of genuine vs. artificial suicide notes. Edelman and Renshaw's (1982) work was one of the first steps in adding some flesh to a theoretical skeleton. They suggested that 'cognitive energy', 'the cognization of finality of life' and 'indications of alienation from the world in general' were features of genuine notes. As Gregory discusses though, even in these studies there was no notion of a central underlying basis, or theoretical causal link between these variations and the decision to die. In Gregory's own study he examined a number of features that had been suggested should discriminate between genuine and false suicide notes. Building upon others' literature and adopting a thematic approach to establishing the broad patterns of suicidal intentions expressed through language, Gregory points out that content features indicative of an 'internalised decision to die' most reliably discriminate between genuine and false notes:

> The high utility of variables measuring at a more thematic content level suggests that content analystical techniques....should perhaps move away from the rigid constraints of the more structural computer based analyses......and instead reconsider the more thematic and contextual aspects of language
>
> p. 150 this volume

Despite Gregory's important first steps in the exploration of this thematic level of analysis, he too is cautious of over interpretation and too ready a willingness to rely on early results. These concerns, which we have pointed out in relation to a number of area, are perhaps nowhere more important than in the investigation of the psychology of deception.

Many of the problems associated with examining presumed deceptive responses is that the features indicative of deception are common to physiological arousal that occurs as a response to being interviewed in an investigation. The response is therefore contextual and not peculiar to guilt *per se*. Further, as Edelman points out in his comprehensive review in chapter 8, individuals may differ in what is known as 'demeanour bias' - individual differences in generally looking as though one is being truthful of fabricating (Bond, Kahler and Paolicelli, 1985)

The detection of deception from apparent 'leakage' cues is also a remarkably unfruitful endeavour, with a whole range of studies showing that the ability to discriminate truth from lies is often no better (and sometimes worse) than chance. Further, only in exceptional cases (see

Ekman and O'Sullivan, 1991) does it appear to be the case that professional lie detectors are able to catch out liars. The majority of studies suggest that there are no differences between experienced individuals and students (e.g. Kohnken, 1987). Edelman suggests that whilst there have been many studies involved in this area the very issues important to deception (i.e. the physiological responses pertinent to having carried out the offence) have been somewhat ignored. That is, too many of the experiments rely on traditional laboratory methods with student samples in highly artificial conditions.

In contrast, the work by Detective Superintendent Murray Kleiner, Dr Eitan Elaad and their colleagues in the National Police Academy of Israel is making great gains in maintaining empirical rigour without compromising external validity. Both their chapters deal with the controversial technique of the polygraph, often mistakenly referred to as 'The Lie Detector'. Two contrasting tests are used with polygraphs. One is the Guilty Knowledge Test (GKT) in which the suspect is examined to see if he or she shows physiological reaction to knowledge that only the guilty person would have. This contrasts with the Control Question Technique (CQT) which relies on the respondent responding more to questions of a potentially criminal nature that have nothing to do with the crime than to matters directly associated with the crime. Thus the GKT relies on the knowledge peculiar to the guilty party evoking a consistently higher response than alternative (irrelevant or false) information during the interrogation. Thus if a guilty subject is asked whether the amount stolen was £3,000, £4,000 or £7,000 then he should 'respond' to £4,000 on the polygraph is that *was* the amount stolen. By asking a number of such questions the guilty subject should consistently 'orient' to the guilty knowledge items. In chapter 9, Kleiner refers to Maltzman's (1979) standpoint that any reinforcer, positive or negative is a signal because it evokes approach or avoidance behaviour. In particular, information processed with reference to the self is more readily recalled than in reference to other schemas (Bower and Gilligand, 1979). Kleiner therefore shows that the use of the polygraph does not indicate lying *per se* but the examinee's ability to process significant information about himself. It is in other words, the private terms of reference of the culprit to his own involvement with the crime that results in the responses evoked in relation to the guilty knowledge items. As a consequence, he makes the challenging proposal that CQT may be on occasion be as valid as the more generally accepted GKT in detecting lying.

In the final chapter, Elaad concentrates on the empirical proof that supports the validity of the GKT by comparing it with a variety of other forensic methods. In particular he notes that the GKT is very successful in protecting against false positives. Ben Shakkar and Furedy's (1990) review, for example shows that innocent individuals were correctly identified in 81 - 100% of cases across 10 studies. Elaad in his own study has developed Widacki and Horvarth's (1978) originally methodologically flawed work and shows that handwriting, fingerprints and GKT were virtually free of false positives - whereas the CQT had a considerable false negative error rate. Elaad's study is not just remarkable in pointing out the potential value of the GKT though. The fact that serious, systematic study is supported and carried out within the police forces suggests that the process of scientific research and criminal investigation are not incompatible bedfellows.

The Final Problem: Utilisation of the Material

The studies reported in the present volume are all at least one step removed from actual applications. They are examples of the very useful studies that the 'back-room boffins' must carry out if they are to give effective advice to those in the thick of an ongoing investigation. The work from the Israeli police force, in particular, shows how valuable such studies can be in contributing to the overall professionalism of police work. The present volume therefore provides a foundation for investigative psychology contributions to the police collection and assessment of accounts of crime.

But the studies reported in the present volume are also very relevant to those psychologists who want to become a direct part of the investigative process. Those individuals who give guidance in the form of 'profiles' to police enquiries. Unfortunately one of the snares that 'offender profilers' are sometimes caught by is to accept the information provided by the police without questioning the aspects of it discussed in this volume. They have worked with the information made available to them without the sort of thorough consideration of its collection, examination and evaluation that is explored in the present volume. Others have claimed they have fool-proof procedures for evaluating the veracity of the information collected by the police in statements or from crime scenes, despite the considerable evidence that their procedures lack any validity.

Thus many of the chapters in the present volume indicate the importance of psychologists taking care not to preach objectivity whilst practising intuition. It may be hard to resist the call of the romantic that probably lies in many psychologists, excited in the whirlwind of activity that surround the investigation of the latest unsolved crime. But unless psychologists hold on to the principles and practices that make their discipline distinct from quackery, romance can quickly turn to tragedy.

Our analogy of the chemist has one very fundamental and essential comparison to the investigative process that is especially relevant to this point. A lack of checks at the collection, examination and evaluation stages can have very serious consequences. Thus, whilst the individual may have very virtuous intentions, meaning well is not enough. For example in the case of the anti-nausea drug thalidomide, the tragic results were a case of a lack of thorough checks at the evaluation stages. These errors lead to very serious consequences. Thus whilst the distribution of an impure solution may be intended to act as a panacea to nausea in the short term, there is no substitute for systematic and thorough analysis at every stage. It is only when the professional has done all in his power to obey strict criteria for appropriate practise that tragedy can be avoided.

References

Bahtia, V.K. (1993). *Analysing Genre: Language use in professional settings.* London: Longman.

Ben-Shakkar, G. and Furedy, J.J. (1990). *Theories and Applications in the detection of deception.* New York: Springer-Verlag.

Bond, C.F. Jr., Kahler, K.N. and Paolicelli, L.M. (1985). The miscommunication of deception: An adaptive perspective. *Journal of Experimental and Social Psychology*, 21, 331-345.

Bower, G.H. and Gilligan, S.G. (1979). Remembering information related to one's self. *Journal of Research in Personality*, 13, 420-432.

Canter, D.V. (1995). Psychology of Offender Profiling in R. Bull and D. Carson (eds), *Handbook of Psychology in Legal Contexts.* Chichester: Wiley.

Canter, D.V. and Brown, J. (1982). Explanatory Roles in C. Antaki (ed), *The Psychology of Ordinary Explanations of Social Behaviour.* London: Academic Press, 221-242.

Edelman, A.M. and Renshaw, S.L. (1982). Genuine versus simulated suicide notes: An issue revisited through discourse analysis. *Suicide and Life Threatening Behaviour,* 12(2), 103-113.

Ekman, P. and O'Sullivan, M. (1991). Who can catch a liar? *American Psychologist*, 46, 913-920.

Fisher, R.P. and Geiselman, R.E. (1992). *Memory Enchancing Techniques for Investigative Interviewing: The Cognitive Interview.* Springfield: Charles C. Thomas.

Grice, H.P. (1975). Logic and Conversation in P. Cole and J. Morgan (eds), *Syntax and Semantics III, Speech Acts.* New York: Academic Press, 41-58.

Kohnken, G. (1987). Training police officers to detect deceptive eye-witness statements. Does it work? *Social Behaviour*, 2, 1-17.

Kohnken, G., Thurer, C. and Zoberbier, D. (1994). The cognitive interview: Are the interviewers' memories enhanced too? *Applied Cognitive Psychology*, 8, 13-24.

Leo, R.A. (1992). From coercion to deception: The changing nature of police interrogation. *America, Crime, Law and Social Change*, 18, 35-59.

Maltzman, I. (1979). Orienting reflexes and significance: A reply to O'Gorman. *Psychophysiology*, 10, 229-234.

Memon, A. and Stevenage, S. (1996). Interviewing witnesses: What works and what doesn't? *Psychology*, 7(6), witness-memory.1.

Mishler, E. (1986). *Research Interviewing.* Cambridge MA: Harvard University Press.

Penrod, S. and Stocklein, J. (1992). *Assessing the impact of production methods on the recognizability of computer-generated facial composites.* Unpublished manuscript, University of Minnesota.

Undeutsch, U. (1982). Statement Reality Analysis in A. Trankell (ed), *Reconstructing the Past, The Role of Psychologists in Criminal Trial.* Stockholm, Sweden: Norstedt.

Widacki, J. and Horvarth, F. (1978). An experimental investigation of the relative validity and utility of the polygraph technique and three other common methods of criminal identification. *Journal of Forensic Sciences*, 23(3), 596-601.

2 The Effectiveness of the Cognitive Interview

MARK R. KEBBELL AND GRAHAM F. WAGSTAFF

Eyewitnesses are an important part of most criminal investigations though they rarely remember as much as the police would like. Consequently, ways of improving eyewitness memory would be very useful to police officers. This chapter evaluates the forensic effectiveness of one of the most successful methods of improving eyewitness memory, the cognitive interview. First, we discuss the limitations of standard police interviewing. Second, we evaluate the effectiveness of the cognitive interview in real investigations. Third, we look at research into police officers perceptions of the cognitive interview. We conclude that the cognitive interview can be a very effective aid to eyewitness memory. However, two main problems are associated with its use. In practice, the components of the cognitive interview are not used equally frequently and police officers often believe that they do not have enough time to conduct a cognitive interview.

Dr Mark R. Kebbell is currently a Lecturer/Research Fellow in Psychology at the University of Liverpool. His research looks at eyewitnesses in the Criminal Justice System. This includes looking at ways of interviewing eyewitnesses to maximise their accuracy, identifying situations when eyewitnesses are accurate or inaccurate, and the influence of court proceedings on witness evidence. His academic achievements have been recognised by the award of a British Academy Postdoctoral Research Fellowship for outstanding younger scholars. He has published a number of journal articles and book chapters, conducted a review of eyewitness performance for the Home Office and received

*Offender Profiling Series: I - **Interviewing and Deception***
Edited by D. Canter and L. Alison. © 1999 Ashgate Publishing, Aldershot. pp 23-39

grants from research bodies such as the Economic and Social Research Council.

Graham F. Wagstaff is a reader in Psychology at the University of Liverpool. He gained his PhD at the University of Newcastle upon Tyne in 1975 and for more than 20 years he has researched widely in areas of hypnosis and law, forensic interviewing and the social psychology of justice. He has published over 100 academic papers and book chapters and is author of *Hypnosis, Compliance and Belief*, which has been widely cited as an authoritative text on the non-state approach to hypnosis. He is also one of the founder members of the British Society of Experimental and Clinical Hypnosis and is on the editorial boards of *Contemporary Hypnosis* and *Experimentelle und Klinische Hypnose.* In addition to his research activities, Dr Wagstaff has given courses on eyewitness testimony to senior police officers, has appeared on radio and television on a number of occasions regarding his views on various topics, and has also acted as a consultant and expert witness in a variety of legal cases.

2 The Effectiveness of the Cognitive Interview

MARK R. KEBBELL AND GRAHAM F. WAGSTAFF

Introduction

When investigating criminal acts, witness testimony is often very important, although witnesses rarely remember as much as the police would like (Kebbell and Milne, in press; Rand, 1975). Consequently, psychologists have tried many ways of enhancing witness recall. However, by far the most extensively used and successful procedure is the 'cognitive interview' (Fisher and Geiselman, 1992):

The 'original' cognitive interview involved four instructions; these required the witness to: 1) *reinstate mental context*; 2) *report everything*; 3) *recall events in different orders*; and 4) *change perspectives* (Geiselman, Fisher, Firstenberg, Hutton, Sullivan, Avetissian and Prosk, 1984). Later, Fisher and Geiselman developed an 'enhanced' cognitive interview (Fisher, Geiselman, Raymond, Jurkevich and Warhaftig, 1987a; Fisher, Geiselman and Amador, 1989). This sought to redress problems that routinely occur in 'standard' police interviews, described later in this chapter. Essentially the 'enhanced' cognitive interview is an original cognitive interview with additional instructions to ensure that: 1) *rapport is established*; 2) *control is transferred* to the witness; 3) questions are *compatible with the witness's mental operations*; 4) the witness is encouraged to use *focused retrieval;* and 5) the witness is encouraged to use *imagery*.

Research indicates that both forms of the cognitive interview have the potential to enhance recall compared to control interviews in laboratory situations. The original version of the cognitive interview produces approximately 25% to 35% more information than controls (Kohnken, Thurer and Zoberbier, 1994), and Fisher et al. (1987a) have found further improvements with the enhanced cognitive interview. These memory enhancements have been shown to occur without adversely influencing accuracy rates (Geiselman, 1996), increasing susceptibility to leading questions (Geiselman, Fisher, Cohen, Holland, and Surtes, 1986), or disrupting confidence-accuracy relationships (Geiselman et al., 1984; Kebbell and Wagstaff, 1997). (For reviews and more detailed descriptions of the cognitive interview see Bekerian and Dennett, 1993; Fisher, 1995; Fisher and Geiselman, 1992; Memon and Bull, 1991; Memon and Kohnken, 1992; Kohnken, Milne, Memon, and Bull, 1994; Memon and Stevenage, 1996.)

The effectiveness of the cognitive interview has meant that most UK police forces have incorporated it into police recruit training and taken steps to train serving officers in its use. This training has been called the 'National Interviewing Package' (Central Planning and Training Unit, 1992). It is also sometimes known as the 'PEACE' approach (PEACE stands for 'planning', 'engage and explain', 'account', 'closure' and 'evaluation') or the 'cognitive' approach. Typically, training lasts for five days; two are spent on cognitive interviewing for witnesses; the remainder is spent on ways of interviewing suspects.

Given this investment of resources, it is obviously important that the cognitive interview should be evaluated not only in laboratory investigations, but also in the field. The aim of this chapter, therefore, is to evaluate the effectiveness of cognitive interviews compared with standard interviews in real investigations.

The 'Standard' Police Interview

To compare cognitive interviews with standard interviews it is first necessary to describe standard interviews and the problems associated with them. Whilst most UK police officers received no formal training in witness interviewing before the introduction of the cognitive interview (George, 1991), police officers did seem to conduct interviews in a similar way (Clifford and George, 1996; Fisher, Geiselman and Raymond, 1987b; George, 1991; Memon, Holley, Milne, Koehnken and Bull, 1994; Yuille, 1984). However, the 'standard police interview' left much to be desired. Fisher et al. (1987b) provide the most detailed description and critique as follows.

Interruption of Witness's Responses

Police interviewing is characterised by frequent interruption of witness's responses by the interviewing officer. After introducing themselves, the interviewer typically asks the witness to tell him or her what happened. However, when the witness starts to provide an account, he or she is frequently interrupted. For instance, in Fisher et al.'s work there were, on average, three open-ended questions requiring an extended answer (e.g. 'describe your attacker') per interview. During the responses to the open-ended questions the interviewer interrupted the witness on average 11 times. In the typical interview the witness was interrupted only 7.5 seconds after he or she had begun to reply.

Interruptions cause two problems. First, they break the concentration of witnesses when they are trying to retrieve information. If the interviewer's questions break the witness's concentration, then the witness must switch attention from trying to recall information, to the interviewer's questions. Then the witness must go back to his or her memory to answer the question. This makes the task much more difficult and such constant shifting of attention prevents optimal recall of the event. This is particularly unfortunate as free recall (i.e. uninterrupted recall) typically produces very accurate information (Yuille and Cutshall, 1986). Further, the increased difficulty of trying to recall information, despite constant interruptions, may prevent the witness from making as much effort later in the interview.

The second drawback is that after the witness has been interrupted several times he or she begins to expect interruption throughout the interview. As the witness expects to have only a short period to respond, he or she shortens responses accordingly. Clearly, any response that is shortened will not produce as much information and may exclude information important to an investigation.

Use of Question-Answer Format

Police interviewing relies heavily on the use of a question-answer format. Most questions used in forensic interviews are closed questions (e.g. "What colour was the attacker's shirt?"). Such questions may have the advantage of eliciting information that the interviewer feels is relevant and prevent the witness from wandering off the point, but they can also cause problems.

Closed questions produce a less concentrated form of retrieval. Witnesses take less time to respond to closed questions than open-ended questions, which may be due (at least in part) to less time being spent actively trying to retrieve information. In addition, both closed and open questions are asked quickly of witnesses; thus, there is only a short time between a question and answer and the next question, giving no opportunity or encouragement to the witness to elaborate or extend an answer. The use of questions also changes the nature of the witness's task from that of free recall. When closed questions are used the interview takes on the format of the interviewer asking a closed question and the witness giving a brief answer, the interviewer asking another closed question, and so on. This means that the interview changes from being directed by the witness to being directed by the interviewer. Fisher et al. comment, “It is difficult enough for the witness to retrieve detailed events from memory when actively trying; it is virtually impossible when he remains passive” (p.181).

Using a question-answer format also means that the only information elicited is that which is requested. Thus, if the interviewer forgets to ask a certain question, no information in that area is recorded.

Inappropriate Sequencing of Questions

The next problem is that, typically, questions are sequenced in an inappropriate manner. This causes problems similar to those associated with excessive use of question-answer format; both impair recall performance through shifts in attention. Many questions asked by interviewers are in a seemingly arbitrary order that may adversely influence witnesses through shifting their retrieval efforts from one area to another. For example, an interviewer may ask a visually orientated question about the suspect's face, then follow with an auditory question about the suspect's voice, then return to a visual target, such as the suspect's clothes. This shift in retrieval attention from one area to another and from one sensory modality to another may impair performance. Indeed, alternating retrieval in this way has been shown in one study to produce a 19% decrease in witnesses’ performance (Fisher and Price-Rouch, 1986).

Further problems can be caused by asking what Fisher et al. term 'general knowledge' questions, such as "Why do you think he did that?", or "Was he married?", "dropped" in amongst questions concerning the crime. Again, shifting from the recall of crime details to general knowledge questions, then back to crime details can decrease the witness's performance.

Other Problems

Other problems occur in some interviews but not all. These include negative phrasing, leading questions, inappropriate language, judgmental comments, lack of following potential leads, and under emphasising auditory cues.

Negative phrasing occurs when questions are asked in the negative form. For example, "You *don't* remember if..?" Phrasing questions in this form may actively discourage the witness from trying hard to retrieve information. Leading questions are questions that subtly suggest that a certain answer is required. Not only are the demand characteristics of the situation likely to produce compliance, but Loftus (1975) found that leading questions may bias witnesses' later recollections of an event.

Inappropriate language is found where interviewers use overly formal sentences or words, which are difficult for the witness to comprehend (e.g., "What was the index number of the vehicle?"). Such language may not only prevent the witness from understanding the question, but also creates a barrier between the interviewer and the witness that is not conducive to optimal performance. Judgmental comments are occasionally made, often about the witness's role in an incident (e.g. "You shouldn't have been carrying so much cash"). These may make the witness defensive or offend the witness, thereby inhibiting any rapport between interviewer and interviewee.

Furthermore, police officers often fail to follow up on leads that they are given. For instance, a suspect may be described as looking like 'a gangster' without any attempt being made to follow up the comment, to elicit why the witness felt that the suspect looked like a 'gangster'. Thus, information that might help produce a more objective description is missed. Finally, auditory clues are often underemphasised. Officers rarely enquire about what a suspect may have said or if they had an accent.

Clearly, the standard police interview has many potential areas for improvement, and any interview procedure that addresses these problems is likely to lead to enhanced recall. It is important to recognise, therefore, that in real-life investigations the cognitive interview may have advantages over standard interviewing procedures that go beyond the use of the specialist mnemonic memory retrieval aids. It also follows that if we are to maximise the effectiveness and efficiency of the cognitive interview in the field, attention must be paid to the relative efficacy of these various components in enhancing recall.

Use of the Cognitive Interview in Real-Life Investigations

Most research on the cognitive interview has been conducted in the laboratory and field studies are rare (see McGurk, Carr and McGurk, 1993; for an evaluation of the PEACE approach as a whole). There are, however, two notable exceptions, one in the USA, and one in the UK.

In the first, Fisher, Geiselman and Amador (1989) conducted a field study with 16 experienced detectives from a robbery division in the USA. Preliminary recordings were made of witness interviews conducted by detectives before any training in the cognitive interview. Subsequent recordings were made after seven officers had been trained in the cognitive interview while the remainder were assigned to a control condition. In all, 88 interviews were recorded before training, and 47 interviews were conducted after training; 24 by officers trained in the cognitive interview and 23 by officers in a control group. Interviews were selected so that each was severe enough that time would be made available to conduct a thorough interview.

Effectiveness of the cognitive interview was tested in two ways; 1) by comparing the number of 'facts' elicited before and after training in the use of the cognitive interview, and 2), by comparing the number of facts elicited by the trained detectives using the cognitive interview and the control group of detectives who were still using standard techniques. There were no significant differences between the two groups before training. However, after training there was a significant improvement; 63% more information was recalled by witnesses interviewed by detectives trained in use of the cognitive interview compared with those interviewed by the 'control' detectives. Moreover, detectives in the cognitive interview trained group showed a 47% increase in the amount of information that they elicited from witnesses compared with their previous performance before training.

However, it could be argued there is no way of definitively establishing whether these increases were due to improved memory, they could reflect an increased willingness to guess. Fisher et al. (1989) therefore estimated accuracy by comparing each witness report with what they term another 'reliable' source, when possible. In 22 cases this source was another witness, in one case a confession, and in one case information was supplied by a video camera. They found a 93% corroboration rate for information produced by detectives untrained in the cognitive interview, and a 94.5% corroboration rate for detectives using the cognitive interview. No significant difference was found between the two. However, as Fisher et al. (1989) note, just because two witnesses reports correlate an item, this does not necessarily mean that they are accurate since both may be wrong. Clearly though, this study shows that the cognitive interview has the potential to lead to dramatic enhancements in witness recall.

However, it is also notable that of the seven detectives trained in the cognitive interview, one produced a *decrease* in performance of 23%. On the basis of such a small sample it is difficult to estimate whether this was a curious anomaly or whether this represents a potential problem. Fisher et al. (1989) comment of this detective:

> Not coincidentally an analysis of the post-training interviews showed that he was the only one of the seven detectives who did not incorporate the recommended procedures into his post-training interviews.
>
> p. 724

However, they provide no details to show how he did not incorporate the recommended procedures. For instance, did he keep interrupting witnesses? Did his method of instructing witnesses to reinstate context cause confusion?

Also, because the cognitive interviews are not described, it is not possible to identify the elements in the cognitive interview responsible for improvements, or even if all the elements of the cognitive interview were used. As we shall see shortly, these are important points. Furthermore, the detectives were aware that they were evaluating a new technique, which they had been specially trained to use. The training for, and use of, a new technique may have produced improvements in the police officers' performance, by motivating them to try harder and in turn, to motivate the witnesses to try harder too.

Of relevance here, is the field investigation in the United Kingdom by George (1991), which is also summarised by Clifford and George (1996). In this study, 28 police officers were evaluated in one of four conditions, seven in each. A recording of an interview performed by each officer was evaluated before each was trained in an interview technique or placed in the control group. The interview techniques were: 1) the cognitive interview; 2) conversation management (a procedure developed to open channels of communication, see Shepherd, 1988); 3) conversation management combined with the cognitive interview and 4) an untrained control group. The results indicated that the cognitive interview showed an improvement when compared to the standard police interview control group of 14% more information. When compared to performance before 'enhanced' cognitive interview training this improvement was 55%. This advantage was for all kinds of information (i.e. who, what, when, where, how and why). Neither conversation management nor the combination of conversation management and cognitive interview produced more information than the untrained group. These results would suggest that it was not 'training' *per se*, or novelty alone that accounted for the improvements that occurred with the cognitive interview.

Clifford and George (1996) provide a detailed account of the form of the cognitive interview. Interestingly, of the four original mnemonic strategies, three were hardly used; instructions to report everything, change orders or change perspectives. A similar pattern of results has been found by Memon, Holley, Milne, Koehnken and Bull, R. (1994) in a laboratory study. George (1991) notes that it is unsurprising that officers rarely used the change of perspective mnemonic as:

> It is not an easy concept to ask someone to put themselves in someone else's shoes to review an event asking them to say what they think they would have seen, and remain confident that there will be no confabulation.
>
> p. 117

Critics have also suggested that the use of the change perspectives mnemonic may make it difficult to use such statements in court, especially if children are interviewed, again because of a danger of confabulation (Boon and Noon, 1994); although it appears to have little impact on jurors' judgements of guilt or innocence (Kebbell, Wagstaff and Preece, in press). The police officers in this study may have had an intuitive grasp of this and so, did not use the technique. Similarly, officers and witnesses may find it difficult to use change order instructions, although it is not clear why officers did not use instructions to report everything.

The fourth mnemonic, reinstatement of context, was used more frequently and to good effect. Information retrieved with an open question was significantly greater when that question was presented with a request to reinstate context. Instructions for focused retrieval (i.e. to work hard) also appeared to significantly increase recall. Imagery, while used relatively frequently in the cognitive interview condition failed to enhance recall on its own.

Importantly, this field study documented the questioning style used by the interviewers. This revealed a dramatic change. Officers in the cognitive interview condition asked far fewer questions. What questions they did ask were more likely to be open and they asked far fewer leading or closed questions. While the number of questions decreased to one third of the pre-training levels, the amount of information elicited from a witness, per ten minutes, increased dramatically. Why, however, the effects of the cognitive interview should be eliminated when it is combined with another procedure (conversation management) remains something of a mystery.

Police Perception of the Cognitive Interview

Whilst the two field studies show that the cognitive interview may enhance witness memory, they tell us little about police officers' perceptions of the cognitive interview. Clearly, officers must have a positive attitude to a technique if it is to be successful, particularly after its novelty value has worn off. To investigate this issue, Kebbell, Milne and Wagstaff (in press) surveyed police officers' perceptions of the effectiveness of the cognitive interview in witness interviews. Ninety-six UK officers trained in the cognitive interview were surveyed as well as a control group of 65 untrained officers. Officers were asked to rate how useful and how frequently they used the components of the cognitive interview. Trained officers were significantly more likely to say that they used instructions to mentally reinstate context, used different orders, changed perspectives and used imagery than untrained officers. The responses of the trained officers also showed that some components of the cognitive interview were used more frequently and were rated as more useful than others. Rated as most useful, and most frequently used, were instructions to establish rapport, report everything, encourage concentration, witness compatible questioning, and mental reinstatement of context. Rated as less useful and less frequently used were different orders, imagery, change perspectives and transfer control. However, it must be borne in mind that officers' reports of how they interview may be very different from how they actually interview (Robson, 1993).

Further data indicated that the cognitive interview was generally perceived to be a useful procedure that increases correct recall; for instance nearly 90% of the officers indicated that the cognitive interview produced 'more' or 'much more' information than a standard interview. These positive perceptions of the cognitive interview do not appear to be simply due to novelty value; the average time since cognitive interview training for the trained group was nearly two years.

Kebbell et al. also questioned officers about their perception of how much incorrect information is generated with the cognitive interview. They found that officers did not have an exaggerated perception of the ability of the cognitive interview to enhance accurate recall; less than 10% felt that the cognitive interview produces much less incorrect information than a standard interview. (This contrasts, for example, with the exaggerated credulity that tends to be shown in interviewing with hypnosis, which may, in fact, have a detrimental effect on overall accuracy, see Wagstaff, 1993; Wagstaff, Vella and Perfect, 1992).

Significantly, however, Kebbell et al. found that many officers reported that they simply do not have the time to conduct a cognitive interview (see also, Kebbell and Wagstaff, 1996). For instance 54% of cognitive interview trained officers reported that they 'never' or 'rarely' had enough time to conduct what they believed was a good interview. This problem was compounded by the fact that 93% of officers believed that the cognitive interview took longer to conduct than a standard interview; a finding supported by the results of some laboratory studies

(Kohnken et al. 1994; Mello and Fisher 1996). Typical comments concerning the cognitive interview were as follows:

> The concept of cognitive interview is and can be very successful. However, for the majority of "street-cops" in uniform, we do not have the luxury of time which is paramount for the success of this style of interviewing.

> Usually do not have enough time to use it properly. Isn't it about time the police hierarchy allowed it's officers to use the tools which it teaches them in Training School? (i.e. time allocated to deal with incidents is far too short).

In fact, of the 74 negative comments, 64 concerned time constraints.

Conclusions

Clearly, the cognitive interview has the potential to enhance witness memory. Furthermore, the importance of witnesses to criminal investigations makes the enhancement of witness evidence extremely worthwhile (Kebbell and Milne, in press; Rand 1975). However, there are two particularly important issues associated with its use in real-life investigations, that require further study.

First, in practice, the components of the cognitive interview are not used equally frequently. Some are used more frequently than others and are perceived to be more useful than others. Second, police officers often do not have as much time as they would like to conduct a cognitive interview. Taken together these factors strongly suggest that time should be spent discovering what parts of the cognitive interview are most effective in recall, and ensuring that officers are trained in those techniques (Bekerian and Dennett 1993; Kebbell and Wagstaff 1996).

For instance, Memon and Stevenage (1996) point out that in many laboratory studies a cognitive interview without mnemonic instructions produces similar recall to a full cognitive interview. In his field study, George also showed that memory enhancements were mainly due to an absence of the problems typically associated with standard police interviews plus instructions to reinstate context. And, significantly, Mello and Fisher (1996) have recently commented:

> The cognitive interview may be a tool that works primarily by facilitating communication rather than or in addition to, one that facilitates memory retrieval.
>
> p. 415

It could be the case, therefore, that valuable training time is perhaps best spent training officers both in the social components of the cognitive interview and context reinstatement. This might be more effective than spending some of that valuable time training officers to use instructions to change orders or change perspectives - devices which are rarely used, and which may have little or no effectiveness in enhancing recall (Boon and Noon 1994; Mello and Fisher 1996).

It is also important that 'quick' interviews are developed (Kebbell, Milne and Wagstaff, in press; Kebbell and Wagstaff 1996). For instance, if a mugger has recently run off and the police wish to search for him in the immediate area it might not be appropriate to conduct a full cognitive interview, all that is required is a brief description. In these situations the problems with standard interviews, described earlier, may not be as clear as they first seem because as a method of conducting a rapid, succinct, interview it may be effective. However, even when time is at a premium, improvements over standard interviews might possibly be achieved through a compromise between standard interviews and the cognitive interview. For example, a full cognitive interview using context reinstatement and uninterrupted free recall may in some situations take too long. A standard interview with frequent interruption and closed questions may take less time but not produce enough accurate information. A compromise might be to ask the witness a direct, open question (e.g., "Describe the mugger in as much detail as you can") and then allow them to respond.

Finally, it is important to emphasise that the interview of a witness provides a good opportunity to enhance police-public relations (Fisher and Geiselman 1992). A well conducted interview with a concerned and genuinely interested police officer is likely to increase the witness's respect for and future willingness to co-operate with the police. The alternative, a poorly conducted interview with an unconcerned police officer, showing little interest in what the witness says, may discourage the witness from future support of the police. As a crime incident is likely to be a talking point for a long period of time, then the witness's impression of the police is liable to be relayed to a large number of people. Thus, it may have a large impact on a locality. Perhaps here, then is an unanticipated benefit of the cognitive interview that may be worthy of future investigation and prove to be one of its most positive contributions to forensic investigations.

Acknowledgements

This chapter was supported by a grant to the first author by the Economic and Social Research Council, UK (Grant R00429234159) and a Research Fellowship by Bolton Institute, UK.

References

Bekerian, D.A., and Dennett, J.L. (1993). The cognitive interview: Reviving the issues. *Applied Cognitive Psychology,* 7, 275-297.

Boon, J. and Noon, E. (1994). Changing perspectives in cognitive interviewing. *Psychology, Crime and Law*, 1, 59-69.

Central Planning and Training Unit (1992). *Investigative Interviewing: A Guide to Interviewing*. London: Home Office, Central Planning and Training Unit.

Clifford, B.R. and George, R. (1996). A field evaluation of training in three methods of witness/victim investigative interviewing. *Psychology, Crime and Law,* 2, 231-248.

Fisher, R.P. (1995). Interviewing victims and witnesses of crimes. *Psychology, Public Policy, and Law*, 1, 732-764.

Fisher, R.P., and Geiselman, R.E. (1992). *Memory Enhancing Techniques for Investigative Interviewing: The Cognitive Interview.* Springfield: Charles C. Thomas.

Fisher, R.P. and Price-Roush, J. (1986). *Question order and eyewitness memory.* Unpublished manuscript, Department of Psychology, Florida International University, USA.

Fisher, R.P., Geiselman, R.E., and Amador, M. (1989). Field test of the cognitive interview: Enhancing the recollection of actual victims and witnesses of crime. *Journal of Applied Psychology*, 74, 722-727.

Fisher, R.P., Geiselman, R.E., and Raymond, D.S. (1987b). Critical analysis of police interview techniques. *Journal of Police Science and Administration,* 15, 177-185.

Fisher, R.P., Geiselman, R.E., Raymond, D.S., Jurkevich, L.M., and Warhaftig, M.L. (1987a). Enhancing enhanced eyewitness memory: Refining the cognitive interview. *Journal of Police Science and Administration*, 15, 291-297.

Geiselman, R.E. (1996). On the use and efficacy of the cognitive interview. *Psycholoquy,* 7 (6), witness-memory.2.geiselman.

Geiselman, R.E., Fisher, R.P., Cohen, G., Holland, H., and Surtes, L. (1986). Eyewitness response to leading and misleading questions under the cognitive interview. *Journal of Police Science and Administration*, 14, 31-39.

Geiselman, R.E., Fisher, R.P., Firstenberg, I., Hutton, L.A., Sullivan, S.J., Avetissian, I.V. and Prosk, A.L. (1984). Enhancement of eyewitness memory: An empirical evaluation of the cognitive interview. *Journal of Police Science and Administration*, 12, 74-80.

George, R. (1991). *A field and experimental evaluation of three methods of interviewing witnesses and victims of crime.* Unpublished Masters Thesis, Polytechnic of East London, London, UK.

Kebbell, M.R. and Milne, R. (in press). Police officers' perception of eyewitness factors in forensic investigations: *The Journal of Social Psychology.*

Kebbell, M.R. and Wagstaff, G.F. (1996, May). Enhancing the practicality of the cognitive interview in forensic situations. [11 paragraphs]. *Psycholoquy*, [on-line serial], 7(6). Available FTP: Hostname: princeton.edu Directory: pub/harnard/Psycholoquy/1996.volume7. File: psych.96.7.16.witness-memory.3.kebbell.

Kebbell, M.R. and Wagstaff, G.F. (1997). Why do the police interview eyewitnesses? Interview objectives and the evaluation of eyewitness performance. *The Journal of Psychology,* 131, 595-601.

Kebbell, M.R. and Wagstaff, G.F. (1997). An investigation into the influence of hypnosis on the confidence and accuracy of eyewitness recall. *Contemporary Hypnosis,* 14, 157-166.

Kebbell, M.R., Milne, R. and Wagstaff, G.F. (in press). Applying the cognitive interview: Police officers' perceptions of its usefulness. *Psychology, Crime and Law.*

Kebbell, M.R., Wagstaff, G.F. and Preece, D. (in press). The effect of testimony elicited with a cognitive interview on jurors' judgements of guilt and innocence. *Psychology, Crime and Law.*

Kohnken, G., Thurer, C. and Zoberbier, D. (1994). The cognitive interview: Are the interviewers' memories enhanced, too? *Applied Cognitive Psychology*, 8, 13-24.

Kohnken, G., Milne, R., Memon, A. and Bull, R. (1994). *A meta-analysis of the effects of the cognitive interview.* Paper presented at the Biennial Conference of the American Psychology Law Society, Santa Fe, New Mexico, USA.

Loftus, E.F. (1975). Leading questions and eyewitness report. *Cognitive Psychology*, 7, 560-572.

McGurk, B.J., Carr, M.J. and McGurk, D. (1993). Investigative interviewing courses for police officers: an evaluation. *Police Research Series*, 4, London: Home Office Police Department.

Mello, E.W. and Fisher, R.P. (1996). Enhancing older adult eyewitness memory with the cognitive interview. *Applied Cognitive Psychology*, 10, 403-418.

Memon, A. and Bull, R. (1991). The cognitive interview: its origins, empirical support, evaluation and practical implications. *Journal of Community and Applied Social Psychology*, 1, 291-307.

Memon, A. and Kohnken, G. (1992). Helping witnesses to remember more: the cognitive interview. *Expert Evidence*, 2, 39-48.

Memon, A. and Stevenage, S. (1996). Interviewing witnesses: What works and what doesn't? *Psycholoquy*, 7 (6), witness-memory.1.

Memon, A., Holley, A., Milne, R, Koehnken, G. and Bull, R. (1994). Towards understanding the effects of interviewer training in evaluating the cognitive interview. *Applied Cognitive Psychology*, 8, 641-659.

Rand, Corporation (1975). The Criminal Investigation Process *Rand Corporation Technical Report R-1777*, 1-3. Santa Monica, California.

Robson, C. (1993). *Real World Research*. Oxford: Blackwell.

Shepherd, E. (1988). Developing interview skills. In P. Southgate (ed.), *New Directions in Police Training*. London: HMSO.

Wagstaff, G.F. (1993). What expert witnesses can tell courts about hypnosis: A review of the association between hypnosis and the law *Expert Evidence*, 2, 60-70.

Wagstaff, G. F., Vella, M. and Perfect, T. J. (1992). The effect of hypnotically elicited testimony on juror's judgements of guilt and innocence. *Journal of Social Psychology*, 31, 69-77.

Yuille, J.C. (1984). Research and teaching with the police: A Canadian example. *International Review of Applied Psychology*, 33, 5-23.

Yuille, J.C. and Cutshall, J.L. (1986). A case study of eyewitness memory of a crime. *Journal of Applied Psychology*, 71, 291-301.

3 Using Cognitive Interviewing to Construct Facial Composites

CHRISTINE E. KOEHN, RONALD P. FISHER AND
BRIAN L. CUTLER

Eyewitnesses are often interviewed shortly after a crime to produce a facial composite of the perpetrator. We reviewed the relevant literature to identify one promising interview technique to maximise memory retrieval (Cognitive Interview) and one computer system to facilitate constructing facial composites (Mac-A-Mug Pro System). An experimental study is described in which witnesses observed a target person and then, two days later, attempted to generate a facial composite. The resulting composites were of very low quality (not at all similar to a photograph of the target) and of no value in selecting the target from a photo array. An analysis of the psychological components of facial memory is presented to explain why the Mac-A-Mug system performs so poorly in realistic eyewitness tasks, in which the target face is constructed from memory. Suggestions are provided to improve facial composite systems by making them more compatible with the psychological processes mediating face recall. Finally, we offer some suggestions to improve the ecological validity of experimental research to evaluate facial composite systems.

Christine E. Koehn, Ph.D. is a graduate of Florida International University. Her Master's and Doctoral work included research on the facial memory of eyewitnesses, effective facial composite construction with various computerised facial construction systems, as well as

*Offender Profiling Series: I - **Interviewing and Deception***
Edited by D. Canter and L. Alison. © 1999 Ashgate Publishing, Aldershot. pp 41-63

interviewing techniques. Currently, she is working as a Research Analyst for the Children's Services Council of Palm Beach County (Florida) where she is researching contracted programs as well as country wide service delivery systems that assist children and families in need. These include children and families in the child abuse and neglect, emergency shelter/foster care, respite care and supervised visitation systems.

Ronald P. Fisher is currently Professor of Psychology at Florida International University, where he has been conducting basic and applied research on memory for the past 14 years. Professor's primary research interests have been on memory retrieval and specifically how to enhance eyewitness memory in a forensically relevant setting. Along with Ed Geiselman, Professor Fisher has developed the Cognitive Interview method of interviewing witnesses, which is used by many investigative agencies (e.g. British Police, FBI). Professor Fisher serves on the editorial board of the journal, *Memory and Cognition*.

Brian L. Cutler is Professor of Psychology and Associate Dean of the College of Arts & Sciences at Florida International University, Miami, Florida, USA. His research and teaching focus on social and cognitive psychological factors affecting human performance in legal settings. His publications address factors affecting eyewitness memory, jury selection, expert psychological testimony, and jury decision making. Professor Cutler also serves as expert witness on the psychology of eyewitnesses memory and as a trial consultant to practising attorneys.

3 Using Cognitive Interviewing to Construct Facial Composites

CHRISTINE E. KOEHN, RONALD P. FISHER AND
BRIAN L. CUTLER

Introduction

During a police investigation, a witness is typically interviewed in three phases. The witness is asked initially to give a verbal description of the events of the crime and of the perpetrator. Several days later, the witness may be asked to construct a facial composite of the perpetrator with the assistance of a skilled artist. Finally, the witness may be asked to identify the perpetrator from a line-up or photo array.

The standard interview protocol typically used by police during the investigation consists of a sequence of short, closed-ended questions (Fisher, Geiselman and Raymond, 1987a; George, 1991). As an alternative to the standard police interview and to assist police in eliciting more information at the description phase of the interview, the Cognitive Interview (CI) was developed. Based on principles of cognitive psychology, the CI has been found to help witnesses recall significantly more information than the standard police interview (Fisher, McCauley and Geiselman, 1994). In considering the CI's potential in the description phase of interviewing, it is reasonable to believe that if used during the composite phase of investigation the CI would elicit more accurate, detailed information and result in more accurate composites.

This chapter examines the CI and some of the composite generation systems currently in use by police agencies. An empirical study is reported that assesses the usefulness of the CI with some modification - for composite generation. Finally, we discuss the implications of this study for constructing composite systems and for related research.

The Cognitive Interview

When an individual witnesses a crime, the police initially ask the witness for a detailed description of the events of the crime and of the perpetrator. The CI was developed as a guided retrieval technique to help witnesses recall more information. The original version of the CI technique utilized four general retrieval mnemonics during recall (Geiselman, Fisher, Firstenberg, Hutton, Sullivan, Avetissian and Prosk, 1984). Two of the interview mnemonics attempt to increase the likelihood of overlap between the encoding and retrieval contexts (encoding specificity principle: Tulving and Thomson, 1973). These include reinstating the environmental and psychological contexts of the event and reporting all information that comes to mind, including fragmentary information. The other two mnemonics encourage witnesses to search through memory using a variety of retrieval paths (Anderson and Pichert, 1978). These include recounting the event in a variety of orders and from a variety of perspectives.

The CI was later revised to emphasize imagery, the importance of establishing rapport between the interviewer and the witness, and communication, especially by making the interviewer's questioning more compatible with the witness's current emotional state and mental representation of the event (Fisher, Geiselman, Raymond, Jurkevich and Warhaftig, 1987b). A thorough description of the CI can be found in the user's handbook (Fisher and Geiselman, 1992).

Research on the CI has shown it to be an effective interviewing technique. In the typical experiment, participants either unexpectedly witnessed a simulated crime in the laboratory or they viewed a film depicting a crime. Several days later, the participants were asked to recall detailed information about the event and the perpetrator. The common finding, across more than 25 experiments, is that participants recalled more correct information with the CI than with the standard police interview, and with no decrease in accuracy (Bekerian and Dennett, 1993; Fisher, McCauley and Geiselman, in press; Kohnken, Milne, Memon and Bull, 1992).

A more realistic test of the CI was conducted in a field study with victims and witnesses of real street crime (Fisher, Geiselman and Amador, 1989). This study utilized experienced detectives from the Metro-Dade Police Department in Miami, Florida, USA. Prior to any training, each detective recorded several interviews with victims and witnesses of crime. Afterward, approximately half of the detectives received training in the (revised) CI. All of the detectives then conducted several additional interviews. The results demonstrated that the CI-trained group elicited 48% more information during the post-training interviews than in the pre-training interviews. Similarly, the CI-trained group elicited 63% more information after training than did the group that received no training. It is noteworthy that the corroboration rates (proportion of statements that were corroborated by another witness) were high and approximately equal for those interviews conducted by CI-trained (.94) and untrained interviewers (.93). This field study of the CI mirrored the results of previous lab studies and demonstrated the practical utility of the CI in real-world settings.

Another field study conducted by George (1991) with British police found similar results. Officers trained to conduct the CI elicited more information in interviews conducted after training than did these same officers before training. Additionally, as in Fisher et al. (1989), more information was elicited by trained than by untrained officers.

In summary, research on the CI has demonstrated its effectiveness for helping individuals recall information in the description phase of a police investigation. Therefore, it seems reasonable that, with some modification, the CI could be more useful than the standard police interview in helping witnesses to recall more information during the composite-generation phase of a police investigation. The resulting CI-enhanced composites should bear a greater resemblance to the suspect and thereby facilitate apprehending the correct suspect.

Composite Generation Systems

Several methods might be used to construct facial composites. The simplest would be to use the witness's verbal description, but such descriptions tend to be vague and uninformative. A preferable alternative is to use a more pictorial representation, which could provide useful information about a suspect that a verbal description does not (Davies, Ellis and Shepherd, 1978). Admittedly, these pictorial facial composites may be only imperfect likenesses of the suspects. Nevertheless, as a screening tool, they may be accurate enough to signal a police officer either to stop and question a potential suspect or to avoid disturbing an obviously innocent individual (Ellis, 1986). Currently, these pictorial facial composites are produced either by police artists, who construct the composite by hand, or by technicians who operate various mechanical or computerized composite systems. We shall focus on the utility of the computerized systems.

Composite production systems that are currently being used by police departments include Photo-Fit (Christie and Ellis, 1981; Davies et al., 1978; Davies, Milne and Shepherd, 1983; Ellis, Davies and Shepherd, 1978; Ellis, Shepherd and Davies, 1975), Identi-Kit (Duggal, Mickus, Daneker and Kassin, 1992; Laughery and Fowler, 1980; Mauldin and Laughery, 1981), Mac-A-Mug Pro (Cutler, Stocklein and Penrod, 1988; Duggal et al., 1992; Penrod, Pappas and Bull, 1992a; Penrod and Stocklein, 1992; Penrod, Thill and Bull, 1992b; Shaherazam, 1986), Compusketch (Visatex Corporation, 1991), FaceKit (InfoTec, 1991), E-Fit (Aspley Limited, 1993), and CD-Fit (Philips, 1992). Although these and other systems are being used by various police departments, very few have been tested rigorously in the laboratory. This chapter will be limited to examining only those systems that have been researched empirically: Photo-Fit, Identi-Kit, and Mac-A-Mug Pro.

The Photo-Fit system is a composite generation system that is composed of black-and-white photographs of five facial features superimposed onto transparencies. The features include forehead and hairline, eyes, nose, mouth, and chin. In the few laboratory tests of the Photo-Fit System, it has been found to have limited utility because of the small number of features it uses (Ellis, Davies, Shepherd, 1978; Ellis, Shepherd and Davies, 1975). In some studies, it has even been found to be less informative than witnesses' verbal descriptions (Christie and Ellis, 1981).

The Identi-Kit system also uses a limited set of features. The features are line drawings superimposed on to transparencies, much like the Photo-Fit System. The transparencies are overlapped to form a facial composite. Additional feature alterations can be made with a special pencil. Like the Photo-Fit System, laboratory testing has revealed that the Identi-Kit is of limited utility because of the small number of features available (Laughery and Fowler, 1980).

A third system is the Mac-a-Mug Pro computerized generation system (Figure 3.1). This system is more flexible than either the Photo-Fit or the

Identi-Kit systems because it can potentially use an unlimited number of features. The features are retrieved from the software's library and can be altered as desired. Alterations can be made by using the program's various editing modes to add or modify features and to shade the resulting composite. The system also contains a wide selection of miscellaneous features, such as hats and eyeglasses.

Research on the utility of the Mac-A-Mug Pro has yielded mixed results. Some studies have shown that it generates effective composites, whereas others have shown that it does not. On the positive side, Cutler, Penrod and Stocklein (1988) found that the Mac-A-Mug Pro was useful for creating composites that are identifiable, whether constructed by a novice or by an experienced operator assisting a novice (see also Duggal et al., 1992).

Other studies, however, suggest that the Mac-A-Mug Pro is somewhat limited in its ability to create good resemblances (Penrod, Pappas and Bull, 1992a; Penrod and Stocklein, 1992; Penrod, Thill and Bull, 1992b). Further, Duggal et al. (1992) demonstrated that other composite generation techniques may have greater utility than the Mac-A-Mug Pro. They compared composites created by sketch artists, the Identi-Kit, and the Mac-A-Mug Pro and found that artists' sketches were chosen most often as the best composites, with Mac-A-Mug Pro composites being chosen only marginally significantly more often than Identi-Kit composites. In summary, the admittedly sparse research suggests that the Mac-A-Mug Pro may have greater potential utility than some of the other available composite generation systems, specifically the Photo-Fit and Identi-Kit systems. In addition, it is flexible, easy to learn, and easy to use, making it particularly valuable for use in applied settings.

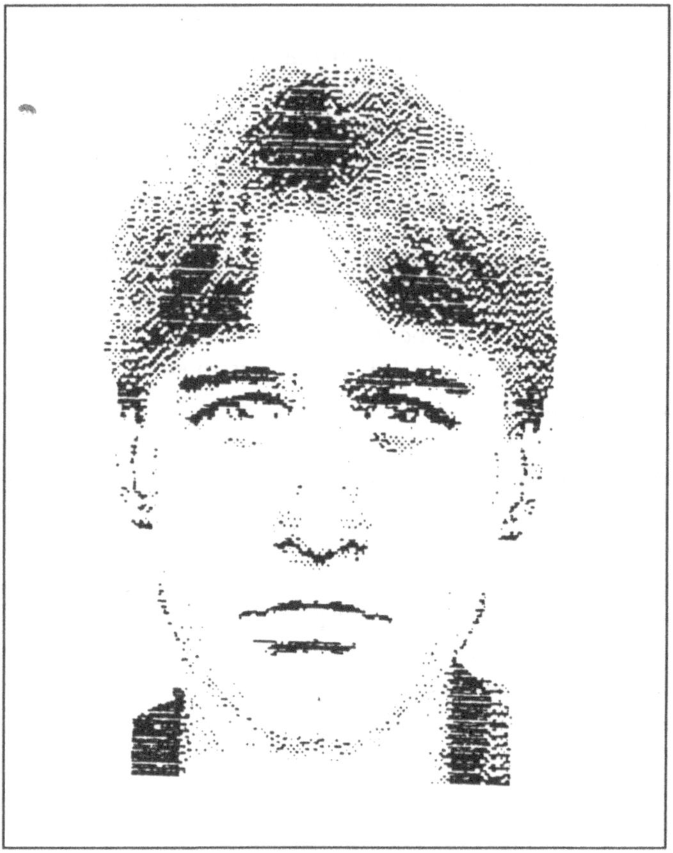

Figure 3.1 Example of Mac-a-Mug Composite Generation System

Interviewing During Facial Composite Production

Studies investigating the usefulness of guided memory retrieval techniques have demonstrated that some retrieval techniques can improve the accuracy of witness-generated composites (Davies and Milne, 1985; Luu and Geiselman, 1993). Davies and Milne (1985) found that subjects who were given a guided memory interview constructed better Photo-Fit composites than did subjects who were asked to spontaneously recall the target face prior to constructing the composite. Luu and Geiselman (1993) found that the CI (original version), when used in conjunction with the Field Identification System (FIS) facial composite generation system, also improved the accuracy of witness-generated composites at least under some conditions.

In the Luu and Geiselman (1993) study, composites were constructed either by adding features one at a time to a developing composite (in the context of a partially-constructed face) or by selecting the features in isolation (not in the context of a partially-constructed face). Presumably the face-context procedure promotes more holistic processing whereas the feature-in-isolation procedure promotes more featural processing. The participants were instructed to construct the composite either by "thinking about the face of the suspect" (Standard) or by using aspects of the CI such as reconstructing the original viewing context, recalling the events in reverse order, changing perspectives, and reporting everything that comes to mind. The results demonstrated that composites made with the CI were significantly better than those made with the Standard Interview in the holistic-processing, condition but not in the featural-processing condition. The authors suggested that the CI enhanced retrieval of the face and that facial images may be processed holistically.

These studies suggest that composite construction may be enhanced by using an appropriate interview strategy in combination with an effective composite-generation system. We therefore combined an interview strategy that has proven to be effective (CI) with a composite production system with some demonstrated potential (Mac-A-Mug Pro).

The CI has been used traditionally with verbal tasks (description) and was therefore revised to be used with the present visual task of composite generation. We revised the CI in two ways. First, based on Schooler and Engstler-Schooler's (1990) findings that verbalization about a stimulus can impair later recognition, the CI was revised to promote more pictorial processing and minimize verbal processing. Second, we encouraged witnesses to search for any trait judgments and/or labels they may have inadvertently made about the target's face at the earlier encoding. Research suggests that such judgments and labels assigned at encoding are helpful at retrieval for recognizing faces (Chance and Goldstein, 1976; McKelvie, 1976; Mueller, Carlomusto and Goldstein, 1978).

The present study assessed which interviewing technique, the current revision of the CI or the standard police interview, would generate better facial composites. The goodness of the composite was evaluated in terms of how similar it was to the actual target and how well one could identify the target while using only the composite as a guide.

Experiment

The participants were 184 male and female undergraduate psychology students from Florida International University: 76 participants constructed facial composites of target people (Phase One) and another 108 participants evaluated these composites (Phase Two).

Before the study began, an experienced Mac-A-Mug Pro operator generated composites of the targets with each target present. These composites were considered the ideal and were used later as the standard to estimate the accuracy of the participants' composites. The study was conducted in two phases. In Phase One, small groups of participants met in a conference room under the guise of participating in another, unrelated experiment. The experimenter (target) spent several minutes instructing the participants about the bogus experiment and made repeated eye contact with each participant. The participants were then dismissed.

Two days later, each participant returned to a different laboratory room and initially did one of four activities. Participants in the Recognition Only condition performed an irrelevant task (not related to describing or constructing a composite of the target); those in the Description condition gave a verbal description of the target; and those in the CI and Standard Interview Composite conditions constructed a facial composite of the target. After this initial activity, all of the participants attempted to identify the target from a sequentially presented target-present or target-absent array containing six photographs.

When constructing the facial composites, participants in the CI group were told that the interview was to be as nonverbal as possible and to concentrate intensely. The participants were encouraged to recreate the context of the earlier experimental session and also to think about the events of that session in both chronological and reverse orders. The participants were then asked to think about when they best saw the target's face. With that image in mind, the participants were asked to think about whether or not the target reminded them of some characteristic type of person (e.g., teacher, plumber). For the remainder of the interview, the participants were asked to close their eyes and to focus in detail on the target's face.

After the participants had this mental image in mind, the interviewer operated the computer and began to construct the facial composite. In the initial stage, the participants were not permitted to view the developing composite; rather, they chose each feature in isolation. The participants chose the features in whatever order they preferred. After all of the features were chosen and the initial composite was completed, the participants examined the composite and indicated whether it needed modification. If the composite was deemed satisfactory, no modifications were made. If modification was necessary, the composite was edited until it was satisfactory.

The standard police interview reflected techniques currently used by various police personnel. This was based on the first author's observation of different police investigators in the Miami area and on field research reported by others (Fisher et al. 1987a; George, 1991). This interview was composed primarily of short-answer and yes-no questions, such as "Which feature would you like to choose next?" There was no attempt to use context reinstatement or guided retrieval. As in the CI, the participants chose the features in the order they preferred. Once all of the features were chosen and the initial composite was completed, the participants examined the composite and indicated whether or not it needed modification. The composites were modified in the same fashion as in the CI condition.

An initial loglinear analysis was conducted to assess the photo array recognition performance of Phase One participants, those people who had actually seen the target. Recognition accuracy was, in general, extremely high: 100% in the Recognition Only condition, 83% in the CI composite condition, 86% in the Standard Interview composite condition, and 81%

in the Description condition. Recognition accuracy was affected only by target presence: accuracy was better when the target was absent than present, $\underline{X}^2(1,\underline{N}=76) = 4.79$, $\underline{p}$ =<.05. The type of task prior to identification (no task, verbal description, CI or Standard Interview composite generation) had no effect on recognition accuracy, $\underline{X}^2(6,\underline{N}=76) = 4.83$, $\underline{p} > .05$.

The composites that were generated by the Phase One participants were evaluated by a different sample of people in Phase Two. One analysis examined the number of features that matched or were common to both the participant's composite and the ideal composite (conducted by an expert with the target in view). The second analysis considered the subjective similarity of the composite to a photograph of the target. In this photograph-comparison method, three people independently rated the composites while viewing a photograph of the appropriate target. They rated on a 1-10 scale how closely the overall composite represented the target in the photograph (1= not a good likeness; 10= good likeness).

The feature-match analysis revealed no effect of the type of interview (CI vs. Standard), all $\underline{X}^2$s ≤ 2.51, $p > .05$. This lack of difference largely reflects a strong floor effect. The number of features that matched the ideal composite was extremely low. Of the 96 composites, 60 had zero matching features, 31 had one match, and 5 had two matches. (The maximum number of possible matching features was 11.)

The analysis of the subjective likeness ratings also revealed no effect of the type of interview (CI vs. Standard), all $\underline{X}^2$s ≤ 6.63, $\underline{p} > .05$. Again the failure to find significant differences probably reflects floor effects. The ratings of almost all of the composites were extremely low: on a 10-point scale, 60% of the ratings were 1's and 24% were 2's.

To assess the utility of the composites and the verbal descriptions, 108 different participants examined one of the composites generated or one of the verbal descriptions given by the Phase One participants and then attempted to identify the target in a photo array. An analysis of these recognition scores revealed that the type of task completed prior to identification (verbal description, CI or Standard Interview composite generation) had no effect on identification accuracy, all $\underline{X}^2$s ≤ 4.86, $\underline{p} > .05$ (see Table 1). Only target presence had an effect: identification accuracy was better when the target was absent than present, $\underline{X}^2(1,\underline{N}=62) = 19.00$, p=<.01. Again, these results may reflect floor-level performance, with only 7% of the target-present participants (although 75% of the target-absent participants) making the correct response.

Table 3.1 Proportion Correct Responses in Phase 2 Using Composites and Descriptions as a Function of Condition and Target-Absent or Target Present Line-up

	Target	
Condition	Absent	Present
Cognitive Composite.	.71(14)	.00(10)
Standard Composite	.80(10)	.08(12)
Description	.72(11)	.20(5)

Note: Frequencies are in parentheses

The results demonstrate that the constructed composites were of poor quality. The component features of the participant-generated composites did not at all match the ideal composite; further, the subjective ratings indicated that the composites were not even remotely similar to a photograph of the target person. Finally, the utility of the composites was very low. When the Phase Two participants used the composites to identify the target from a target-present photo array, they were rarely correct.

Why was photo array identification so poor? Were the composites of low quality or was the photo array task inherently difficult (e.g., because of similar-looking photos)? It appears that the photo array task was not particularly difficult, as the Phase One participants who directly observed the target and identified him from memory, not from the composite were very accurate. Rather, it appears that the composites were of low quality. In fact, the composites were no more valuable than a verbal description of the target.

Conclusion

In our experiment, using the Mac-A-Mug Pro system, the constructed composites were of low quality, and we failed to find an advantage of the CI over the Standard interview. Just the opposite was found by Luu and Geiselman (1993) who used the FIS composite-construction system and found (a) high-quality composites and (b) improved composite production when using the CI. We suspect that the difference between the two systems is responsible for both the difference in quality of the composites and also of the (in)effectiveness of the CI. That is, the composites generated by the Mac-A-Mug Pro system were of such poor quality that they would be of little use no matter what interview was conducted during composite construction.

The results reported here are in contrast to Cutler et al. (1988) in which the composites generated by the Mac-A-Mug Pro were useful for identification. One critical difference between the present study and Cutler et al. is the conditions under which the composites were constructed. In the present study, the witnesses described (a) *from memory* and (b) to another person (computer operator) the characteristics of the target. In Cutler et al. the composites were generated by an experienced operator himself/herself and *while viewing* a photograph of the target.

Other studies using the Mac-A-Mug corroborate the idea that effective composites can be generated only when the target is present. In Experiment 1 of Penrod, Pappas and Bull (1992a) composites generated from memory but *edited with the target's photograph present* were good resemblances of the targets. However, in Experiment 2, composites constructed from memory but *not edited with the photograph present* were not good resemblances of the targets. The resulting composites were not useful for selecting the target from a photograph lineup (see also Penrod, Thill and Bull, 1992b).

The common finding, both across studies and within studies, is that the Mac-A-Mug is capable of generating useful composites when the target is immediately available to the operator of the system; however, when the target is not immediately available so that the source of the composite is the witness's memory, the Mac-A-Mug appears to be incapable of generating useful composites. As the latter condition (composite constructed from witness's memory) is the more likely in a typical eyewitness situation, this bodes poorly for the Mac-A-Mug Pro's utility in real-world investigations.

What accounts for the Mac-A-Mug's ability to construct effective composites when the target is present but not when it is absent, i.e., when it is constructed from memory? One simple explanation is that the memory record of the target's face is less accurate or less detailed than is the actual target itself. That is, the limitation stems from the impoverished information contained in the source of the composite, the memory record of the target. This source-related explanation suggests that effective composites cannot be constructed reliably when the witness relies on his/her memory of the target. There are instances, however, in which effective composites can be generated when the target is not present (Luu and Geiselman, 1993). Apparently, the Mac-A-Mug's inability to construct effective composites when the target is absent cannot be explained either by (a) the composite system (Mac-A-Mug) alone--as the Mac-A-Mug is effective in some instances - or by (b) the memory requirement alone - as effective composites can be constructed from memory when other composite systems are used. It appears that there is something unique about the *combination* of the Mac-A-Mug system and the necessity to construct the composite from memory that gives rise to the poor-quality composites.

We shall examine this interaction between the Mac-A-Mug composite system and the memory requirement and offer a hypothetical explanation of the results. Following this analysis, we shall offer practical suggestions as to how to modify a composite-production system in order to be compatible with the cognitive requirements of constructing a face from memory.

To review, some studies demonstrate the Mac-A-Mug's utility whereas others do not. Penrod et al. (1992a) suggest that the various results can be explained by the Matching Hypothesis. They suggest that when an individual is permitted to view a person or photograph during composite construction or knows that he/she will need to memorize a face for later construction, the individual may study and encode the face in terms of its featural properties. If, at retrieval, featural processing also predominates, then there is a match between the processes used to encode the target's face and those used to retrieve and construct the target's face and the resulting recollection will be accurate. With its format of selecting individual features, the Mac-A-Mug Pro system represents such a featural retrieval task. Therefore, when the processes at both encoding and retrieval match (both are featural) a high quality composite is constructed. In Cutler et al. (1988), recognizable composites were generated when the system operator was permitted to view a photograph of the target during composite construction. Recognizable composites also were generated by witnesses in Penrod et al. (Exp.1, 1992a). These participants were not only aware that they would later need to construct a facial composite of the target from memory but were also given a photograph of the target to look at while making final modifications.

However, the format for everyday facial perception is holistic (Berman, Cutler and Foos, 1991; Wells and Hryciw, 1984). In an everyday situation, then, the featural task of composite generation represents a mismatch between the encoding and retrieval processes and should result in ineffective composites. This appears to characterize the situation in Penrod et al. (Exp. 2, 1992a) in which observers encoded the target face incidentally and then attempted to construct a composite from memory. The resulting composites were not recognizable (see also Penrod et al., 1992b).

The results of the study reported here are also compatible with the matching hypothesis. They reflect the limitation of retrieving a facial image that has been encoded holistically with a composite production system that is based on featural processing. The mismatch between the natural holistic encoding of the target's face and the featural retrieval dictated by the Mac-A-Mug system accounts for the poor quality of the facial composites.

This pattern of results suggests a grim outlook for using composite generation systems in real-life situations. Most actual witnesses probably encode faces holistically rather than featurally, because they are unaware at the time that they will be asked later to reproduce the criminal's face. They do not perceive their immediate task as one of intentional learning in preparation for a later facial composite construction. And most assuredly, they will not have the perpetrator's picture in front of them while constructing the composite. As a result, their mental representation of the assailant's face is likely to reflect mainly its holistic properties. Composite systems that are based primarily on a featural output, such as the Mac-A-Mug Pro system, can then be expected to be ineffective.

The FIS composite system used by Luu and Geiselman (1993), by comparison, did produce effective composites when composite generation emphasized holistic retrieval. These results are promising because they suggest that a composite system that works holistically can help individuals to generate an effective composite after they have encoded a face holistically.

One question that remains is whether the interviewing technique used during composite generation can influence the effectiveness of composites. Luu and Geiselman (1993) found that composites generated with the CI were more effective than composites generated with the Standard Interview when the composites were constructed in a holistic-to-specific fashion. With the CI's focus on the holistic retrieval of facial images, a match may have occurred between the natural, holistic encoding of the face and the holistic retrieval processes in both the interviewing technique and composite construction system. The results of this study suggest that, indeed, using a holistically-based interview can facilitate the quality of the composite constructed, but only when a holistically-based composite construction system is used. We know of only one exception to this rule, which we cannot explain. Davies and Milne (1985) found that a guided interview procedure enhanced facial composites (cf. spontaneous recall) even when a feature-based composite system was used (Photo-Fit). Despite this one exception, the present study and the bulk of the research argue in favor of a more holistic-based composite system.

Recommendations

Our analysis suggests that composite generation systems that promote retrieval of holistic properties will probably be found to have the greatest utility. Furthermore, if a holistically-based composite can be constructed, then principles of the CI should be incorporated into the interview-construction process. Based on these ideas, we offer the following specific suggestions.

(1) Begin the composite construction by recreating the context of the original event, and encouraging the witness to focus on his/her mental image of the target face.

(2) Request the witness to provide an initial description of the target face, concentrating on the holistic properties of the face, e.g., overall face shape, position and size of individual features relative to the whole face. Similarly, encourage the witness to provide subjective comments about the target face (e.g., old, angry, looks like my brother).

(3) Develop a procedure whereby subjective comments can be converted into specific, objective alterations. These may be based on known, normative properties of face type or on idiosyncratic knowledge. For example, old faces may contain age lines or being more pear-shaped. Idiosyncratic descriptions (my brother) can be converted into specific physical properties by follow-up probing: What about the person made him look like your brother? (see Fisher and Geiselman, 1992).

(4) Following this initial description, the witness should indicate any salient features that were particularly distinctive. These should be followed by other features that the witness can easily recall and describe.

(5) A complete starting facial composite should be constructed by the computer from this initial description. The computer can search through its database for those features that best match the witness's description. Features that do not appear in the witness's description are given default values, which will be either the middle value along a given dimension (e.g., medium-size nose) or the modal value. All of these features will be assembled to create the starting face.

(6) All editing of this starting composite should be done within the context of the entire face.

Other suggestions that may increase the effectiveness of the composite system are as follows:

(1) Simplify the system so that it can be manipulated as much as possible by a novice (the witness) without extensive training. The expert operator should serve as the middle man only to implement the more sophisticated components of the system or when the witnesses requests assistance.

(2) All preliminary versions of the composite prior to the final version should be stored temporarily. These preliminary versions can be removed from storage after the final composite is indicated by the witness. This allows witnesses to resurrect earlier-selected features easily, and also minimizes the damage created by glitches in the system that cause it to shut down. This can be particularly devastating with a victim who may be too upset, drained, or frustrated to reconstruct the composite.

Some composite generation systems have recently been developed that do make use of some of these suggestions. As of yet, however, there has been no published research on these systems. Naturally, we encourage others to test these and other suggestions empirically before placing them on the market for consumption.

With the recent development of some holistically-based facial composite systems, such as E-Fit (1993) and FaceKit (1991), future studies might examine some of the more interesting theoretical approaches to face recollection. For example, the Matching Hypothesis can be examined by manipulating featural and holistic processes at encoding and retrieval. Similarly, we might test the verbal-overwriting hypothesis, that the pictorial representation of the face is converted to a more verbal code (Schooler and Engstler-Schooler, 1990). If the overwriting hypothesis is supported, a face that had been previously described verbally might be better constructed by a featural composite system whereas a face that had only been seen might be better constructed by a holistic composite system.

Finally, we might examine how variations in face types affect the mental representation and the preferred method of construction. That is, whereas the typical face may be represented primarily in terms of its holistic properties, faces with more distinctive individual features may be better represented in terms of specific features. If so, some faces may be better constructed with a featural composite system and other faces better constructed with a holistic system.

The utility of interviewing strategies during composite construction should also be further assessed. Our expectation is that the utility of the interview strategy will depend upon the specific composite system that is being used. Interviewing strategies that are successful with one composite system will need to be modified by the structural constraints of another system. Similarly, the utility of an interviewing strategy may vary across different types of face. For example, a featurally-distinctive face may be better described when questions focus on specific features, whereas a more typical face may be better described from a more holistically-oriented interviewing strategy. One may wish to examine this issue by examining the utility of a preliminary question that probes whether the target face is better described in terms of holistic properties or in terms of one or two salient features.

We end this chapter with two research suggestions to improve the ecological validity of research on facial composites. We believe that many studies, including our own, err by asking judges to evaluate composites by comparing them to people they do *not* know. For instance, in Cutler et al. (1988) judges evaluated a composite by searching through a photo array of unfamiliar faces; in Laughery and Fowler (1980) judges rated the composites against photographs of unfamiliar faces; and in Ellis, et al. (1975) judges rated the composites against faces randomly constructed by the composite system. In real police investigations, however, composites are most useful when the police officer who looks at a composite knows the target. The composite may be similar to, and therefore remind the police officer of, someone he/she knows from previous encounters. Alternatively, the composite may appear so different from a known suspect that it excludes the suspect from the investigation. Rarely can a police officer make use of a composite when he or she is unfamiliar with the suspect. We suggest therefore that, in laboratory experiments, judges be asked to evaluate the composites by comparing them against people whom they are familiar with, not against people whom they do not know. For example, judges might be asked to indicate which of several famous personalities (entertainers, political figures) is depicted in the composite.

Finally, when facial composites are used in a police investigation, they typically accompany a verbal description. The verbal description may refer to the criminal's physical attributes or other relevant aspects of the crime. The value of the facial composite then is the degree to which it enhances the investigation *beyond that of using only the verbal description*, not whether the facial composite, by itself, can lead to an identification. We believe that many laboratory tests, again including our own, err by asking judges to evaluate the facial composite in isolation. Demonstrating that facial composites, by themselves, can lead to a correct identification may be of theoretical value. If we wish to apply laboratory results to police investigations, however, the critical comparison should be between a verbal description only and a verbal-description-plus-composite.

References

Anderson, R.C. and Pichert, J.W. (1978). Recall of previously unrecallable information following a shift in perspective. *Journal of Verbal Learning and Verbal Behavior*, 17, 1-12.

Aspley Limited. (1993). *E-Fit.* Aspley Limited, United Kingdom.

Bekerian, D.A. and Dennett, J.L. (1993). The Cognitive Interview. Reviving the issues. *Applied Cognitive Psychology*, 7, 275-298.

Berman, G. L., Cutler, B. L., and Foos, P. W. (1991). Attempts to improve face recognition accuracy by inducing holistic processing at retrieval. In D. F. Ross and M. P. Toglia (Chairs), *Current trends in research on adult eyewitness memory and identification accuracy. Symposium conducted at the meeting of the American Psychological Society,* Washington, D.C.

Chance, J. E., and Goldstein, A. G. (1976). Recognition of faces and verbal labels. *Bulletin of the Psychonomic Society*, 7, 384-386.

Christie, D. F. M. and Ellis, H. D. (1981). Photofit constructions versus verbal descriptions of faces. *Journal of Applied Psychology*, 66, 358-363.

Cutler, B. L., Stocklein, C J. and Penrod, S.D. (1988). Empirical examination of a computerized facial composite production system. *Forensic Reports*, 1, 207-218.

Davies, G. and Milne, A. (1985). Eyewitness composite production: a function of mental or physical reinstatement of context. *Criminal Justice and Behavior*, 12, 209-220.

Davies, G., Ellis, H. and Shepherd, J. (1978). Face recognition accuracy as a function of mode of representation. *Journal of Applied Psychology*, 63, 180-187.

Davies, G., Milne, A. and Shepherd, J. (1983). Searching for operator skills in face composite reproduction. *Journal of Police Science and Administration*, 11, 405-409.

Duggal, S., Mickus, L., Daneker, E. and Kassin, S. (1992). *Computerized facial composites and eyewitness recognition.* Poster presented at the Eastern Psychological Association, Boston. Williams College.

Ellis, H. D. (1986). Face recall: A psychological perspective. *Human Learning*, 5, 189-196.

Ellis, H. D., Davies, G. M. and Shepherd, J.W.(1978). A critical examination of the Photofit technique for recalling faces. *Ergonomics*, 21, 297-307.

Ellis, H. D., Shepherd, J. and Davies, G. (1975). An investigation of the use of the Photofit technique for recalling faces. *British Journal of Psychology*, 66, 29-37.

Fisher, R. P. and Geiselman, R. E. (1992). *Memory Enhancing Techniques for Investigative Interviewing: The Cognitive Interview*. Springfield, Ill: Charles C. Thomas.

Fisher, R. P., Geiselman, R. E. and Amador, M. (1989). Field test of the cognitive interview: Enhancing the recollection of actual victims and witnesses of crime .*Journal of Applied Psychology*, 74, 1-6.

Fisher, R. P., Geiselman, R. E. and Raymond, D. S. (1987a). Critical analysis of police interview techniques. *Journal of Police Science and Administration*, 15, 177-185.

Fisher, R. P., McCauley, M. R. and Geiselman, R. E. (1994). Improving eyewitness testimony with the cognitive interview. In D. Ross, J. D. Read and M. Toglia (eds.), *Adult eyewitness testimony: Current Trends and developments*. London: Cambridge University Press.

Fisher, R. P., Geiselman, R. E., Raymond, D. S., Jurkevich, L. M. and Warhaftig, M. L. (1987b). Enhancing enhanced eyewitness memory: Refining the cognitive interview. *Journal of Police Science and Administration*, 15, 291-297.

Geiselman, R. E., Fisher, R. P., MacKinnon, D. P., and Holland, H. L. (1985). Eyewitness memory enhancement in the police interview: Cognitive retrieval mnemonics versus hypnosis. *Journal of Applied Psychology*, 70, 401-412.

Geiselman, R. E., Fisher, R. P., MacKinnon, D. P. and Holland, H. L. (1986). Enhancement of eyewitness memory with the cognitive interview. *American Journal of Psychology*, 99, 385-401.

Geiselman, R. E., Fisher, R. P., Firstenberg, E., Hutton, L. A., Sullivan, S. J., Avetissian, I. V. and Prosk, A. L. (1984).Enhancement of eyewitness memory: An empirical evaluation of the cognitive interview. *Journal of Police Science and Administration*, 12, 130-138.

George, R. (1991). *A field and experimental evaluation of three methods of interviewing witnesses/victims of crime*. Unpublished manuscript. Polytechnic of East London, London.

InfoTec. (1991). *FaceKit*. InfoTec, Virginia.

Kohnken, G., Milne, R., Memon, A. and Bull, R. (1992). *A meta-analysis on the effects of the cognitive interview*. Paper presented at the European Conference of Psychology and Law. Oxford, England.

Laughery, K. R. and Fowler, R. H. (1980). Sketch artist and Identi-kit procedures for recalling faces. *Journal of Applied Psychology*, 65, 307-316.

Luu, T. N. and Geiselman, R. E. (1993). Cognitive retrieval techniques and order of feature construction in the formation of composite facial images. *Journal of Police and Criminal Psychology*, 9, 34-39.

Mauldin, M.A. and Laughery, K.R. (1981). Composite production effects on subsequent facial recognition. *Journal of Applied Psychology*, 66, 351-357.

McKelvie, S. J. (1976). The effects of verbal labeling on recognition memory for schematic faces. *Quarterly Journal of Experimental Psychology*, 28, 459-474.

Mueller, J. H., Carlomusto, M., and Goldstein, A. G. (1978). Orienting task and study time in facial recognition. *Bulletin of the Psychonomic Society*, 11, 313-316.

Penrod, S., Pappas, C. and Bull, M. (1992a). *Preparation and recognition of known targets using the Mac-A-Mug Pro composite production system*. Unpublished manuscript, University of Minnesota.

Penrod, S. and Stocklein, J. (1992). *Assessing the impact of production methods on the recognizability of computer-generated facial composites* Unpublished manuscript, University of Minnesota.

Penrod, S., Thill, D. L. and Bull, M. (1992b). *Identification of facial composites from a sequentially presented photographic lineup*. Unpublished manuscript, University of Minnesota.

Philips. (1992). *CD-Fit*. Philips Interactive Media Systems, United Kingdom.

Schooler, J. W. and Engstler-Schooler, T. Y. (1990). Verbal overshadowing of visual memories: Some things are better left unsaid. *Cognitive Psychology*, 22, 36-71.

Shaherazam (1986). *The Mac-A-Mug Pro Manual*. Milwaukee, Wisconsin: Shaherazam.

Tulving, E. and Thomson, D. M. (1973). Encoding specificity and retrieval processes in episodic memory. *Psychological Review*, 80, 352-373.

Visatex Corporation. (1991). *Compusketch*. California: Campbell.

Wells, G. L. and Hryciw, B. (1984). Memory for faces: Encoding and retrieval operations. *Memory and Cognition*, 12, 338-344.

Author Notes

This chapter is based on Christine Koehn's Master's Thesis research (Florida International University).

We would like to thank Mr. Peter Bennett for his helpful comments on using facial composites in police investigation.

4 British and American Interrogation Strategies

LYDIA SEAR AND TOM WILLIAMSON

Although the American criminal justice system is based on English law, the interrogation methods of British and American police are vastly different. Since the introduction of the Police and Criminal Evidence Act 1984 (PACE) and following the shock of a number of miscarriages of justice, police forces in England and Wales have developed a new ethos of "open-mindedness" in police interrogations. Officers are trained to adopt a neutral position to facilitate the gathering of accurate and reliable information. However, the change from an inherent confession-driven police culture to one of a "search for the truth" has proved difficult as officers are still expected to function within an adversarial system.

In stark contract American police are trained to use sophisticated psychologically-manipulative techniques such as trickery and deceit in order to induce confessions. These techniques are sanctioned by the courts with the belief that the safeguard of "due process" of the criminal justice system will deflect any possibility of a miscarriage of justice. However, it may only be a matter of time before America is forced, from the aftermath of a major shock to their judicial system, to review their existing investigative framework and to adopt a more neutral "search for the truth" ethos similar to that provided by PACE.

Lydia Sear completed her degree at the University of Kent, Canterbury in 1996, having spent one year in the USA undertaking research on the interrogation of American police. Other published research investigates the personality characteristics and interviewing skills of British police officers. Lydia is presently training in Forensic Psychology and is

*Offender Profiling Series: I - **Interviewing and Deception***
Edited by D. Canter and L. Alison. © 1999 Ashgate Publishing, Aldershot. pp 65-81

continuing her postgraduate research into various issues of police interviewing.

Tom Williamson completed his Honours Degree in Psychology at York University in 1982. In 1992 he was awarded a Ph.D. for his research into Police Interrogation. He is the Deputy Chief Constable of the Nottinghamshire Police. He chairs the Behavioural Science Committee of the Association of Police Officers. Tom is a Visiting Professor of Criminal Justice at the Institute of Police and Criminological Studies, University of Portsmouth.

4 British and American Interrogation Strategies

LYDIA SEAR AND TOM WILLIAMSON

The interviewing of suspects is regarded by most police officers as a critical stage in criminal investigation (Baldwin, 1994), yet a confession obtained as a result of coercive police interrogation practices is likely to be inherently unreliable.

There is no doubt that being interrogated by the police is a coercive situation (Irving, 1980), and can be highly stressful, presenting possible psychological problems for interviewees. In 1980 Irving and Hilgendorf described the police interview as a 'closed social interaction':

> *The room is closed, the participants close to each other, interruptions are avoided as far as possible, and in keeping with the general character of the interaction, that is of a person in control .... suspects are discouraged from initiating conversation, asking questions, answering back ordemonstrating any kind of outright rejection of the interviewing officer's authority....*

This situation has been ameliorated recently in the United Kingdom where legislation has resulted in defence lawyers being present in up to 80% of interviews and the record of the interview being kept on an audio or video tape with a copy being provided to the suspect or the suspect's lawyer. Although American criminal justice is based on English law, the police methods of interrogation of the two countries are now starkly different. Since the introduction of the Police and Criminal Evidence Act 1984, and as a result of miscarriages of justice that have come to light since, police forces in England and Wales have developed a new ethos. Interrogation is now defined as a 'search for the truth' with the emphasis on the 'open-mindedness' of police officers whilst conducting interrogations. In contrast, American police are trained to use manipulative techniques with the prime objective of obtaining confessions, which are sanctioned by the judiciary. This chapter compares these differing styles of police interrogation and explains the principles and rationales behind them.

Police Interrogation in England and Wales

The Police and Criminal Evidence Act (PACE) and its Codes of Conduct were introduced in 1984 (revised April 1995) to regulate practice in respect of the detention, treatment and questioning of persons by police officers (Code C), including compulsory audio taping of all police interviews to eliminate allegations of fabrication of evidence. They prohibit the use of oppression to obtain a statement or confession, defining it as 'torture, inhuman or degrading treatment, and the use of threat or violence'. However, what they fail to define is that 'oppression' may be induced 'implicitly' through the very nature of the interrogation and the expectancies of the interrogating officer. The mere authority of the police, the isolation of the individual, and the uncertainty and anxiety surrounding the interrogation 'situation', may ultimately lead to false confessions (Gudjonsson and Clark, 1986).

The British judiciary has now finally come to accept the risk of false confession occurring under certain circumstances (Gudjonsson, 1993), and are more aware that some police tactics can result in unreliable statements being obtained, including false confession. Examples of police behaviour resulting in unreliable confession statements are the circumstances surrounding the cases of the 'Guildford Four' and the 'Birmingham Six', where the emphasis was on police impropriety as well as on the psychological vulnerabilities of the appellants (Gudjonsson, 1992). The case of the 'Tottenham Three' made the courts recognise the role of psychological factors in producing unreliable confession evidence particularly in the case of juvenile suspects or those who are vulnerable e.g. through low IQ or learning difficulties.

In the light of these factors, a Home Office Circular 22/1992, followed by another, 7/1993, introduced a new training package for basic interviewing skills. The principles of 'investigative interviewing' were to provide an ethical foundation for the police in questioning suspects. They were to ensure that what was said during police questioning was said freely and recorded accurately. Officers adopting oppressive questioning styles would not only be out of step with nationally agreed guidelines on questioning but would find judges adopting a more robust position with regard to admitting confession evidence than was the case in the past. Judges would also be paying particular attention to confessions from those whom expert psychologists could show were likely to be unreliable (Gudjonsson, 1992).

Rules governing the acceptance of confession evidence in England and Wales were first drawn up in the 19th Century and were known as the 'Judges Rules' and they held that in order to be accepted a confession had to be 'voluntary'. In Section 76(2) of PACE, 'voluntariness' has been replaced by the concept of 'reliability', which means that confessions are excluded when it can be shown that they were obtained by such means or in conditions which are likely to render them unreliable, but the burden of proof lies with the prosecution.

Inherent psychological factors, such as a suspect's disturbed mental state or learning disability, are particularly relevant to inadmissibility under Section 78 and may cause a judge to consider a confession from such a person to be 'unreliable' and therefore in the circumstances of the case, not to allow the confession evidence to go to the jury (Gudjonsson, 1993).

Code C of the Codes of Practice offer important provisions for interviewing 'special groups' such as juveniles, and persons who are mentally disordered or handicapped (Home Office, 1991). The legal provision is the presence of an 'appropriate adult', a responsible adult called in by the police to offer special assistance to the detainee, who can be a relative of the detainee, or a professional person such as a social worker. The role of the appropriate adult is to advise the person being questioned and to observe whether or not the interview is being conducted properly and fairly, and secondly, to facilitate communication with the person being interviewed (Home Office, 1991).

The pressure for change has built up slowly over recent years. The transition from coercive questioning practices to a new ethos of 'searching for the truth' has been difficult for some police, as was shown in the *Heron* case (1994), where Mr Justice Mitchell found the interviewing officers had deceived the suspect regarding identification evidence and had engaged in repetitive verbal pounding alleging the certainty of the defendant's guilt. Sear (1996) in a study on police personalities and interviewing behaviour found that 'openness' is an important factor for successful interviewing, but one which police officers find difficult to put into effect. 'Openness' may be at odds with the very adversarial nature of the criminal law and the police culture that operates within it, as research has confirmed a gap between police training and its practical implementation. Supervisors have blamed 'cultural' issues as a barrier to effective implementation of supervising their officers' interviewing performance, suggesting that quality is not highly rated as a performance indicator, and is an issue 'only when something goes wrong' (Stockdale, 1993). Some senior police managers feel that the 'new agenda' of neutrality is seen as a sign of weakness, in direct conflict with a police culture based on 'tradition' and 'discipline' and a macho image (Stephens and Becker, 1994).

During the 1980s the police service was heavily influenced by American approaches to questioning, which in turn probably reflected the lack of any suitable indigenous training material (Williamson, 1994). The model of interviewing described by Inbau, Reid and Buckley (1986) was particularly influential with its emphasis on persuasive questioning techniques including misrepresenting the strength of the evidence in order to obtain a confession. Decisions by English courts made such training untenable and have consistently nipped such practices in the bud. For example, in the case of *R v Mason* (1988) 86 Cr App R 349, the Court of Appeal held that evidence was not acceptable where an officer had lied that the suspect's fingerprints had been found. This is in stark contrast to decisions in American courts which actively support and legitimise a doctrine of deception as a means of gaining evidence or confessions through police questioning (Leo, 1992).

The Principles of 'Investigative Interviewing'

The new ethical framework on which the national training programme in investigative interviewing is based has not been widely understood (Williamson, 1994). The first principle is intended to shift the police service from its traditional prosecution orientation and to encourage it to see its task as a search for the truth. This is a departure from the traditional adversarial nature of police investigative encounters and an adoption of a more neutral position as gatherers of accurate and reliable information from suspects, witnesses or victims. However, although this was accepted by the Royal Commission on Criminal Justice, they were not prepared to alter significantly the accusatorial nature of our system of justice and make it more of an inquiry for the truth. That is, the police may aspire to be independent seekers of truth, but they must continue to work within an accusatorial framework. In an adversarial system, the inquisitorial function is conducted only by the police. Many miscarriages of justice have arisen from an unduly adversarial and partisan position adopted by the police (Williamson, 1994).

The second principle is intended to encourage officers to approach an investigation with an open mind instead of their focus on 'interrogation' of suspects. Information obtained is to be tested against what the officer already knew or could establish. Research studies indicated that a more successful approach to interviewing of suspects would be based on more thorough interviewing of victims and witnesses (Baldwin, 1992). It was recognised that good evidence was going to take time, which was in marked contrast to the expediency of contemporary interviewing practice. Research has also shown that confession is closely correlated with the strength of the evidence in the case which should encourage a switch of strategy away from focusing on a confession and towards obtaining more information from victims and witnesses (Moston, Stephenson and Williamson, 1990).

The third principle is intended to encourage officers to be fair placing policing in an ethical framework.

The principles of 'investigative interviewing' are designed to help police officers in any subsequent judicial proceedings where their actions are being examined to show that they had behaved 'fairly'. They also underline the importance of recognising the difficulties of those with special needs, including those with low IQs, learning difficulties and others who may be at risk and liable to make false confessions.

However, there is still no agreed procedure for identifying people who may be at risk. The onus of identifying when an 'appropriate adult' is required lies with the police, who are also responsible for finding a suitable person to act in this capacity. Most commonly, the police will ask a relative to act as an appropriate adult, particularly in the case of juveniles (Gudjonsson, 1993). Studies indicate that there may be serious difficulties involved in identifying, by behavioural observation alone, persons with a mental handicap prior to their being interviewed by the police, and there is strong evidence to indicate that offenders typically have IQs that fall well below the normal population mean of 100 (Eysenck and Gudjonsson, 1989). This highlights the fact that the police are commonly interviewing persons of low IQ that are not immediately apparent to the police.

Training

A new training programme which addresses each of these issues has been implemented following Home Office Circulars 22/1992 and 7/1993, and training materials have been developed to create a learning culture where interviewers are continually learning from their experience. However, at present, despite every interview being tape-recorded, monitoring of interviews is not generally carried out, either by the police hierarchy and supervisors, or other members of the judiciary. Janet Stockdale (1993) states in her report for the Royal Commission on the state of police interviewing, that supervisors were reluctant to 'check up' on their officers, and the quality of interviewing was not of prime importance, 'except if anything goes wrong'.

Police Interrogations in America

In stark contrast to the legal system in England, deception is considered by the American police, and the courts also, to be a natural part of detecting. The detective deceives in order to establish grounds for convicting and punishing. The detecting process is informed and controlled by notions of fairness and dignity, but these notions are often unclear both in outcome and justification. The law in America almost always supports police deception (Skolnick, 1982), but they often work within a contradictory system which demands certain kinds of fidelities and insists upon other kinds of betrayals. For instance, the law permits the detective to pose as a consumer or purveyor of vice, but does not allow him to employ ruses to gain entry without a search warrant.

American police are permitted by the courts to engage in trickery and deception and are trained to do so by the police organisation. The philosophy is that the criminals do not have the monopoly on lying. Like has to be used with like. Detectives, for example are trained to use informers or to act themselves as informers or agent provocateurs when the criminal activity under investigation involves possession or sale of drugs.

The line between acceptable and unacceptable deception is 'entrapment' in American law, the definition of which is hazy and unclear (Leo, 1992). A subjective approach focuses on whether the person would have been predisposed to committing the crime, even without the participation of the agent. An objective approach focuses on the 'conscience of the community'. However, both legal tests of entrapment - objective and subjective - permit police to employ a vast amount of routine deception. Judicial acceptance of deception in the investigation process enhances moral acceptance of deception by detectives in the interrogatory and testimonial stages of criminal investigation, and therefore increases the probability of its occurrence (Skolnick, 1982).

Interrogation Training

The training of interviewing and interrogation techniques of American police is generally carried out by outside commercial training organisations, such as The Reid School of Interviewing and Interrogation, an independent organisation founded by John E. Reid, an ex-police officer, who, according to the company sales literature, offer '*a systematic, common-sense approach to a successful interrogation through extensive research and practical experience over the past 50 years*'. The focus of the training is based on the use of manipulative methods. The use of trickery and deceit by interviewers is at its core, with the emphasis on obtaining confessions its main goal. As the training book states:

> *The vast majority of criminal offenders are reluctant to confess and must be psychologically persuaded to do so, and unavoidably by interrogation procedures involving elements of trickery or deceit. The legality of such procedures is well established.*
>
> (Inbau, Reid and Buckley, 1986)

Police officers and other members of the judicial system in the United States, viewed trickery and deceit as an acceptable, and indeed, a necessary part of the interrogation; a view which is reinforced by the decisions of many court cases. In one leading case, *Frazier v Cupp,* 394

(1969), a conviction based in part on a confession obtained by the use of a 'substantial piece of trickery and deceit' was upheld by the U.S. Supreme Court. The defendant, whilst under interrogation as a murder suspect, was told falsely that a suspected accomplice had confessed. The court stated that although the misrepresentation about the accomplice's confession had been relevant, it had not rendered the otherwise voluntary confession inadmissible as evidence. The court then stated that cases of this nature were to be decided upon in 'the totality of the circumstances'. This decision has subsequently been used to ratify the use of trickery and deceit in criminal investigations by the entire USA

In addition to the leading case of *Frazier v Cupp,* many other cases, state and federal, have upheld the legal validity of trickery and deceit in the interrogation process. They include decisions legitimising lying by saying that fingerprints have been found when this is untrue, placing blame upon and condemning the victim, lying to a murder suspect that the victim was still alive, and other similar tactics. This judicial precedent has, however, been contested at certain times. For example, in *People v Payton, 1984* the appellate court stated that 'a suspect grossly and intentionally misled as to the amount and strength of the evidence against him might well be induced to confess as a direct result of those misrepresentations'. However, in reply, Judge Steigmann of the sixth judicial circuit, attacked this line of thinking, suggesting that the end justifies the means, by stating:

> *If the defendant believes the police representations to be true, how logically can it matter whether those representations were true or not when a court determines whether the defendant's admissions were voluntarily made?*
>
> (Inbau, Reid and Buckley, 1986)

However, the use of trickery and deceit is not without its qualifications, with the Supreme Court stipulating that their use by investigators 'must not be of such a nature as to 'shock' the conscience of the court or community, for instance where an interrogator misrepresents himself as a defence attorney to procure a confession. Nor can it be of the type that is apt to 'induce a false confession'. Here, however, the decision for the latter qualification is a purely subjective one of the investigating officer, the sole criteria of which is to ask himself :'*Is what I am about to do or say apt to make an innocent person confess?'*.

Detectives are trained to build a rapport with suspects in order to lower their anxiety levels. They are advised that the goal of an interview is either *investigative* (e.g. establishing a suspect's alibi) or *behavioural,* (non-verbal and verbal reactions of the suspect). Investigative information primarily represents physical or circumstantial evidence which establishes the facts used to identify the guilty suspect; behavioural information is elicited solely to determine whether or not the person being interviewed is telling the truth. To understand the concepts of these guidelines, investigators are taught how to understand the *psychological dynamics* of an interrogation, but 'following the letter of the law and the intent of the law'. As the Reid training manual (Inbau, Reid and Buckley, 1986) states:

> *We will say or do nothing that would cause an innocent person to confess to something they did not do.*

Officers are told that they must become 'skilled actors' in an interrogation situation, and to use their skills to influence the behaviour of the suspect *physically, mentally,* and *emotionally.* They are taught how to 'read' the suspect to determine if he is truthful or deceptive, if the interrogation is going to be easy or difficult, and where the interrogation process is at any time. Among the techniques taught are the following:

'Justification' Theme Development

The principle is to present 'moral justification' for the suspect's criminal behaviour. It is a monologue presented by the interrogator in which he offers reasons and excuses that will serve to psychologically (not legally) justify, or minimise, the moral seriousness of the suspect's criminal behaviour. The idea behind this is that it will save the suspect's 'self-respect', allowing them to put the blame onto someone or something else. For example:

Robbery:	Blame the victim - 'He was asking for it. Why was he walking there at 4 am?'
Theft:	The company is rich; stealing to support family;
Rape:	Slam female sex; blame victim.

Officers are advised not to give the suspect any time to deny the charge, that is, he must continue with a monologue of the theme, thereby weakening the suspect's denials. They are told that an innocent suspect *never* moves past the denial stage, but remains steadfast in the assertion of his innocence. 'Justification' also involves 'feigning understanding' of sex crimes, using themes such as:

'I would have done the same thing...... '.
'Her mother dresses her in those little tiny pants, deliberately turning you on.... '

in order to elicit an admission. Obviously, the officers are asked to say things that may be against their personal moralistic thinking, but they are told that although it is difficult, the end justifies the means.

'Minimisation' Theme Development

This provides a face saving circumstance for the crime, but must appear credible to the suspect for him to accept it. For example:

'This was the first time, wasn't it?'
'She led you on originally, didn't she?'

In essence, the officers are making it 'psychologically easy' for the suspect to confess to the crime.

Training emphasises using the anxiety levels of the suspect to the interrogator's best advantage. That is, to maximise the suspect's internal anxiety associated with the deception, and to decrease the suspect's perception of the consequences of an admission or confession. This could include sympathetic phrases from the interrogator such as:

'You'll feel better if you just tell me..... '
'If she wasn't dressed in that slinky little blouse and mini skirt this would never have happened'.

The philosophy behind this psychological concept is that the suspect will reduce his 'perception' of his culpability, and therefore, by making an admission he can reduce his anxiety level.

However, there is a frightening naiveté about the conceptual thinking behind these psychological techniques. The police consider that the methods they use are within the framework of the law, which, of course, is correct. They consider them as using 'sales psychology', paving the way for suspects to confess because they feel it is their best course of action, based on compassion and understanding.

A paradox to the sanctioning of these techniques by the judicial system is that in most States the recording of interrogations is not normally carried out, because of the fact that defence lawyers may use the tape to demonstrate to the jury just what transpires in an interrogation. That is, the public might not understand the psychological concepts behind the techniques. Final statements of interrogations contain only the admission, if any, not what transpired to obtain it.

The American police are convinced of the effectiveness of this style of interrogation, and this is exacerbated because the judicial system makes little, if any, provisions for mentally handicapped, or mentally subnormal individuals during interrogation. In a cross-cultural study in England and the U.S. Sear (1995) found that in the U.S. there were no guidelines, statutory or supervisory, for interviewing such persons, and an appropriate adult is only required to accompany a child who is less than twelve years old. In one interrogation she observed a male of 29 with a mental age of about 14 being 'convinced' by the detective that he had committed rape, by suggesting that if he did not confess, the judge would lock him up and throw away the key! (Sear, 1995).

Due Process

America's answer to the possibility of a miscarriage of justice through the use of deceptive techniques by the police is 'due process', a belief that at some stage in the justice system, any mistakes will be discovered. A primary part of 'due process' of the criminal justice system in America is *corpus delicti*. That is, a confession must be accompanied by corroborating evidence, although this merely has to be 'circumstantial'. In England, this is not the case, a person may go to prison on a confession-basis only, although the judge should give a strong warning to the jury that care is needed before convicting on the basis of confession alone (Uglow, 1995).

American defence attorneys will often try to suppress confessions as being obtained by 'coercive measures'. In Federal courts this takes place in a 'suppression hearing' where defence will try to suppress evidence, including a confession being obtained because of improper police activity. During these pre-trial motions, the defence attorney usually bears the burden of proving that the confession was coerced. However, most judges appear to accept the veracity of police officers statements, and the interrogation techniques used are known and accepted by the judicial system (Underwager and Wakefield, 1992).

In spite of the inherent acceptance by the legal system of the interrogation techniques used by American police officers there is a struggle in confessions law between the protection of constitutionally-based individual rights and the facilitation of effective law enforcement. The problem is that the courts have not agreed upon a single, uniformly applied definition of the term 'coercion'. Police trickery, while relevant to a finding of coercion, is not unconstitutional in, and of, itself (Sasaki, 1988). The decision is based upon an individual's own 'perspective' of that system of justice. Interrogators are counselled to separate permissible interrogation tactics from impermissible ones by asking themselves: '*Is what I am about to do, or say, apt to make an innocent person confess?*' (Inbau, Reid and Buckley, 1986). Given the prevailing ignorance and lack of concern regarding false confessions the answer to the question is rhetorical. This is a long way from the opinion of the late Chief Justice Earl Warren, from whose court came the Miranda decision (*Miranda v Arizona, 1966)*:

> *The abhorrence of society to the use of involuntary confessions does not turn alone on their inherent untrustworthiness. It also turns on the deep-rooted feeling that the police must obey the law while enforcing the law; that in the end life and liberty can be as much endangered from illegal methods used to convict those thought to be criminals as from the actual criminals themselves.*

Despite the rhetoric, Supreme Court decisions on confessions have continually failed to condemn police trickery (Sasaki, 1988). Nevertheless, false confessions are known to exist, although little recognition is made of them (Skolnick and Leo, 1992). A study in 1986 of wrongful conviction in felony cases, conservatively estimated that nearly 6,000 false confessions occur every year in the United States (Huff, Rattner and Sagarin, 1986). However, the American police alone cannot be held responsible for the use of the coercive and manipulative techniques in interrogation when there is no overt opposition from the judiciary. Driven by their caseloads, and from the 'successes' confessions bring, officers view their methods as indispensable investigative tools and do not question their efficacy or ethicacy. Like their counterparts in England and Wales it is a part of a shared police culture.

Conclusion

Investigative interviewing in England and Wales shows how new processes may be developed but that they require an enormous shift in police culture away from the over-reliance on confession evidence required by common law adversarial systems of justice. Hammer (1993) argues that some shock or major threat must be present to precipitate the shift of culture and systems which is required to re-engineer whole processes. In the UK these were achieved by a series of Court of Appeal decisions and a tight regulatory framework brought about by two Royal Commissions of Inquiry. As a result it is clear that the American and British police interrogation techniques are now vastly different. It may only be a matter of time before similar shocks hit the American criminal justice system, bringing with it the recognition of the need to change the ethos of investigations from an over-reliance on confession evidence into a clear 'search for the truth' within a legal framework similar to those which the provisions in PACE offer.

References

Baldwin, J. (1992). *Video Taping Police Interviews with Suspects: An Evaluation.* Police Research Series Paper 1. London: H.O. Police Research Group. Home Office.

Baldwin, J. (1994). Police Interrogations: What Are the Rules of the Game? In D. Morgan and G. Stephenson (eds) *Suspicion and Silence: The Right to Silence in Criminal Investigations.* London: Blackstone.

Birch, D. (1989). The PACE hots up: confessions and confusions under the 1984 Act. *Criminal Law Review.* 95-116.

Eysenck, H.J. and Gudjonsson, G.H. (1989). *The Causes and Cures of Criminality.* NY: Plenum Press.

Gudjonsson, G.H. (1992). *The Psychology of Interrogations, Confessions and Testimony.* Chichester: Wiley.

Gudjonsson, G.H. (1993). Confession evidence, psychological vulnerability and expert testimony. *Journal of Community and Applied Social Psychology,* 3, 117-129.

Gudjonsson, G.H. and Adlam, K.R.C. (1983). Personality Patterns of British Police Officers. *Personality and Individual Differences,* 4 (5), 507-512.

Gudjonsson, G.H. and Clark, N.K. (1986). Suggestibility in Police Interrogation: A Social Psychological Model. *Social Behaviour,* 1, 83-104.

Hammer, M. (1993). *Reengineering the Corporation* London: Harper Collins Publishers.

Home Office (1985a). *Police and Criminal Evidence Act 1984.* London: HMSO.

Home Office (1991). *Police and Criminal Evidence Act 1984 (s.66). Codes of Practice.* London: HMSO.

Home Office (1995). *Police and Criminal Evidence Act 1984.* (s.60(1)(a) and s.66) Codes of Practice, Revised.

Huff, Rattner and Sagarin (1986). Guilty until proven innocent: wrongful conviction and public policy. *Crime and Delinquency,* 32, 518-544.

Inbau, F.E., Reid, J.E. and Buckley, J.P. (1986). *Criminal Interrogation and Confessions,* 3rd ed. Baltimore, MD: Williams and Wilkins.

Irving, B. (1980). Police Interrogation. *A Case Study of Current Practice.* Research Studies No.2. London: HMSO.

Irving B. and Hilgendorf, L. (1980). *Police Interrogation: The Psychological Approach.* Research Studies No.1. London: HMSO.

Leo, R.A. (1992). From coercion to deception: the changing nature of police interrogation in America. *Crime, Law and Social Change,* 18, 35-59.

Moston, S., Stephenson, G.M. and Williamson, T.M. (1990). *The effects of case characteristics on suspect behaviour.* Paper presented at the British Psychological Society Annual Conference, Swansea University, April 5th.

Neubauer, D. (1992). *America's Courts and the Criminal Justice System.* 4th ed. Belmont: Wadsworth Publishing Company.

Royal Commission on Criminal Justice (1993) *Report Cmnd 2263.* London: HMSO.

Sasaki, D.W. (1988). Guarding the guardians: Police trickery and confessions. *Stanford Law Review,* 40, 1593-1616.

Sear, L.R. (1995). *An ethnographic study of the Spokane Police Department's Interviewing and Interrogation Techniques: The means justifies the end and the end justifies the means.* Paper presented at the DCLP Conference, York, September 1996.

Sear, L.R. (1996). *An investigation into whether the personality traits of police officers have a causal effect on their interviewing behaviour.* Unpublished undergraduate project, University of Kent.

Sear L.R. and Stephenson, G.M. (1997). Interviewing skills and individual characteristics of police interrogators. *Issues in Criminology and Legal Psychology,* 29, 27-34.

Shepherd, E. (1996) The trouble with PEACE. *Police Review 26th July 1996,* London: Police Review Publishing Co.

Skolnick, J.H. (1982). Deception by Police. *Criminal Justice Ethics,* 1 (2), 40-54.

Skolnick, J.H. and Leo, R.A. (1992). The ethics of deceptive interrogation. *Criminal Justice Ethics.* 11 (1), 3-12.

Stephens, M. and Becker, S. (eds). (1994). *Police Force, Police Service: Care and Control in Britain.* Basingstoke: Macmillan.

Stockdale, J. (1993). *Management and Supervision of Police Interviews.* Police Research Group Paper 4. London: Home Office.

Uglow, S. (1995). *Criminal Justice.* London: Sweet and Maxwell.

Underwager, R. and Wakefield, H. (1992). False confessions and police deception. *American Journal of Forensic Psychology.* 10, 49-66.

Williamson, T. (1994). Reflections on Current Police Practice. In D. Morgan and G. Stephenson (eds) *Suspicion and Silence: The Right to Silence in Criminal Investigations.* London: Blackstone.

5 Statement Validation

BRYAN TULLY

The major premise of statement analysis stems from empirical evidence that the recall of real events differs noticeably from fabricated accounts in (Undeutsch, 1954; Trankell, 1972; Wegner, 1989). Udo Undeutsch pioneered the technique of credibility assessment to develop relatively precise, definable criteria, that may help discern valid statements from artificial ones. This chapter outlines the original "Undeutsch Hypothesis" (Undeutsch, 1954), highlighting its complexities, limitations and its developments into Criteria Based Content Analysis (CBCA), (Stellar and Kohnken, 1989). After much empirical testing CBCA is generally considered the most systematised aspect of the overall Statement Validity Analysis procedure.

This chapter looks at the development of credibility assessment, and emphasises the difficulties apparent to researchers when evaluating the technique. These include setting up of adequate field studies using real cases, problems of cognitive and motivational issues affecting the reliability of statements and the possible variations in the use of the criteria available to statement analysis. Although often discredited as being a relatively subjective technique, this chapter concludes that statement analysis is a means of applying psychological knowledge, not a conclusion generator in its own right.

Bryan Tully is a Chartered Clinical, Occupational and Forensic Psychologist. He was trained and worked in various NHS settings and was a Research Fellow for the Police Foundation UK in the early 1980s. Following this he was appointed Head of a newly created Psychology Unit for the Royal Hong Kong Police Force. Through that appointment, Dr Tully developed his interest and specialist knowledge of the problems and techniques for obtaining reliable and robust testimony from

*Offender Profiling Series: I - **Interviewing and Deception***
Edited by D. Canter and L. Alison. © 1999 Ashgate Publishing, Aldershot. pp 83-103

vulnerable victims and suspects in the legal system. He was trained in "*Statement Validity Assessment*" by the original developer of this methodology, Professor Udo Undeutsch of the University of Cologne. Since then he has met and consulted with most of the internationally leading researchers in this area. From the early 1990s Dr Tully has practised as an expert witness Psychologist and he is one of the six members of the Psychologists at Law Group based in London and Bristol. A major theme in many of the legal cases undertaken in the question or questionability of credibility of memory or reports, ranging from personal psychological injury claims to disputed confessions and so called recovered memories of childhood sexual abuse.

5 Statement Validation

BRYAN TULLY

Original Work and Conceptualisation

At the beginning of the twentieth century both European and American Psychologists regarded child witnesses as "dangerous". i.e. more likely than not to render unreliable and misleading eyewitness accounts of events which they had been asked to remember (Stern 1910, Whipple 1913). To a great extent this conclusion was grounded on early experiments which rather than examine what children did remember, tested what they could and could not recall when faced with scores of questions concerning some experimentally set up eyewitness event. The number of "errors" dutifully generated by these procedures varied in almost direct relation to the number of questions put. Stern first appeared in Court as an expert witness in 1903 and it was not very surprising that whilst Courts on both sides of the Atlantic continued to rely on adult eyewitness accounts of at least the essential matters they claimed to recall, it was considered that children and young people were not to be trusted to render reliable accounts. This was not only based on notions of the supposedly poor cognitive powers of children. It was also because a witness needed to appreciate the need to tell the truth. A child could surely not be trusted in that respect as much as a respectable and responsible adult. Further this principle was extended so that women in general, and especially those of "dubious moral character" could not be trusted to give reliable accounts where those might be in conflict with a man with a reputation and standing in society. Needless to say, where alleged victims belonged to one of these untrustworthy categories it was unlikely that Courts would find for them or that the Prosecuting authorities would even bring cases as far as Court.

Not long after the second world war, Professor Udo Undeutsch of the University of Cologne had begun to develop a radically different view. In 1953 he told the 19th Congress of the German Psychological Association that it is not the veracity or reputation of witnesses which mattered and needed evaluation, but rather the truthfulness of the particular statements they made. The statements could and should be evaluated independently for their authenticity regardless of the reputation for trustworthiness or lack of trustworthiness of the witness. Witnesses with reputations for unreliability of lack or morality may tell the truth on a particular occasion, whilst highly respectable and worthy Citizens might have the greatest incentive to lie in respect of issues of sexual victimisation. Thus Undeutsch's method was to challenge the assumption of unreliability in respect of certain categories of witnesses such as young persons, and be extended beyond them. There were, according to Undeutsch, certain relatively exact definable descriptive criteria that form a key tool for the determination of the truthfulness of statements. This possibility arises out of what has come to be known as the "Undeutsch Hypothesis" i.e. that statements based on memories of real (self experienced) events are different in quality from statements which are not based on experience but are mere products of fantasy, invention, distortion or coaching. The contents of reality thus reported (the "Realitatsgehalt") formed the basis of a new approach to credibility assessment, called by Undeutsch "Statement Reality Analysis".

In 1954 Undeutsch had an opportunity to demonstrate his views to the German Supreme Court. He had recently given evidence at a retrial of three young men who had been found guilty of raping a girl. The girl was from a middle class family and was considered to be of a very good reputation. After the initial conviction of the three young men, the girl had begun to change some aspects of her story. The three defendants appealed against their conviction. Undeutsch interviewed the girl as part of the proceedings for the re-trial. Undeutsch exposed the fact that the girl was not drawing on a real and credible memory. She was having to inconsistently invent details. He cross examined her closely and challenged her story when it did not fit his "Undeutsch Hypothesis". He suspected correctly that having lied initially to excuse the fact that she was late home one evening (her parents being very strict about her behaviour and reputation) she found that she had set in motion a criminal prosecution which was entirely unintended. As matters progressed it became increasingly difficult to backtrack without exposing herself in a highly public fashion as someone who had not only departed from her strict moral sexual code, but who had lied and been believed by everyone thereby resulting in the most serious of consequences. Until Undeutsch's interview she had found no way of resolving this dilemma. It was Undeutsch's tape recording of these interviews which impressed the Supreme Court. The conviction of the three young men was quashed and the Court commissioned Undeutsch to conduct a formal inquiry into what "other and better resources" were needed for an out of Court expert to examine witness statements, particularly in sexual offence cases, and especially where there was little other evidence than the testimony of the alleged victims. In these circumstances the Court held that an expert in child psychology must be called upon to testify as to the credibility of such witness accounts. This then was how the role of "Witness Psychology" ("Aussagepsychologie") became institutionalised into the German legal procedural system.

Undeutsch's original set of criteria were complex and it was not always obvious what standard should be used to determine whether a criterion had been met and what weight should be put upon one criterion or another. A formal list is given below. (Undeutsch, 1989):

A. Criteria Derived from Single Statements

I. General Fundamental Criteria

1. Anchoring (embodiment) in time and place
2. Concreteness
3. Wealth of reported details
4. Originality (individual depiction, more than clichés, trite and stereotyped phrases)
5. Internal consistency
6. Mentioning of details, specific of the particular type of sex offence

II. Special Manifestations of the Aforementioned Criteria

7. Reference to details which exceed the probable capacity of the witness
8. Reporting of subjective experiences, supplement: Trankell's "Bilateral emotion criterion"
9. Mentioning of unexpected complications
10. Spontaneous corrections, specifications, complements

11. Self-disserving interspersions

III. Negative or Control Criteria

12. Lack of internal consistency
13. Lack of consistency with the laws of science and nature
14. Lack of external consistency (discrepancy with other incontrovertible facts).

B. Criteria Derived from a Sequence of Statements

1. Lack of persistence (stability, steadfastness).
2. Prior inconsistent statement.

Criteria Relating to Reporting Behaviour

The report should be typical for someone with the background and psychological characteristics of the witness, should be rendered spontaneously but the details fit as a mosaic into a consistent whole.

Other German psychologists varied the criteria in some respects, but in essence they covered a number of core areas. The sequence of statements gathered over time was considered important. Of course some variation would be expected but significant denials of matters originally recalled clearly would be suspicious. Some criteria related to the way or style with which the story was told and whether it fitted with what, would have been expected from a child of a certain age and whether the emotional expression or "commentary" fitted the child's emotional makeup and the alleged impact of the offence. Most important were what Undeutsch considered the fundamental criteria as applied to the content of the statement collected. These criteria covered the originality and degree of detail, details of the offender-victim relationship, the embedding of the offence in the context of the life situations of the alleged offender and victim, the reference to details whose significance could not be fully understood, the variation in the course of events and how complications were handled. Other criteria dealt with the psychological reactions of the alleged victim to what was said to have happened and the experience of trying to remember details when that was not easy. At the end of all this, the data had to be related to a forensic assessment of the other relevant information in the case.

Undeutsch himself had begun to co-operate closely with the distinguished Swedish Psychologist, Arne Trankell at the Laboratory of Witness Psychology in Stockholm. Trankell himself and his associates had developed a system of "investigative reasoning" which was similar in many respects to Undeutsch's method of "Statement Reality Analysis". In some ways Trankell's system, which he called "Formal Structure Analysis" went further by requiring the Psychologist to examine all statements in a case, and generate hypotheses which would be tested by collecting more data, conducting further interviews etc. Indeed in examples which Trankell has published, the Psychologist is the virtual investigator on the case rather than an examiner of certain aspects of witness statement production (cf Trankell, 1972).

Statement Reality Analysis encompasses, what for some is a fundamental weakness, in that the way the examination data are brought together to establish a conclusion is not well specified. Having identified certain criteria as being met to some extent, there still required a considerable exercise of well informed judgement to determine if this means that authenticity has been established or not. Experienced practitioners developed a "feel" for recognisable real instances of criteria being met, rather than referring in each case to a fixed standard of decision. Wegener (1989) stated recently "explicit combination rules as well as an experimentally obtained weighting system for each of the existing criteria is presently non existent". This fact hinders establishing which criteria are more reliable than others, or which could be productively modified or elaborated. Undeutsch's (1989) "rules" for evaluation are undoubtedly of the fuzzy sort. He states that the examiner must consider the intensity of each criterion's manifestation and how pronounced it is. The number of details meeting one or more of the criteria is clearly important and must take into account the capacity of the reporting person (including, knowledge, experience, motives and so on), and the complexity of the event with which the analysis is concerned. These matters cannot be reduced to completely clean metrics yet without risking losing some of the understanding which underpins some aspects of the judgement or recognition of criteria referred to above. This is an essential element of the practice of statement analysis as much as the limited theory from which it springs. That limited theory is basically the "Undeutsch Hypothesis". What that lacks in theoretical elaboration it makes up for in the diversity of empirical implications. Together, these three elements, (Hypothesis, Judgement, Empirical Implications) constitute the particular "informed psychology" which underlies the process of statement analysis. Consequently, it is unlikely that a fixed formula for application will be established in the near future. However this does not mean that there is not considerable scope for defining, systematising and testing some aspects of the process, and this is just what has been done in the last decade. This has undoubtedly been prompted by the dissemination of this method into the Anglo-American world, where both legal systems and the more empirical/experimental approach to the subject of psychology has put the method to different tests.

Pre-Experimental Evaluations of Statement Analysis

In legal matters there is no absolute determination of ground truth. Therefore, it has not been possible to state what percentage of cases have been proved to have been determined correctly or in error. Undeutsch (1982) has pointed out that by that date the method had been submitted to unremitting scrutiny by trial courts in Germany for a quarter of a century. He makes the remarkable claim that in what has been a collective caseload of over 40,000 in Germany and Sweden, there had not been one case where the Court found in accordance with the method's indication of truthfulness, and later a conviction was overturned. On the other hand, the method has often been the mean of demonstrating unreliability in other statements or even other kinds of preliminary evidence such as medical "findings". Wegener (1989), in spite of his clearest statement about the lack of explicit rules for drawing conclusions, has pointed nevertheless to the high degree of consistency in procedures and final judgements from different experts, at least from within the German speaking area. This includes managing tricky matters such as where a victim distorts an essentially truthful account of assault in order to escape blame or shame, or recants afterwards.

Wegener himself has carried out one interesting evaluation procedure in relation to some 350 of his own assessments over a period of 10 years.

Most of the examined alleged victim witnesses found the procedure worthwhile and affirming. However a small number, some 6% experienced the assessment negatively, expressing disappointment and bitterness that the expert was siding with the defendant, or because of the "additional pressure" which Wegener justified, on the grounds that the truth was discovered and confirmed at trial. It is worth noting that many practitioners in the UK and US who have welcomed Statement Analysis as a useful assessment procedure, may not realise the active role the Germans play in challenging and testing what appear to be non credible accounts. Having gone through a text of an initial account and considered the surrounding circumstances, it is part of the German practice to cross examine and challenge the alleged victim in areas that appear inauthentic. The examiner will be particularly aware of the gains and reasons which might lie behind an alleged victim's falsification. They will seek to spell out the consequences of a false report and try to help the interviewee to deal with the consequences of admitting distortions. There is no doubt these can be tough and confrontational encounters, which to British child centred sensitivities feel like mini interrogations. They are justified by the fact that often a false account is clearly established, as is why and how it came to be made. The more child centred approach in the English speaking world may be more sensitive to the child, but leaves more doubts as to the truth in many cases. In the Anglo-American system the method is even more of a truth confirming versus lie detection method than it is in Germany. In the UK the main issue in child victim interviewing has been in safeguarding against interviewers contaminating or distorting a child's memory whilst failing to obtain all there was to tell. In other words, it has focused on the cognitive problems of the child, rather than motivational ones (cf Tully and Tam 1987, Home Office/Department of Health Memorandum on Good Practice 1992).

Developments of Criterion Based Content Analysis and the Wider Process of Statement Validation

The exposure of Statement Analysis to the English speaking legal and psychological world, and the development of criticism that "...previous approaches lacked systematic organisation and precise definitions (and distinctions).." led Steller and Kohnken (1989) to recreate what they considered an integration of the various Undeutsch derived systems. They separated out the criteria and deciding that "reality criteria" had been used in so many different ways, decided to use the term "content criterion". "Criterion Based Content Analysis" ("CBCA") thus emphasised that the criteria were used for judging the content of a statement. They then employed the term "Statement Validity Analysis" to cover the overall assessment which would draw on all the other forms of information apart from the statements. Their list of newly reorganised criteria is as follows:

Table 5.1 Content Criteria for Statement Analysis
(From Steller and Kohnken, 1989)

General Characteristics

1 Logical Structure
2 Unstructured Production
3 Quantity of Details

Specific Contents

4 Contextual Embedding
5 Descriptions of Interactions
6 Reproduction of Conversation
7 Unexpected Complications During the Incident

Peculiarities of Content

8 Unusual Details
9 Superfluous Details
10 Accurately Reported Details Misunderstood
11 Related External Associations
12 Accounts of Subjective Mental State
13 Attribution of Perpetrator's Mental State

Motivation Related Contents

14 Spontaneous Corrections
15 Admitting Lack of Memory

16 Raising Doubts about One's Own Testimony
17 Self-Depreciation
18 Pardoning the Perpetrator

Offence Specific Elements

19 Details characteristic of the Offence

Validity Checklist

Psychological Characteristics

1 Appropriateness of Language and Knowledge
2 Appropriateness of Affect
3 Susceptibility to Suggestion

Interview Characteristics

4 Suggestive, Leading or Coercive Questioning
5 Overall Adequacy of the Interview

Motivation

6 Motives to Report
7 Context of the Original Disclosure or Report
8 Pressures to Report Falsely

Investigation Questions

9 Consistency with the Laws of Nature
10 Consistency with other Statements
11 Consistency with Other Evidence.

The validity checklist is employed to test the plausibility of various alternative hypotheses by examining particular aspects of the information. It often reveals where the investigation has been lacking in respect of information either incomplete or bearing other evaluative implications. The interview procedure is a key area for this procedure. The interview has to be "adequate" for the task of statement analysis. If the interviewer introduced distractions or failed to establish rapport, or did not adequately attempt to elicit a free narrative, or used leading and closed questions, or failed to ask appropriate follow up questions to resolve ambiguities, or ignored possible alternative hypotheses throughout then this will affect final evaluation of a victim's account.

Motivational factors are obviously important. The attitude of a child e.g. to his or her parents engaged in acrimonious divorce proceedings may be relevant to the production of an accusation against one parent.

Simulation and Laboratory Studies

An early and rather limited simulation study has been reported by Kohnken and Wegener 1982 (cited by Steller 1989). A 10 minute film of a family argument was shown to one group of subjects, whilst others only received a detailed description. The subjects were interviewed in a standard way and transcriptions were assigned to trained raters. The film group produced more detail, but the other group were rated as giving more unstructured production. Members of both groups were reasonably consistent over repeated questioning. These were the only criteria put to the test. Yuille (1988) had children tell both made up and true stories. The children often found it hard to make up completely false stories and they tended to be innocuous. The raters identified true and false stories well above chance level, but again the study was a limited test on limited material. Steller, Wellershaus and Wolf (1988) also used children and had them telling stories of what had really happened to them or not. The researchers tried to find experiences which had something in common with sexual abuse.

They settled on some medical procedures, being beaten by another child, or attacked by an animal. These all entailed direct involvement by the child, feelings of loss of control, and negative emotional tone. This study showed that even an hour and a half of training could produce very good inter-rater reliability on the presence or absence of criteria. However, it was plain that some criteria such as "Raising Doubts about One's Own Testimony" were much more likely to be agreed upon to a much greater degree than one such as "Contextual Embedding". Some kinds of stories or topics lent themselves to being differentiated more than others. It is evidently easier to fabricate authentically some topics rather than others. Other research has also shown that the raters find it more difficult to reliably discriminate between "Description of interactions" and Reproduction of conversions" (Hofer, Kohnken Hanewinkel and Bruhn, 1993, cited in Kohnken et al., 1993). Considering this boundary issue for the "Undeutsch hypothesis", Steller (1989) notes that there are some rather specific aspects of psychological experience in sexual offences. Further, the Undeutsch hypothesis would be more likely to differentiate true versus false accounts where the matter in question cannot be observed frequently in everyday life, and a more or less intimate manipulation of the body of the person affected is part of the described event. The power of each of the criteria to differentiate singly, or in combination, is likely to be affected by the special features of the incident, the extent the victim has been involved how much of an account is produced and whether it has been collected with the "special care" needed to preserve authentically remembered details (Tully, 1985).

Field Study

It is extremely difficult to set up an adequate field study using real cases. Esplin, Boychuk and Raskin (1988) set up interviews with children who have had sexual abuse confirmed or have had a case dismissed, and where there was really no supporting evidence. The two groups were however similar in terms of age and type of alleged sexual abuse. In spite of there only being one scorer (who was blind to group membership), and there not being any absolute way of being certain sexual abuse had not occurred in the "unconfirmed" group, the results showed that every criterion measure except one was much more present in the confirmed abuse group as compared with the unconfirmed group. The exception was "Accurately reported details misunderstood", which occurred in only one case in each group. It should be noted however that when this criterion is fulfilled in real life cases, this can be a very telling criterion, and this is especially so for very young children. Seven criteria were not found in the Unconfirmed group. This then represents very good support for the underlying system of Criterion Based Content Analysis.

Cognitive and Motivational Issues Affecting Reliability of Statements

The chief issue which has preoccupied the German psychologists working in the field of Statement Analysis has been motivated falsification or distortion of remembered accounts. They may make allowance for cognitive and mnemonic capability when evaluating the significance of the presence or absence of criteria. On the other hand British and American Psychologists have been preoccupied with cognitive failure and the social effects of suggestive or leading interviewing style on accounts of sexual abuse elicited by interviewers. This climate in the Child Protection services is partly compensatory for failing to believe children in the past. It has now been established that children can be very suggestible and that "special care" is needed in conducting the interview in which the testimonial "statement" is gathered. Further, a child can mislead himself or herself by not perfectly distinguishing the sources of "remembered" events which may arise in part from other memories unrelated to an incident in question, or from the exercise of imagination or thinking. In a recent and particularly thorough review, Ceci and Bruck (1993) write:

> Source monitoring studies suggest that children could be vulnerable to a range of confusions between actual events and suggested events when they are perceptually and semantically similar. However, because the locus of children's greater misattribution is unclear, and there are no data that link children's suggestibility and source monitoring difficulties...these claims are speculative at this stage.

Ceci and Bruck have tried to unravel the cognitive, social (influence) and motivational factors in suggestibility and lying i.e. providing deliberate falsehoods. These are many and complex. Optimising testimonial accuracy requires attention to any and all the variables which may be critical in any case. This raises the question as to whether certain procedures designed to accomplish one aim will affect another with a differing purpose. Kohnken, Schimossek, Aschermann and Hofer (1994) set out to see if utilising a "cognitive interview", designed to maximise accurate output from memory (Fisher and Geiselman, 1992) would have an adverse effect on the criteria used to differentiate truthfulness in accounts. They were aware that Steller and Wellershaus (1992) had shown that with particular instructions some of the criterionised differences between true and false accounts were eroded. Kohnken et al (1994) had some subjects view a 12 minute film on blood donation and others only had a verbal description. They had to fabricate their testimony of having really seen the film. The "cognitive interview" produced significantly more accurately recalled details and more errors. Although the proportion was comparable to the non "cognitive interview", this was a key finding since it has been a frequent claim of "cognitive interview" researchers that enhanced output of accurate details is accomplished without commensurate rise in errors (cf Fisher and Geiselman 1992). In this case there was no significant interaction between interview type and the discriminability of truthful from fabricated accounts. Thus in this study, the use of a "cognitive interview" did not erode the discriminating ability of the Criterion Based Content Analysis. One problem with drawing generalisations from this approach is that it is not entirely defensible to treat one example of the "cognitive interview" as if its effects can be expected to be invariant across differing situations. This makes an unwarranted assumption that one particular experimental arrangement and the test of its effects on one CBCA procedure is "representative" of the interaction of two variables. The underlying psychology makes it quite impossible that in the Steller and Wellershaus study, the cognitive interview instructions brought out more criterion fitting statements, whilst in the Kohnken et al. study, the "cognitive interview" exposed the lack of real memory for those subjects who had not seen the film, whilst providing those who had with more real recollections to be truthful about. Much would depend on the amount and quality of memory. The effects of one procedure on results from another could be enhanced, eroded or mutually cancelled out. The "cognitive interview" cannot be treated like a standard drug dose expected to have predicted interaction or not with a standard dose of another drug on a standard biological organism.

Variations of Content Criteria

Kohnken et al (1993) used a variation of the new systematised 19 criteria re-developed by Steller and Kohnken (1989). This was in part to meet the problems raters had experienced with making reliable distinctions between some categorisations, and in part in recognition that their particular memory materials did not involve certain content criteria. However, these researchers also tried out a half dozen newly invented criteria, "not part of the CBCA system". Two of these correlated with their canonical discriminate function significantly. One of these was "Display of Insecurity" - which in fact obtained the highest correlation with the discriminant function. The other was what was termed "Reporting Style". "Display of Insecurity" was defined as being unsure or stating that a recollection was a belief only. "Lack of Memory" was applied only when an interviewee spontaneously expressed being unable to remember a particular item at all, particularly during the questioning part of the interview. "Reporting Style" was defined as being more issue related and less long winded. Truthtellers were found to exemplify this characteristic in their accounts as compared to fabricators. They also tended to "Provided (more) reasons for lack of memory" concerning e.g. detailed descriptions, also to "Use less clichés", and, contrary to the researchers' expectations, to "Repeat elements already described without additional details". Some of these experimental variations are of limited value and can only be easily applied when comparing two groups recollecting allegedly identical material. In a single sample, it would be impossible for this example to determine just how many clichés are needed to reach the criterion involved. Individual differences would be a major factor. Other writers who have been trained in Statement Analysis and in wider forensic approaches to the evaluation of child abuse have produced criterion like characteristics of contrasting accounts of actual abuse compared with unreliable or fictitious allegations. Rogers (1989) points out that unreliable accounts may include self serving details, be extraordinarily dramatic, describe alleged perpetrators taking no steps against discovery, include sudden claims not to remember when caught out in inconsistencies, or deny that earlier matter was ever said. On the other hand, these findings outside one formal system surely show that the Steller-Kohnken systematisation of CBCA now permits more controlled, indeed more systematic variation of CBCA. This is to be welcomed as there is no reason at all to consider that the present approach is not open to much improvement. In addition it shows that whilst the principles of Statement Analysis may be relatively systematic and well grounded, it does not follow that any particular formula for conducting the examination will have merit across all or most situations. Excessive empiricism is not likely to prevent practitioners finding good and even scientific reasons for varying the method as it is applied in each particular set of circumstances. Experimental tests are however important in checking assumptions in the light of the lack of conceptualisation and theory. Take for example Kohnken et al.'s prediction that fabricators would provide more repetitions than truthtellers. This assumption seemed reasonable, in that under a cognitive interview protocol, fabricators may have less real memory to draw on. The cognitive load of inventing answers and remembering those invented answers which the demand characteristics of that situation requires, makes repetition a rational strategy. However, truthtellers trying genuinely to remember more about an event they have really experienced may adopt a retrieval strategy of repeating their own productions as self prompts to new retrievable material. The "cognitive interviewer" is after all applying a similar technique to them by going over the ground again. There appears to be a limit as to what can be predicted on a theoretical, primarily empirical basis. The point is that Statement Analysis has neither been developed, systematised, nor applied under the influence of major psychological theories of memory. The area of psychological theory and research activity derived therein from, which would appear to be most relevant is "reality or source monitoring" (Johnson and Raye, 1981, Lindsay, 1990, Johnson, 1991). This is concerned centrally with how externally derived, perceptual, "real", experiences are differentiated from internal experience itself. Research based on this area of theory has been applied to dreams, delusions, brain damage, and the effects of suggestibility on witnesses' recall. We still await however a theory influenced approach to Statement Analysis. Undeutsch's original conviction that truthful accounts differ from fabrications, he traced back to Goethe's prescription that writing good poetry had to be based on real experience and not plucked out of the blue. It remains to be seen when Statement Analysis will be developed through other insights as well. It is surely time.

The Scope of Statement Validity Analysis

The application of Criterion Based Content Analysis is the most systematised aspect of the overall Statement Validity Analysis procedure. The list of matters considered within the framework in which CBCA is to be evaluated is almost as broad as that undertaken by any investigation cum trial proceedings into an alleged crime. Apart from the list drawn up by Steller and Kohnken (1989); see Table 5.2 earlier, Rogers (1989) has pointed out differing characteristics of a parent supporting a report of true child molestation as opposed to promoting an exaggerated or false allegation. German psychologists have shown very little interest in the characteristics of the alleged perpetrator, save insofar as the victim-witness report details are consonant with known typical criminology. This reflects their role as "Witness Psychologists" rather than "Forensic Psychologists" as understood in the American tradition especially. Rogers (1989), an American Forensic Psychologist, includes how far suspect behaviour fits a profile she considers to be characteristic of Guilty Perpetrators who Deny, Guilty Perpetrators who Admit, and those who are Not Guilty and Deny. Included in these profiles are observations of suspect responses to interviews, psychological test findings, attitude of the suspect towards the alleged victim, and attitudes to law enforcement. These would all be added to the overall validation process. In some ways this is closer to Trankell's Swedish approach to the whole investigation.

Statement Analysis is a very transparent method. Once completed the results tend to compel agreement rather than the result relying on the say so of some expert. Like a good dissection or archaeological dig, the expertise lies in the method of revealing what all can see then and interpret. Apart from some re-organising, the protocols used currently are not much different to those originally developed. Theory driven research has only just begun. The results may well lead to some radical further developments.

Recent studies have shown that most of the criteria of Content Based Criteria Analysis are rated reliably across well briefed judges and from one time to another (Horowitz et al., 1997). These researchers however found a few to be not so reliable. These were "superfluous details", "admitting lack of memory", and "spontaneous corrections". Also related external associations and unusual details failed to reach a statistical level of "acceptability". All of this should be borne in mind by practitioners, but these findings have a great capacity to mislead. The authors of this research wrongly conclude that the criteria need to be more tightly defined or eliminated. This problem with this slavishly numerical operational definitional approach to the use of the criteria is that it loses sight of the underlying nature of the narrative. Not all matters to which some criteria refer are expressed clearly. If some subjects on some occasions express themselves with lack of clarity, then judges required to determine if a criterion applies or not will demonstrate a mixed or lowered interjudge reliability. However, often that criterion can be seen to apply clearly. On those occasions inter judge reliability would be much higher. That is when it matters of course. Practitioners should not put weight on unclear or uncertain judgements and they do not need research to tell them that is sensible. Another problem is that some things mentioned by children might be classified as either an example under one criterion or another, and there may be a tendency for a judge to prefer one interpretation to another. Another judge may see it the other way round. From the point of view of the psychology of real experience being expressed in certain known ways, it really does not matter if, as has been known all along, the criteria are not discrete and some judges might prefer one to another when classifying a topic of narrative This only becomes important if conclusions are drawn on mechanical and statistical grounds only. To put this another way, the instrument is a means of applying psychological knowledge not a conclusion generator in it's own right.

References

Ceci, S. J. and Bruck, M. (1993). Suggestibility of the Child Witness: A Historical Review and Synthesis, *Psychological Bulletin*, 113, (3), pp. 403 - 439.

Esplin, P. W., Boychuk, T. and Raskin, D. C. (1988). *A Field Validity Study of Criteria Based Content Analysis of Children's Statements in Sexual Abuse Cases.* Paper presented at the NATO Advanced Study Institute on Credibility Assessment, Maratea, Italy.

Fisher, R. P. and Geiselman, R.E. (1992). *Memory-Enhancing Techniques for Investigative Interviewing*, Springfield, Illinois: Charles C. Thomas.

Home Office and Department of Health (1992*) Memorandum of Good Practice On Video Recorded Interviews with Child Witnesses for Criminal Proceedings,* London: H.M.S.O.

Horowitz, S. W. (1991) Empirical Support for Statement Validity Analysis, *Behavioural Assessment*, 13, pp. 293-313.

Horowitz S. W., Lamb, B., Esplin, P., Boychuk, T., Krispin, O. and Reiter-Lavery, L. (1997). Reliability of criteria-based content analysis of child witness statements. *Legal and Criminological Psychology* 2, 11-21.

Johnson, M. K. (1991). Reality monitoring: Evidence from Confabulation in Organic Brain Disease Patients. In G. Prigatan and D. Schacter (eds.) *Awareness of Deficit after Brain Injury*, pp 124-140, New York: Oxford University Press.

Johnson, M. K. and Raye, C. L. (1981). Reality Monitoring, *Psychological Review*, 88, pp 67-85.

Kohnken, G., Schimossek, E., Aschermann, E. and Hofer, E. (1994) *The Cognitive Interview and the Assessment of the Credibility of Adults Statements*, Unpublished Manuscript.

Lindsay, D. S. (1990). Misleading Suggestions can Impair Eyewitnesses Ability to Remember Event Details, *Journal of Experimental Psychology, Learning, Memory, and Cognition* 16 pp 1077-1083.

Rogers, M. (1989) *Coping with Alleged False Molestation: Examination and Statement Analysis Procedures*. Paper presented to Fifth Annual Symposium in Forensic Psychology, of the American College of Forensic Psychology.

Steller, M. (1989). *Recent Developments in Statement Analysis in Credibility Assessment*, ed. John Yuille. The Netherlands: Kluwer.

Steller, M. and Kohnken, G. (1989). Criteria Based Statement Analysis In D. C. Raskin (Ed.) *Psychological Methods for Criminal Investigation and Evidence*. New York: Springer.

Steller, M. and Wellerhshaus, P. (1992). *Information Enhancement and Credibility Assessment of Child Statements: The Impact of the Cognitive Interview Technique on Criteria Based Content Analysis*. Paper presented at the 3rd European Conference of Law and Psychology, Oxford, England.

Stern, W. (1910) Abstracts of Lectures on the Psychology of Testimony and the Study of Individuality. *American Journal of Psychology*, 21, pp 270-282.

Tully, B. (1985). "Special Care Questioning", *FBI Law Enforcement Bulletin*, Nov, pp 9 - 15.

Tully, B. and Tam, K-O. (1987). Helping the Police with their Inquiries: the Development of Special Care Questioning Techniques, *Children and Society*, 1, (3) pp 187-197.

Trankell, A. (1972). *Reliability of Evidence, Methods for Analysing and Assessing Witness Statements*. Stockholm, Sweden: Beckmans.

Undeutsch, U. (1982). Statement Reality Analysis In A. Trankell (ed.) *Reconstructing the Past, The Role of Psychologists in Criminal Trials*, Stockholm, Sweden: Norstedt.

Undeutsch, U. (1989). The Development of Statement Reality Analysis. In J. Yuille (ed) *Credibility Assessment*. The Netherlands: Kluwer.

Wegener, H. (1989) The Present State of Statement Analysis. In J. Yuille (ed) *Credibility Assessment*. The Netherlands Kluwer.

Whipple, G. M. (1913). The Psychology of Testimony and Report *Psychological Bulletin*, 10, 264-268.

Yuille, J. (1988) The Systematic Assessment of Children's Testimony, *Canadian Psychologist,* 29, pp 247-262.

6 Forensic Application of Linguistic Analysis

MALCOLM COULTHARD

This chapter focuses on the growing use of linguistic analysis in criminal investigations and the practical application of forensic linguistics. A variety of areas of analyses are discussed, with examples from real cases revealing how examination of written text may reveal consistent grammatical differences to identify the author. Methods used to investigate claims that statements have been falsified are then discussed. The first of these examines how spoken and written English differ, and how this influences the inference that a statement may be false. Subsequently, conversational rules and register features are discussed in the same context. They describe how falsified statements cannot truly reflect real speech. The consistency of statements are examined showing how linguistics can find whether different parts of statements were written at different times and in different contexts.

Malcolm Coulthard is Professor of English Language and Lingusitics at the University of Birmingham, where he has been for the whole of his academic career. He is best known for his publications on the analysis of discourse, An Introduction to Discourse Analysis (1977, 1985) and Advances in Written Text Analysis (1994). He was the founding Chair of the International Association of Forensic Linguistics and the founding Editor of Forensic Linguistics: The International Journal of Speech, Language and the Law. He has acted as an expert witness in over 100 cases and has given evidence in Northern Ireland, Scotland, Hong Kong and the Appeal Court in London.

*Offender Profiling Series: I - **Interviewing and Deception***
Edited by D. Canter and L. Alison. © 1999 Ashgate Publishing, Aldershot. pp. 105-125

6 Forensic Application of Linguistic Analysis

MALCOLM COULTHARD

Introduction

Thirty years ago Jan Svartvik (1968) published The Evans Statements: A Case for Forensic Linguistics in which he demonstrated that disputed parts of a series of four statements, which had been dictated to police officers by Timothy Evans and incriminated him in the murder of his wife and daughter, had a grammatical style measurably different from that of the uncontested parts. A new discipline was born. Initially its growth was slow: in unexpected places there appeared isolated articles in which the author, often a distinguished linguist, analysed disputed confessions, commented on the likely authenticity of purported verbatim records of interaction; assessed the ability of ordinary people, particularly non-native speakers, to understand the written legal language used in contracts, insurance proposals and the official police warning which is read out to those accused of crimes; identified and evaluated inconsistencies in the non-native-like language attributed to immigrants or aboriginals, in challenged police records of depositions (see Levi, 1994a, an annotated bibliography).

There was, however, in the early days no attempt to establish a discipline or even a methodology for forensic linguistics - the work was usually undertaken as an intellectual challenge and almost always required the creation, rather than simple application of a method of analysis. By contrast, in the past five years there has been a rapid growth in the frequency with which Courts in a series of countries have called on the expertise of linguists and, in consequence, there is now a developing methodology and a growing number of linguists who act as expert witnesses, a few even on a full time basis (see Levi, 1994b). The International Association of Forensic Linguists was established in 1993 and the journal, Forensic Linguistics: the International Journal of Speech,

Language and the Law appeared for the first time in 1994.

What do Forensic Linguists do?

Forensic language analysis can be divided into three sub-areas; forensic handwriting analysis, forensic phonetics and forensic linguistics. Forensic handwriting analysts are concerned with the marks left by writing on a page. They may be asked by whose hand or with which typewriter or printer a text was produced (Davis, 1986) or, more recently, to decipher, by means of a technique called Electro-Static Deposition Analysis (ESDA), the impressions left on a given page by what was written on the sheet(s) above and then to use that knowledge to express an opinion about the authenticity, date and/or timing of the writing on the page in question, (Davis, 1994).

Forensic phoneticians focus on the sounds produced when someone speaks; sometimes they are called on simply to identify the accent of an unknown voice tape-recorded while making obscene or threatening phone calls, but much more often they are asked to compare tape-recorded samples of known speakers, who are usually already suspects, with samples of an unknown voice. Occasionally, they may be asked simply to transcribe crucial phrases or even single words from tape, or to offer an opinion as to whether a tape has been interfered with either physically or instrumentally; (see Baldwin and French, 1990; French, 1994; Hollien, 1990; and Nolan, 1983).

The analysis of what was said or written, that is questions of orthography, lexis, grammar, text structure and meaning, is the province of the forensic linguists. In the main, forensic linguists evaluate a claim, or more usually conflicting prosecution and defence claims, about the origin, authorship and/or contextual significance of (parts of) documents, though occasionally they are asked to express an opinion on the 'common sense' meaning of individual words, phrases or parts of texts.

Linguists analysis, by its very nature, requires much more data than the analysis of handwriting and speech because the features it typically focuses on occur much less frequently. Whereas a given subject might write the letter 'e' once every two or three words, and produce the sound /I/ every couple of seconds, he may write or say "then I" less than once a week and 'immodest' less than once a month. In other words, there are many more options and therefore many fewer instances of each option. For this reason, although linguistics already works with the concept that every speaker has a slightly different version of the language, his own idiolect, and asserts that if one had enough data it would be possible to identify every speaker uniquely, at the moment there are neither the data banks nor the computational resources to undertake this task. Linguistic fingerprinting, although theoretically possible, is still a gleam in the linguist's eye, despite the claims made by (Morton, 1991) for the CUSUM technique, (see, Canter, 1992 and Sanford et al., 1994). However, for forensic purposes, there is no need of a technique as accurate as fingerprinting because, for other non-linguistic reasons, it is almost always possible to reduce the list of possible authors to a very small number, in many cases to only two, and then the linguist needs only to evaluate the likelihood of one of them being the author.

In what follows I will exemplify by reference to real cases - all the extracts quoted are authentic, although sometimes the names of people and places have been changed to preserve anonymity when there is a possibility of an appeal.

The Linguistic Bases of Analysis

a) Idiolectal Evidence

It is a basic tenet of linguistics that not only is language rule-governed although, of course, any spoken or written text may display items which break the rules of the standard language. Linguists divide rule-breaking into two categories, 'performance' mistakes, where the speaker/writer knows that he has broken a rule, which, of course, does not prevent him from breaking it again, (and again, as learners of foreign languages know to their chagrin), and 'competence' errors where the speaker/writer is working with a non-standard set of rules, but rules which he nevertheless follows consistently even though he may still make performance mistakes which break his own rules. In short texts it is usually only possible to focus on the grammatical features of an idolect, because in order to examine characteristic vocabulary choices one needs a great deal more textual data.

Theoretically the most difficult author-identification cases for the forensic linguist to handle are those involving anonymous letters, as there is usually a fairly large number of potential authors and only a small amount of written text to analyse. For this reason, success is in the main limited to those cases which involve semi-literate authors, who necessarily provide a comparatively large number of idiolectal mistakes and errors in a comparatively small amount of text. (Obviously all intending anonymous letter writers should use the (American) spell-checking and style-improver options available in the latest word-processing programmes in order to homogenise and thereby disguise their idiolect.)

Below I reproduce a few short extracts from a typed anonymous letter, which the addressee-company suspected was written by one of its own employees, with the words containing non-standard features in italic; (there are many more instances in the rest of the letter of the particular phenomena I have chosen to focus on):

> ....*I hope you appreciate that i am enable to give my true idenitity as this wolud ultimately jeopardize my position....*
> ....*1 would like to high light my greatest concern ....*
> ....*Have so far deened it unnecessary to investegate these issus....*

There are several interesting non-standard features immediately evident, although one of the problems of dealing with a typewritten text is that error and mistake may be confused and compounded - one may not know, for a given item, particularly if it only occurs once, whether the 'wrong' form is the product of a mis-typing or a non-standard spelling or grammatical rule - for instance if the text includes the word 'color' is this a typing mistake or a (British English) spelling error? In examining the non-standard items above we note: firstly, the writer is an inexperienced typist the first person pronoun "I" appears not only as "I" but also as "i" and the very unusual "1"; secondly, some of the words have metathesized(reversed) letters and others additional or omitted letters; thirdly the writer has serious problems when spelling words containing the reduced (unstressed) vowel schwa- thus we have the following spellings "enable" = "unable", "investegate" = "investigate" and elsewhere "except" = "accept". Fourthly, the writer is unsure about when to write certain sequences of morphemes as a single word and when as two separate words - thus “high light” and “with out”. In addition, but not exemplified here, there are homonym problems, “weather” appears for “whether” and “there” for “their”. Finally, the writer has some grammatical problems: the frequent omission of markers of past tense and of the 3rd person singular present tense and even of articles - “have now (a) firm intention”. Collectively these mistakes and errors are idiosyncratic and idiolectally distinctive and proved to be instanced in the authenticated letters of only one of the eight employees who the Company knew had access to the information contained in the threatening letter. This letter writer turned out to be the employee suspected by the Company.

There are many occasions when someone claims that a text is in part or entirely falsified - i.e. that the real author is different from the purported author. In this context the fabricator, whether he is creating an interview record, a confession statement or a suicide note is acting as an amateur dramatist and imagining what the purported speaker/author would have produced in the same circumstances. As with any fabrication, be it bank notes or texts, the quality of the finished product will depend on the degree of understanding that the falsifier has of the nature of what he is falsifying. Depending on the nature of the text being fabricated different linguistic approaches are suitable. I will give a few examples.

b) Spoken v Written English

The first case concerns a disputed statement, in which the accused apparently confessed to involvement in a terrorist murder. He himself claimed that he had said some of what was contained in the statement and that this had indeed been fairly accurately recorded, but he denied in particular having dictated the first and very incriminating sentence of the statement which he claimed had been invented by the police officers.

It is now well established within linguistics (Halliday, 1989) that spoken and written language have different principles of organisation and can usually be distinguished both grammatically and lexically. As a generalisation spoken language tends to have short clauses, a low ratio of lexical to grammatical words and to present what happened as processes by verbs, whereas written language tends to have longer clauses, a higher lexical density and to present what happened as products by the use of nominalisations. Thus, for example, the following sentence from the disputed statement, which the accused admitted to having said, displays the co-ordinated clauses and very low lexical density typical of spoken narrative:

> *I drove down to the flats & I saw him up on the roof and I shouted to him and he said that he would be down in a couple of minutes.*

We notice that there are thirty two words, only seven of them lexical items per clause. The disputed first sentence, presented below, is in marked contrast to this uncontested sentence consisting, as it does, of only two clauses which contain forty seven words (conservatively treating '1987' and 'ABC' as single words), 25 of which are lexical, giving a clause length of 23.5 and a lexical density of 12.5:

> *I wish to make a further statement explaining my complete involvement in the hijacking of the Ford Escort van from John Smith on Monday 28 May 1987 on behalf of the A.B.C. which was later used in the murder of three person (sic) in Newtown that night.*

In other words this sentence has the high lexical density, massive subordination and frequent nominalisation - for example statement, involvement, hijacking and murder - typical of written texts. On cross examination the police officer/scribe conceded that the statement may not after all have been verbatim, but continued to maintain that all the words were indeed spoken by the accused, though "perhaps not in that order"!

c) Conversational Rules on Explicitness and Detail

Some cases require reference to the socio-linguistic rules for the production of texts. Grice (1975) in his seminal article 'Logic and conversation' observed that one of the controls on speaker's contributions is the *quantity maxim*, which he summarised as:

> *a) Make your contribution as informative as is required (for the current purposes of the exchange),*
> *b) Do not make your contribution more informative than is required.*

What Grice is concerned with here is the fact that all utterances are shaped for a specific addressee on the basis of the speaker's assumptions about shared knowledge and opinions, and in the light of what has already been said earlier, both in the ongoing interaction and in previous interactions. This appeal, to what Brazil (1985) has called 'common ground', makes conversations frequently opaque and at times incomprehensible to overhear, as we can see in the question/answer sequence below:

> *PC: Why did you do it?*
> *A: Well he told me if I didn't it would be worse for me...*

It is for this reason that truly 'authentic' conversation would be impossible between actors on the stage: the real addressee of any stage utterance is in fact the audience. Thus, there has arisen the dramatic convention of over-explicitness, which allows characters to break the quantity maxim and say to each other things they already 'know' and even things that are strictly irrelevant, in order to transmit economically essential information to the audience. This is a convention which the dramatist Tom Stoppard parodies in the opening scene of *The Real Inspector Hound*:

> *Mrs Drudge (into phone): Hello, the drawing room of Lady Muldoon's country residence one morning in early spring... Hello! -- the draw -- Who? Who did you wish to speak to? I'm afraid there is no one of that name here, this is all very mysterious and I'm sure its leading up to something, I hope nothing is amiss, for we, that is Lady Muldoon and her house guests, are here cut off from the world, including Magnus, the wheelchair-ridden half-brother of her ladyship's husband, Lord Albert Muldoon, who ten years ago went out for a walk on the cliffs and was never seen again -- and all alone for they had no children.*

When we come to consider the fabricator of forensic texts, we can see that he is in a situation directly analogous to that of the dramatist - he is creating his text with the overhearer, in this case the judge and jury in Court, in mind, and is anxious to make incriminating information as unambiguous as possible. Thus, at times, the fabricator, just like the dramatist, will break the maxim of quantity, though rarely as extremely as in this extract from the beginning of a fabricated telephone conversation. A convicted defendant is trying to incriminate one of the prosecution witnesses:

A: *Hello*
B: *Hello, can I speak to Mr A please?*
A: *Speaking*
B: *Are you surprised I've phoned you instead of coming down and seeing you as you asked in your message over the phone yesterday?*
A: *No I'm not surprised. Why are you phoning me here for? Why don't you come in to see me if you want to see outside?*
B: *Well you've dragged me through a nightmare and I don't intend to give you an opportunity to set me up again for something else or beat me up again and abandon me miles away as you did outside Newtown Prison with the two detectives; and for your information, as you may know, I've filed an official complaint against you and the two C.I.D. detectives*
A: *The detectives and I beat you up and C.I.D. they denied, they didn't beat you up and you cannot do anything because you got no proof.*

Over-explicitness can be realised in the choice of noun groups as well. In the disputed confession attributed to William Power, one of the Birmingham Six, (see Coulthard 1994a) there was frequent reference to "white plastic (carrier) bags"

Walker was carrying... two white plastic carrier bags....
Hunter was carrying ... three white plastic carrier bags...
Richard was carrying ... one white plastic carrier bag...
Walker gave me one of the white plastic bags...
Hughie gave J. Walker his white plastic bag...

Our knowledge of the rules of conversational composition tells us that it is unlikely that Power would have used the combination 'numeral + white + plastic + carrier + bags' even once. Firstly, it represents a degree of detail that does not seem to have any importance in the story as he tells it and it is very unusual for narrators to provide detail which has no relevance to their story. Finally, it is a noted feature of speech that speakers do not normally produce long noun phrases of this kind; rather they assemble complex information in two or three bits or bites. For comparison we can compare the way the information came out in Power's interview with the police, which has a ring of authenticity:

Power:	*He's got a holdall and two bags*
Watson:	*What kind of bags?*
Power:	*They were white, I think they were carrier bags*

Even then there was nothing about 'plastic'. The extract below taken from cross-examination during the trial shows clearly that, once a full form of a referring expression has been used, a speaker's normal habit is to employ a shortened version on subsequent occasions.

Mr Field-Evans:	*And did you say 'two white plastic carrier bags?'*
Power:	*Yes Sir*
Mr Field-Evans:	*Whose idea was it that Walker was carrying two white carrier bags? Were those your words or the Police Officers' words?*
Power:	*They were the Police officers'. They kept insisting that I had told them that they carried plastic bags into the station.*
Mr Field-Evans:	*Does the same apply to what Hunter was carrying?*
Power:	*I don't know what you mean sir.*
Mr Field-Evans:	*I am sorry. Whose idea was it that you should say that Hunter was carrying three white plastic bags?*
Power:	*Well, sir, I said that.*
Mr Field-Evans:	*But was it your idea?*
Power:	*No. They kept saying that I had already told them that they were carrying plastic bags into the station. When I said that, they said "who was carrying them? who was carrying them?" They threatened me, I said "They were all carrying them?" They asked me how many*

were they carrying and I just said
one, two, three, one and one.

d) Register Features

Linguists have long recognised that the language that any given individual uses varies according to the contexts in which and the topics for which he is using it - this is called register variation. Thus, at its simplest a policeman at work will have a series of linguistic options which mark him as a policeman, as indeed will a doctor, an economist etc. When a text is being falsified there is always the possibility that the real author will allow features of his own usage to enter into the text; these features may be idiolectal, as we saw above, but may also be due to register.

To illustrate this I will focus on a text from the 1950's from the well-known Derek Bentley and Chris Craig case. Bentley and Craig were apprehended by the police as they were trying to break into a warehouse; Bentley was quickly arrested while Craig, in resisting arrest, shot and killed a policeman. Two hours after his arrest Bentley made a statement which, as he was functionally illiterate, was written down by one of the interviewing police officers. At his trial Bentley claimed that his statement was in fact a composite document, i.e. not only transcribed but in part also written by the police. I will focus on one small linguistic feature simply to illustrate how a register analysis works, obviously a full analysis would focus on a whole series. (I reproduce the whole statement as an appendix).

"then"

One of the marked features of Derek Bentley's confession is the frequent use of the word "then". In its temporal meaning -- 10 occurrences in 582 words. This may not, at first, seem at all remarkable given that Bentley is reporting a series of sequential events and that one of the obvious requirements of a witness statement is accuracy about place and time. However, a cursory glance at a series of other witness statements suggested that Bentley's usage was at the very least untypical, and thus a potential intrusion of a specific feature of police register which is related to a professional concern with the accurate recording of temporal sequence.

To test this I created two small corpora, the first composed of three ordinary witness statements, one from a woman involved in the Bentley case itself and two from men involved in another unrelated case, totalling some 930 words of text, the second composed of statements by three police officers, two of whom were involved in the Bentley case and one in another unrelated case, totalling some 2270 words, (cf Fox, 1993).

The results were startling: whereas in the witness statements there is only one occurrence of "then" in 930 words. In contrast "then" occurs 29 times in the police Officers' statements, that is on average once every 78 words. Thus, Bentley's usage of temporal "then" groups his statement firmly with those produced by the police officers.

In this case I was fortunate in being able to check the representativeness of my 'ordinary witness' data against a reference corpus, the Corpus of Spoken English, a subset of the COBUILD Bank of English, which, at the time, consisted of some 1.5 million running words collected from many different types of naturally occurring speech. "Then" in all its meanings proved to occur a mere 3,164 times in the whole corpus. That is, on average, only once every 500 words, which supported the representativeness of the witness data and the claimed specialness of the police and Bentley data.

What was perhaps even more striking about the Bentley statement was the frequent post-positioning of "then", as can be seen in the two sample sentences below, selected from a total of 7 occurrences in the 582 word text:

Chris then jumped over and I followed
Chris then climbed up the drainpipe to the roof and I followed.

This has an odd feel because not only do ordinary speakers use "then" much less frequently than policemen, they also use it in a structurally different way -- for instance, in the COBUILD spoken data they use "then I" ten times as frequently as "I then". Indeed the structure "I then" occurs a mere 9 times in the whole of the spoken sample, in other words only once every 165,000 words. By contrast the phrase occurs 3 times in Bentley's short statement, once every 194 words, a frequency almost a thousand times greater than that instanced in the spoken corpus. In addition not only does this "I then" structure, as one might predict from the corpus data, not occur at all in any of the three witness statements, but also there are, by contrast, 9 occurrences in one single 980 word police statement, as many as in the entire 1.5 million word spoken corpus. Taken together the average occurrence in the three police statements is once every 119 words. In other words, the structure "I then" does appear to be a feature of police (written) register.

More generally, it is in fact the structure Subject (+ Verb) followed by "then" which is typical of policeman's register; it occurs 26 times in the statements of the three officers and 7 times in Bentley's statement. Interestingly, Svartvik (1968:29-32) had made the same discovery, but had not actually made it explicit, because the analytical category he had used was 'clauses with mobile relator', with a gloss to the effect that 'such clauses include then and also'. What he did not emphasise, obviously because he did not have access to corpora and therefore did not realise its significance, was the fact that in each and every one of the 23 examples of the category in his corpus the 'mobile relator' was realised by "then".

When we turn to look at yet another corpus, the shorthand verbatim record of the oral evidence given in court during the trial of Bentley and Craig, and choose one of the police officers at random we find him using the structure twice in successive sentences, "shot him then between the eyes" and "he was then charged". In Bentley's oral evidence there are also two occurrences of "then", but at this time the "thens" occur in the normal preposed position: "and then the other people moved off", "and then we came back up". Even Mr Cassels, one of the defence barristers, who one might expect to have been influenced by police reporting style, says "then you". Recently other linguists, working on a whole series of British police and witness statements, have confirmed the use of postposed "then" to be a marked feature of police register.

e) Consistency

This is a strange case. A man was arrested and charged with armed robbery. He denied the offence but accepted a police invitation to go out with them in a patrol car and show them where he had actually been at the time of the robbery. A police officer made contemporaneous notes of this journey on both sides of a sheet of lined paper attached to a clip-board resting on his knee. When they returned to the police station the accused was asked to sign the paper as a true record of the journey, which he did after asking for one minor correction. The accused, and now convicted man claims that after he had signed the document the first third of which is presented below, it was interfered with. There is no doubt that the whole test is in the same hand, i.e. it was written by the same person, but the suggestion is that the original was written on alternate lines and that these spaces were filled in afterwards. What the accused claims to be authentic is presented in bold and the lines have been numbered for ease of reference:

1.1	5:00 pm	**O/S P. Station**
1.2		I/think/came past here yesterday I then
1.3		turned left. Up there (towards Nortonway).
1.4		but I'll know for sure after
1.5	5:06 pm	**At Mercury towards Wimslow (not**
1.6		**Little Norton)** as I first said
1.7		this morning
1.8		**Left on A5302, Gloucester Rd**, Whitby
1.9		and went towards town centre
1.10		**Through T/L (Underton Rd)**
1.11		and carried straight on
1.12		**Stopped near Hopleys** + looked at
1.13		some of the cars down left side and some of the
1.14		**Cars down right hand side,** I got back
1.15		into car then.
1.16		**(Pointed out Patsy Ang.)** that's where
1.17		I get my dinner
1.18		**Pointed out Halifax,** I might have
1.19		looked in the window there.
1.20		**Stopped on Gunman car park** and
1.21		that's where I walked back.

After studying this text for some time it becomes clear that the utterances fall into two groups with different grammatical composition rules: the claimed authentic notes have what one might call note-taking grammar, which has no articles, no continuous tenses, verbs with subjects and occasionally clauses with no verb at all:

1.10	**Through T/L/ (Underton Rd)**
1.18	**Pointed out Halifax**
1.20	**Stopped on Gunman car park**

Whereas most of the claimed additions composed in tranquillity, have the full range of choices of the grammar of standard written English:

1.2/3	I then / turned left
1.4	but I'll know for sure after
1.14/15	I got back / into car then
1.18/19	might have / looked in the window there
1.21	that's where I walked back

In fact all the criminating items in the two page text are in full grammar, are linguistically and semantically dependent on the note-taking grammar items and incidentally, although in the same hand, in smaller letters. There is thus no doubt that the text was written on two separate occasions; what the linguistic analysis cannot demonstrate, of course, is whether the full text was on the paper when it was signed or whether, as the accused claimed, the additions were made after the document had been signed.

Interpretation

The meaning of phrases or even individual words can be crucial in some trials. Perhaps the most famous example comes from the case of Derek Bentley already referred to above. Bentley, already under arrest at the time was said to have shouted to Craig, who had a revolver, "let him have it, Chris", shortly afterwards Craig fires several shots and killed the policeman. There was a long debate in court, without any linguist being consulted, over the interpretation of the ambiguous utterance. It was resolved in favour of the prosecution's incriminating interpretation, "shoot him"; this made Bentley an accessory to murder, for which he was convicted and later hanged.

More often, the dispute is not over what an item was intended to mean by the producer of the message but rather what a non-expert, the Ordinary man-in-the-street, might reasonably have interpreted it to mean. For example, at the moment there are cases coming to the American courts about the meaning of warnings on cigarette packets and advice given to women contemplating breast implants. The problem for the linguist is how to discover and then to argue what the 'ordinary' meaning of an item actually is. One fairly new method is to argue on the basis of evidence of actual usage taken from computerised collections of millions of words of spoken and written texts.

My colleague John Sinclair was asked to give an opinion on the ordinary man's understanding of the word *visa.* Apparently in law a visa is not an 'entry permit' but rather ' a permit to request "leave to enter" '. Sinclair was asked to provide evidence that this is not the commonly understood use and meaning of the word. He based his evidence mainly on a 5 million word corpus of The Times Newspaper, although he supplemented the detailed analysis with the reference to the whole of the Birmingham Bank of English, totalling, at that time, some 28 million words and now approaching 200 million. The Times corpus included 74 instances of "visa" and "visas" in the sense under consideration, of which over 50 collocated with common verbs like "grant", "issue", "reuse", "apply for" and "need" and Sinclair noted that, although the commonest modified of "visa(s)" is "exit" it also co-occurs with "entry" and "re-entry":

> *You cannot enter an Arab country with an Israeli visa stamped in your passport;*
> *British passport holders do not require visas;*
> *Non-Commonwealth students who require an entry visa will need a re-entry visa, even if you only leave the country for a couple of days.*
>
> (Sinclair 1991)

Thus he concluded that

> *The average visitor, encountering everyday English of the type recorded in the corpus, would deduce that a visa was a kind of permit to enter a country ... There is nothing ... in these examples to suggest that a person who is in possession of a valid visa, or who does not require a visa, will be refused entry. The implication is very strong that a visa either ensures entry, or is not needed for entry. The circumstances of someone requiring "leave to enter" in addition to having correct visa provision does not arise in any of the examples, and the word "leave" does not occur in proximity to "visa(s)" except in the meaning "depart". (ibid)*

This is an example of what can be achieved with a fairly common word and a reasonably small corpus and demonstrates very clearly the usefulness of the method. However, it also shows that it is essential to have a substantial number of instances of the word in question and is therefore in itself a justification for the collection of very large corpora - if for instance one was interested in the word "pimp" which occurs in the existing corpora a mere once every 2 million words, one would ideally need to consult a corpus of some 200 million words.

Concluding Remarks

What I have attempted is to give an idea of the ways in which current linguistic techniques can be applied to forensic texts. The methodologies are still being developed and refined - there is now an International Association of Forensic Linguists whose members are working together to create and evaluate new techniques and divulge them in their recently founded journal Forensic Linguistics. However, although many cases are still intractable, the achievements already are, as I hope to have shown, exciting and suggestive.

Appendix

Derek Bentley 'Statement'

I have known Craig since I went to school. We were stopped by our parents going out together, but we still continued going out with each other - I mean we have not gone out together until tonight. I was watching television tonight (2 November 1952) and between 8 pm and 9 pm Craig called for me. My mother answered the door and I heard her say I was out. I had been out earlier to the pictures and got home just after 7 pm. A little later Norman Parsley and Frank Fazey called. I did not answer the door or speak to them. My mother told me that they had called and I then ran after them. I walked up the road with them to the paper shop where I saw Craig standing. We all talked together and then Norman Parsley and Frank Fazey left. Chris Craig and I then caught a bus to Croydon. We got off at West Croydon and then walked down the road where the toilets are - I think it is Tamworth Road.

When we came to the place where you found me, Chris looked in the window. There was a little iron gate at the side. Chris then jumped over and I followed. Chris then climbed up the drainpipe to the roof and I followed. Up to then Chris had not said anything. We both got out on to the flat roof at the top. Then someone in a garden on the opposite side shone a torch up towards us. Chris said: 'It's a copper, hide behind here'. We hid behind a shelter arrangement on the roof. We were there waiting for about ten minutes. I did not know he was going to use the gun. A plain clothes man climbed up the drainpipe and on to the roof. The man said: 'I am a police officer - the place is surrounded.' He caught hold of me and as we walked away Chris fired. There was nobody else there at the time. The policeman and I then went round a corner by a door. A little later the door opened and a policeman fell down. I could see he was hurt as a lot of blood came from his forehead just above his nose. The policeman dragged him round the corner behind the brickwork entrance to the door. I remember I shouted something but I forget what it was. I could not see Chris when I shouted to him - he was behind a wall. I heard some more policemen behind the door and the policeman with me said: 'I don't think he has many more bullets left'. Chris shouted 'Oh yes I have' and he fired again. I think I heard him fire three times altogether. The policeman then pushed me down the stairs and I did not see any more. I knew we were going to break into the place. I did not know what we were going to get - Just anything that was going. I did not have a gun and I did not know Chris had one until he shot. I now know that the policeman in uniform is dead. I should have mentioned that after the plain clothes policeman got up the drainpipe and arrested me, another policeman in uniform followed and I heard someone call him 'Mac'. He was with us when the other policeman was killed.

References

Baldwin, J. and French, J. (1990). *Forensic Phonetics.* London: Pinter.

Brazil, D. C. (1985). *The Communicative Value of Intonation.* Birmingham: English Language Research.

Canter, D. (1992). An Evaluation of the 'Cusum' Stylistic Analysis of Confessions, *Expert Evidence*, I,ii.

Coulthard, R. M. (ed) (1986). *Talking about Text.* Birmingham: ELR.

Coulthard, R. M. (1992). 'Forensic Discourse Analysis', in R. M. Coulthard (ed), *Advances in Spoken Discourse Analysis*. London: Routledge, 242-57.

Coulthard, R. M. (1993). '*Beginning the Study of Forensic Texts: Corpus, Concordance, Collacation', Data Description Discourse*, London: Harper Collins, 86-97.

Coulthard, R. M. (1994a). 'Powerful Evidence for the Defence: an Exercise in Forensic Discourse Analysis', in J. Gibbons (ed), *Language and the Law*, London: Longman, 1441-42.

Coulthard, R. M. (1994b). 'On the Use of Corpora in the Analysis of Forensic Texts', *Forensic Linguistics*, 1,1, 27-43.

Davis, T. (1986). 'Forensic Handwriting Analysis' in R. M. Coulthard (ed) *Talking about Text.* Birmingham: ELR, 189-207.

Davis, T. (1994). 'ESDA and the Analysis of Contested Contemporaneous Notes of Police Interviews', *Forensic Linguistics: the International Journal Of Speech Language and the Law*, l,i, 71-89.

Fox, G. (1993). 'A Comparison of "Policespeak" and "Normalspeak": a Preliminary Study' in J.M. Sinclair, M. Hoey and G. Fox (eds*) Techniques of Description: Spoken and Written Discourse, A Festschrift for Malcolm Coulthard*, London: Routledge 183-95.

French, J. P. (1994) An Overview of Forensic Phonetics with Particular Reference to Speaker Identification. *Forensic Linguistics: the International Journal of Speech Language and the Law*, 1, 2, 169-181.

Gibbons, J. (ed) (1994). *Language and the law*, London: Longman.

Grice, H. P. (1975). Logic and Conversation. in P. Cole and J. Morgan (eds) *Syntax and Semantics III, Speech Acts*, New York: Academic Press, 41-58.

Halliday, M. A. K. (1989) *Spoken and Written Language*, 2nd edition, Oxford: OUP.

Hollien, H. (1990) *The Acoustics of Crime* London: Plenum.

Kunzel, H. (1987). *Sprechererkennung: Grudzuge Forensischer, Heidelberg: Kriminalistik-Verlag.*

Levi, J. (1994a). Language as Evidence: the Linguist as Expert Witness in North American Courts, *Forensic Linguistics*, 1,i,1-26.

Levi, J. (1994b). Language as Evidence: the Linguist as Expert Witness in North American Courts, *Forensic Linguistics: the International Journal of Speech Language and the Law*, 1,I, 1-26.

Levi, J. N. and Walker, A. G. (eds) (1990). *Language In the Judicial Process*, London: Plenum.

Morton, A. Q. (1991). *Proper Words in Proper Places*, Glasgow: University, Department of Computing Science.

Nolan, F. (1983). *The Phonetic Bases of Speaker Recognition* Cambridge: CUP.

Sanford, A. J., Aked, J. P., Moxey, L. M. and Mullin, J. (1994). A Critical Examination of Assumptions Underlying the Cusum Technique of Forensic Linguistics. *Forensic Linguistics: the International Journal of Speech Language and the Law*, 1, 2, 151-167.

Sinclair, J. McH. Unpublished expert opinion on the ordinary man's understanding of the word "visa".
Sinclair, J. McH. (1991). *Corpus, Concordance, Collacation*, Oxford OUP.
Svartvik, J. (1968). *The Evans Statements: A Case for Forensic Linguistics*, Goteborg, University of Gothenburg Press.

7 The Decision to Die: The Psychology of the Suicide Note

ADAM GREGORY

This chapter examines the content of "genuine" and "simulated" suicide notes. Through the use of a multivariate approach, it shows how 66 suicide notes may be discriminated with respect to nine variables. Where the analysis facilitated the separation of these variables into two groups. The first broadly reflects measures of content whilst the other is characterised by measures of structure. A second anlaysis demonstrated that the five measures of content best discriminated between genuine and simulated notes. It is proposed that collectively these five variables reflect the degree to which an individual has internalised the decision to die. Further analysis suggests that within content measures there exist two sub-divisions, whereby genuine notes may be identified through an analysis of lexical components with respect to psychological themes deemed characteristic of a genuine wish to die.

Adam Gregory has been an employee of the Behavioural Science Section (BSS) of Surrey Police since completing his B.Sc (Hons) in Psychology at the University of Surrey in 1994. His role within the BSS, as a Behavioural Consultant, is to provide investigative support to Police personnel across a wide range of policing issues. These issues include tackling violent crimes such as sexual assault and homicide as well as higher volume crimes like burglary, autocrime and drug related offences. The Section is headed by Mr Rupert Heritage having grown out of the Offender Profiling Unit which he established in 1993. Profiling work is still undertaken by the section at a national and international level.

*Offender Profiling Series: I - **Interviewing and Deception***
Edited by D. Canter and L.Alison. © 1999 Ashgate Publishing, Aldershot. pp 127-156

7 The Decision to Die: The Psychology of the Suicide Note

ADAM GREGORY

Introduction

The Suicide Note is a potentially rich, yet largely ignored, primary source of information, about suicide and about language. Since the notes will be typically written just prior to the suicide attempt, the information accessed is likely to reflect the state of mind which underlie the decision to take one's own life, as well as the aspects of language common to these states.

If it is possible to look at features of life which are either consistent or inconsistent with a suicidal individual, an approach utilised by Psychological Autopsy, a procedure used with varying success in America to help resolve equivocal deaths (See Ebert, 1987; Dregne, 1982) it may be feasible to determine how these features manifest themselves in the language used in a suicide note.

A Genuine and Simulated Suicide Note Corpus

If, as postulated here, there exist common features in the language of genuine suicide notes, it would seem sensible to compare them with notes written by non-suicidal individuals, as a means of clearly identifying the subtle features that distinguish them.

Shneidman and Farberow (1957) provide a corpus of 33 pairs of suicide notes, where each pair has one genuine suicide note and one which was written by a non-suicidal individual, termed a simulated suicide note. The Authors' intention was to provide a corpus for subsequent study by themselves, (and by others) since they felt that the examination and study of such notes would provide clues to the affect, conflicts and motivations of the suicidal person. The details of this corpus made it very appropriate for use in the present study.

The 33 genuine suicide notes of the 66 note corpus, as presented in Clues to Suicide (1957), edited by Edwin S. Shneidman and Norman L. Farberow, were obtained from the Office of the Coroner, Los Angeles County, between the years 1945 and 1954. Each of these writers was matched man-for-man with a simulated note writer of similar chronological age (within 5 years), and of the same occupational level, thus giving a total of 66 notes. All 66 subjects were male, Caucasian, Protestant and between the ages of 25 and 59. The simulated note writers were screened to ensure that no one showed any sign of personality disturbance or tendency towards morbid thought.

In line with the intentions of the above authors, the present study hypothesised that it would be possible to identify a number of linguistic features which, in combination, would allow discrimination between the two groups of notes; genuine and simulated. In this way it would be possible to deduce just what it is about a genuine suicide note that makes it authentic, as well as identifying the features of a suicidal state of mind which non-suicidal individuals are perhaps unable fully to comprehend.

The Language of Suicide

A number of studies have utilised the Shneidman and Farberow corpus of notes, in a variety of ways. There were three major studies which closely followed the publication of the suicide note corpus: Osgood and Walker (1959); Gottschalk and Glesser (1960); and Ogilvie, Stone and Shneidman (1966). The common objective of these studies was to generate criteria which would permit a researcher or clinician to analyze a particular piece of text and from it assess a suicidal state. All three of these studies looked directly at the notes in the corpus, using content analytic measures, such as Type/Token ratio (number of different words/number of total words), Noun/Verb ratio, and other measures drawn largely from the General Inquirer (Stone et al., 1966). The methods were either applied by hand or by the use of computer analysis packages. For example, Ogilvie, Stone and Shneidman, (1966) used a computer based linguistic analysis procedure called the Harvard II Psychosociological Dictionary which breaks language down using two categories of what are called Tags. First order tags are further divided into Things Roles and Objects, or Processes: Emotional States and Actions, whilst Second order tags refer to Institutions, Statuses, Qualities and Symbolic Referents. Differences in the frequency of these Tags were noted between the two types of suicide notes using the same 66 note corpus as was used in the present study. A number of conclusions were drawn.

More references to things and less references to processes were found in the genuine notes, compared to the simulated notes (a finding supported by Gottschalk and Glesser), as well as a higher frequency of the word love. In contrast the simulated notes had an emphasis on references to processes rather than things, and showed evidence of problem solving, in contrast to evidence suggesting that problems had already been solved, as was found in the genuine notes.

In addition to these findings, Osgood and Walker found that the use of indices such as stereotyping, and the use of distress words differed significantly between genuine and simulated notes. They also concluded that the genuine note writer uses more nouns and verbs, and shorter sentence segments.

More recently, an important study by Edelman and Renshaw (1982), criticises this group of studies at three levels.

Firstly, no attempt was made to explore the relationship between any of the measures identified, or to combine them in order to provide a statistically significant multivariate model for use as a quantitative and predictive tool for accurately and consistently making discriminations. Secondly, no unified theory of discourse analysis methodology was generated or used. It is therefore the task of the researcher or clinician to judge which measures should be used, and when. Finally none of the studies are able to provide what Edelman and Renshaw refer to as being a consistent language profile. Therefore no unified theory of the suicidal person can be determined.

Edelman and Renshaw, performed their own study (a discourse analysis) of the 66 note corpus of Shneidman and Farberow. They sought to verify the findings of the previous research, and to provide a discriminatory tool for assessing language indicants in the pathological state of suicide. They also hypothesised that it would be possible to develop a general language profile of the cognitive state of a person who writes a suicide note, prior to committing the act. The details of their methodology are given below.

By using the Syntactic Language Computer Analysis (III) package, Edelman and Renshaw attempted to derive a 'map' of an individual's cognitive states by examining that individual's verbal behaviour. SLCA-III is based upon three types of lexical classification:

Information units (Nouns)
Relational units (Verbs)
Qualifiers (Adjectives and Adverbs)

each of which can have eight qualities which apply in different ways to the three categories: These included:

Time - past, present or future
Sensation - abstract or concrete
Existence - perceived to exist or not exist
Motion - to indicate activity or a state.

A total of 36 variables were generated.

They used t-tests (2-tailed, $p<0.05$) to decide which of the variables discriminated between the genuine and the simulated notes in the sample. Nine variables satisfied this criteria: Total word usage, Total Information Units (nouns), Negative Audience (the word you), and Negative Existential Density (asserting the word not). A subsequent multiple discriminant analysis of all 36 variables also identified the measure Future Time. This discriminant function was used to classify the notes, and showed an accuracy of 80% (27 genuine and 26 simulated noted classified correctly).

The authors do therefore attempt to provide a language profile of the suicidal individual, which draws upon notions of Cognitive Energy, Cognization of the finality of life, and Alienation from the world in general to provide the theoretical framework. However, the emphasis still seems to be on the observed changes in language themselves, rather than the explanation of why these changes occur. Any underlying processes are mentioned to explain particular features and observations, rather than truly accomplishing a unifying theory underpinning the suicide process, as was their objective.

Although the hypotheses proposed are perhaps less than satisfied and the arguments supporting them are by no means definitive, the development of some of the ideas presented by Edelman and Renshaw may still prove fruitful.

In contrast to the methods utilised above, there has been research which has looked at the problem of discriminating between genuine and simulated suicide notes from the perspective of the judge and the criteria he/she uses (Arbeit and Blatt, 1973; Leenaars, 1991; Leenaars and Lester, 1991). The objectives in these studies were to identify what it was about suicide notes (again from the Shneidman and Farberow corpus), which convinced people that they were genuine (or simulated).

Leenaars, (1991) attempted to define observable protocol sentences which were representative of a number of theoretical formulations to be tested. Although these sentences were found to reliably predict the content of the notes in general, when they were subsequently reduced to a meaningful empirical nosology using cluster analysis (eight discrete clusters being identified), none of the clusters were able to discriminate between the two groups (genuine and simulated) of notes. Leenaars and Lester (1991) further suggest (from their phenomenological analysis of the same notes) that although people typically look for evidence of a prior traumatic event in the notes, no other generalisations of the criteria used by people seem to exist. Indeed, the authors conclude that people hold strikingly opposite views of suicide; often both are wrong.

However this approach has been more successfully utilised by Arbeit and Blatt (1973), who focused on peoples' (primarily clinicians) capacity to detect and understand the communication of suicidal intent. Their principle goals were given as being, to assess whether discrimination could be made between the notes of suicidal and non-suicidal people, what criteria or particular features of the notes were used in the process, and whether the level of clinical training affects the ability to make such distinctions. The procedure used was as follows.

The authors randomly divided the 33 pairs of notes (from the Shneidman and Farberow corpus) into 3 groups. They then asked 93 subjects of differing clinical ability (ranging from undergraduates to practising clinicians), to decide which of the 11 pairs of suicide notes, allocated to them, were genuine. They also asked the subjects to decide which factors in the notes were indicative of a genuine suicide and which were not. Finally the subjects rated each of these factors in terms of its importance weighting, indicating how strong a predictor (of a genuine or a non-genuine note) each factor was considered as being. Whilst (perhaps surprisingly) finding no significant differences between the abilities of each subject group in identifying the genuine note from each pair, differences were found across the sample as a whole. Therefore the sample was divided purely in terms of their accuracy on the task and each group was analyzed with reference to the factors chosen by each, and the importance weighting attributed to them.

Accuracy of judgment was significantly related to the use of 10 factors and to the degree of importance placed upon 4 factors. Some of these factors are listed below; the first group are deemed to be more likely to indicate a genuine suicide note, whilst the second group are more indicative of a simulated note.:

Group 1
Longer notes.
More positive affect.
Presence of instructions to survivors.
Higher awareness of reflection of action on others.

Group 2
Higher sense of despair.
Increased relief from tension.

Although this second approach is, empirically, not as useful as the first, it is still able to yield some interesting and potentially useful findings. By looking at the criteria used by accurate judges, (as done by Arbeit and Blatt) it is possible that further measures of discrimination may be identified.

Limitations of Previous Research

When taken as a whole, the literature concerning suicide notes is relatively poor. At present a large number of variables have been identified by various studies, which seem to discriminate between genuine and simulated notes, but this array of findings is almost completely without structure. The principal explanation for this observation is derived from the nature of the majority of research and the scarcity of research taking a multivariate approach. The objectives and hypotheses given in many studies relate directly to the goal of discrimination, with little concern to any theoretical framework to explain the findings or relate the measures used to each other or to explicit psychological process that may underlie the decision to take ones own life. Probably the most comprehensive and therefore noteworthy account is that of Edelman and Renshaw (1982) as detailed above. However even their proposed model may be faulted, largely due to the constraints put upon it by the reliance upon computer based content analytic procedures. Such methods dictate that the analysis be concerned exclusively with the more structural aspects of language, with little provision for more thematic content; an aspect possibly of some importance in gaining a complete understanding of the cognitive, psychological processes which underlie the suicidal state of mind.

A Holistic Multivariate Approach

This study attempted to build upon the findings of previous research, by devising a multivariate model of the suicidal individual. The model utilises a broader and more diverse selection of variables, which whilst being largely drawn from previous findings, define and relate more completely, the range of psychological processes that underlie the decision to die.

An Appropriate Range of Variables

The selected range of variables were derived in a number of ways. The majority were taken from the above literature and past research concerning suicide notes themselves and consist of measures that have been successfully utilised before, either directly or in a form that lent itself well to adaptation or modification. The remaining variables were derived more loosely from literature on suicide in general (eg. Atkinson, 1978; Shneidman, 1976; Choron, 1972; Wekstein, 1979) and the hypothesised processes that are said to underlie it, or were the result of more intuitive psychological expectation and experience of suicide notes themselves.

The Detailed Hypothesis

The nine variables selected are listed below, along with a brief note of the underlying theory for each, and an indication of the direction in which each was expected to vary. It should be noted that there exists an order to the variables in terms of their 'nature', such that they constitute a range which becomes progressively less characteristic of the notes' Structure and more characteristic of their Content. The former are therefore direct measures of the linguistic structure of the suicide note and could have been applied to any sample of written text, whilst the latter relate to the more thematic content of the note, and are therefore more contextualy based, being specific to the language of suicide, rather than to language in general.

1 Percentage of Nouns

This identified trend is possibly related to the concept of cognitive energy (i.e. the degree of mental activity) of an individual, as proposed by Cummings and Renshaw (1979). This is likely to be higher for the genuine note writer and could manifest itself in language as an increased lexical density of which the percentage of nouns is a measure. Almost all relevant research has indicated that high noun usage is more likely to be most common in genuine suicide notes. This was directly measured by Osgood and Walker, (1959) and by Edelman and Renshaw, (1982) whilst Gottschalk and Glesser, (1960) noticed that genuine notes had more references to people places and things and the hypothesis used in this study was in line with these findings.

2 Percentage of Verbs

It may be suggested that the genuine note writer is likely to be more concerned with actions, both before (his) and after (others) the suicide act, rather than with feelings (for example, see Left Instructions). The hypothesis was therefore that the proportion of verbs in the writings of genuine suicide note writers would be higher than their simulated counterparts. Although predictively not as strong or robust as the nouns measure, some research (notably that of Osgood and Walker, 1959) has indeed given support to this hypothesis.

3 Average Sentence Length

Another implication of increased cognitive energy of the suicidal individual, may be his/her ability to express more ideas in a more concise manner.

Although research shows that the mean length of genuine suicide notes, in terms of the total number of words, is greater, there is also some evidence that the language segments which make up the note are on average, shorter. This again seems to reflect the apparent increase in lexical density for the genuine note writer, as mentioned in variable 1. Osgood and Walker (1959), identified this trend in terms of clause length but this study took the sentence as the unit of measurement for simplicity, the hypothesis being that similar findings would result i.e. the mean sentence length of genuine note writers would be shorter than that of the simulated note writers.

4 Total Number of Words

Logically, it may be suggested that an individual truly on the brink of taking their own life, is likely to have more to say due to the increased availability and salience of information to draw upon, when actually writing the note. It may be that this finding is a further manifestation of increased cognitive energy. For these reasons the total number of words used by the individual was hypothesised as being greater for the genuine note writer.

5 Percentage of Cognitive Process Verbs

Gottschalk and Glesser, (1960) indicate that the proportion of references to cognitive processes decreases as the complement of references to people, places and things, for the genuine note writer. These findings were supported by Ogilvie, Stone and Shneidman in 1966. It is likely that by the time the genuinely suicidal individual actually comes to write the note, all or most of his thoughts, doubts and decisions would have already been resolved, whilst this is unlikely to apply to the rather false reasoning of the non-suicidal note writer. It was hypothesised that these processes will be reflected in the proportion of verbs which have a cognitive component, ie. greater for the simulated note writer. Examples of such verbs include, to Feel, Want, Forgive, Hope, etc.

6 Positive Affect

If emotion is expressed in genuine suicide notes, it is proposed that, generally it will be positive, giving support and praise to survivors, and reflecting on the positive aspects of the past. It is likely that there will be a failure, by the simulated note writers, to appreciate this, since it does not fit with their more stereotyped ideas of anger, blame or revenge. It was suggested by Arbeit and Blatt, (1973) that positive affect is seen as being an important indicator of a genuine note by accurate judges whilst Ogilvie, Stone and Shneidman, (1966) noted that the word love had a higher frequency in the genuine suicide notes than in the simulated ones. This particular variable combined these two findings using a framework common to normal note writing (whereby Dear.... and Love....... are seen as being the typical opening and close of a letter) and therefore reflects the degree of positive emotional content expressed within the language of the suicide notes. Such words included Love, Loving(ly), Dear(ly), Dearest, Darling, Beloved and Bless, the hypothesis being that the amount of positive affect found in the genuine notes would be greater than that of the simulated.

7 Left Instructions

It is likely that the genuine suicide note writer has a strong need to communicate with survivors by means of last instructions, (see particularly, Lester and Leenaars, 1988). These may take the form of requests for particular burial arrangements, final wishes for family or friends, or the designation of the receiver of items in a will. Whichever form they take they are always more likely to appear in the language of the genuine rather than the simulated note writer, which was the hypothesis in this case.

8 Reasons/Explanation Given

Whether or not an individual provides the reader of the note with an explanation of the reasons for their action (real or imagined), and if so, how specific these reasons are, are both likely to discriminate between genuine and simulated note writers. It was hypothesised that genuine note writers will firstly be less likely to give any explanation for their action (as this may not be the purpose of the note, particularly if the individual feels that he has already made his intentions clear), and secondly if reasons are provided they are likely to be highly specific (since they would be able to draw their reasons from real life events which had actually occurred prior to their decision to commit suicide). In contrast, the simulated note writer was hypothesised to be more likely to provide the reader with explanations for their action (reflecting the stereotyped expectation of the primary purpose of the note), and also to exhibit a decreased specificity within these explanations (due to the relatively low availability and salience of specific reasons compared to those of a stereotypical and therefore general nature). Finally, suicide decisions based (explicitly) upon the loss of mind were also hypothesised to have been provided by non-suicidal individuals, characterising their stereotypical perceptions and expectations of the mental processes which underlie the decision to die. General reason notes and loss of mind notes were therefore grouped together as being more characteristic of the simulated note writer, whilst specific or no reason notes were grouped as being more likely to be written by the genuinely suicidal individual.

9. Locus of Control

It may be expected that genuine note writers are more likely to have an external locus of control, thus rendering themselves devoid of responsibility and leaving themselves no option, whilst the simulated note writer may well perceive themselves as having control, (ie. internal) reflecting their inability to empathise with the true feelings of the suicidal individual. This variable was therefore designed to discriminate between (hypothesised suicidal) individuals who perceive that they no longer have control of the situation or their own destiny and instead attribute the blame to external, usually social forces, (eg. "The world is too cruel, this is the only way out for me") from those (hypothesised non-suicidal) individuals who attribute control as being internal, almost independent of outside factors, (eg. "I have chosen to end my life").

The above variables were subject to a number of criteria, the main one of which was that they must be strictly objective and verifiable. This was deemed essential for a truly empirical study of written text and language. For this reason any variable in the list above deemed subjective in nature, was coded using two independent raters who scored such variables in parallel with the researcher according to set guidelines. As with all variables, no judge was aware of the nature of the source of any note, be it genuine or simulated. A content analysis of the 66 notes was performed and the variables were measured according to the above hypotheses.

Smallest Space Analysis of the Selected Variables

Since the problem is clearly a multivariate one, a Smallest Space Analysis (SSA) was performed, in order to examine the relationships between the nine variables and therefore provide an insight into the processes which underpin the decision to die.

Figure 7.1 shows the 2 dimensional solution of the SSA using the monotonicity coefficient. Variables highly correlated with each other are represented as being close to each other in the space, whilst variables with low (or negative) correlations are to be found some distance apart. For example, Total number of words is highly correlated (r=0.89) with Positive Affect and so these two points are in close proximity of each other. In contrast, the correlation of Total number of words with Nouns is very low at 0.01 and therefore the distance between these two variables is much larger. This plot has a coefficient of alienation of 0.128, which means that it is an accurate graphical representation of the relationships between the variables.

The SSA indicated that a clear distinction of the variables into two groups was appropriate, a line has been added to the plot to illustrate this. This distinction is clearly based upon the 'nature' of the variables as explained earlier.

The closely packed group of variables on the right of the plot was broadly comprised of variables concerned with note Content:

1) Locus of Control, Reason/Explanation, Positive Affect, Left Instructions and Total Words:

whereas the second group of variables, those spread more widely over the left hand side of the space, were more indicative of the Structure of the notes, consisting of:

2) Sentence Length, Nouns, Verbs and Cognitive Process Verbs.

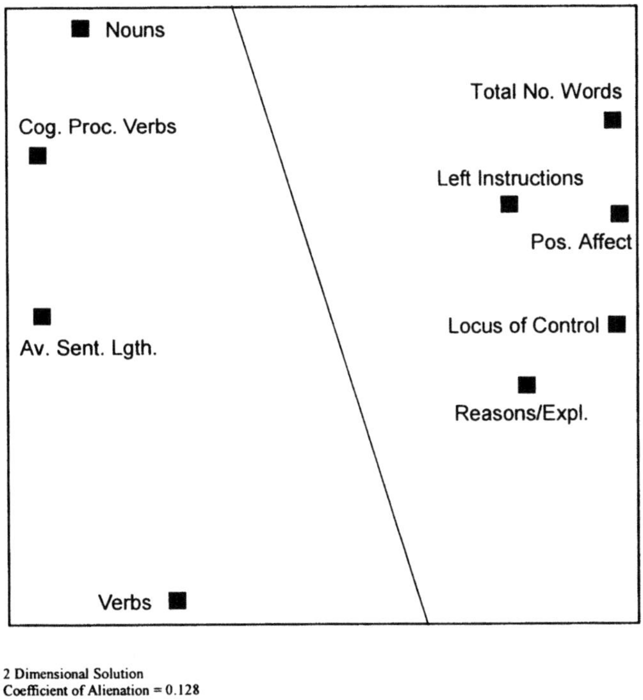

Figure 7.1 SSA of 9 Variables Over the 66 Suicide Notes

The only anomaly in these groupings was the presence of, Total Number of Words in Group 1, the Content group. This measure of note length had been considered as being a measure of structure by all previous research as well as by this study; an explanation is therefore required. The explanation of this finding is only apparent when the variable is considered with respect to other measures in the same (content) group. If, as has been hypothesised, genuine suicide notes may be characterised by the inclusion of left instructions as well as a greater emphasis on specifics, it is then a logical step to expect that such features would result in an increase in the number of words used in these genuine notes, and therefore explain why Total Number of Words is actually more closely associated with measures of content than with measures of note structure.

The Discrimination of Genuine and Simulated Suicide Notes

Partial Order Scalogram Analysis, or POSA was used as a means of discriminating between the suicide notes themselves, rather than between different types of variables. According to Shye (1985), POSA is essentially a technical procedure for fitting observed profiles into a two dimensional space, subject to the condition that order relations, including incomparability, are preserved. For POSA to work effectively a number of preliminary criteria needed to be met. In contrast to SSA which is based upon correlations, and the similarity between variables, POSA utilises profiles and is based upon differences in these profiles across subjects (a profile being simply a sequence of values attained by each note from variable 1 to variable n, where n is the last variable in the series). It is therefore essential to maintain a common order in the variables, ensuring that they all vary in the same direction as well as minimising the total number of possible profiles which may be achieved within the data set. In line with these demands, the re-coding of the nine variables such that they all took values from 1 to a maximum of 4, where high values were expected to be more indicative of genuine note writers, provided POSA with a particularly suitable data set.

Since SSA had produced a clear definition of two distinct groups of variables, two POSAs were performed, one using the group of content variables, and a second, with the four more structural variables, as a means of comparison.

POSA on 5 Content Variables

The plot generated by the first POSA is illustrated in Figure 7.2. Each different profile is represented by a point in space, this point however may represent more than one note since it is possible for notes to share the same profiles. The dotted lines have been drawn on to indicate particular regions of the space for which certain values are achieved.

These regions are labelled A, B, C, and D, for ease of reference, such that:

A = Low X and Low Y.
B = High X and Low Y.
C = Low X and High Y.
D = High X and High Y.

From the monotonicity coefficients of the variables with the axes, it is evident that the space is divided largely by the X and Y axes. The variables Locus of Control and Reason/Explanation have coefficients with the X axis of 0.94 and 1.00 respectively, whilst Total Words, Positive Affect and Left Instructions have coefficients of 0.98, 0.87 and 0.72 (respectively) with the Y axis. Whilst the spatial distribution is obviously more complicated than this, it is useful to think in these terms to allow a clearer interpretation. The regions A, B, C and D therefore broadly represent the following:

C	D
A	B

A: An internal locus of control, and general reasons/explanation for action. AND; A relatively short note (in terms of words), little expression of positive affect and no instructions for survivors.
B: An external locus of control, and specific or no reasons/explanations given. AND; A short note, little positive affect and no instructions left.
C: An internal locus of control, and general reasons/explanation. AND; A longer note, a higher degree of positive affect and instructions for survivors.
D: An external locus of control, and specific or no reasons/explanation for the decision. AND; A longer note, an increased positive emotional content and instructions left..

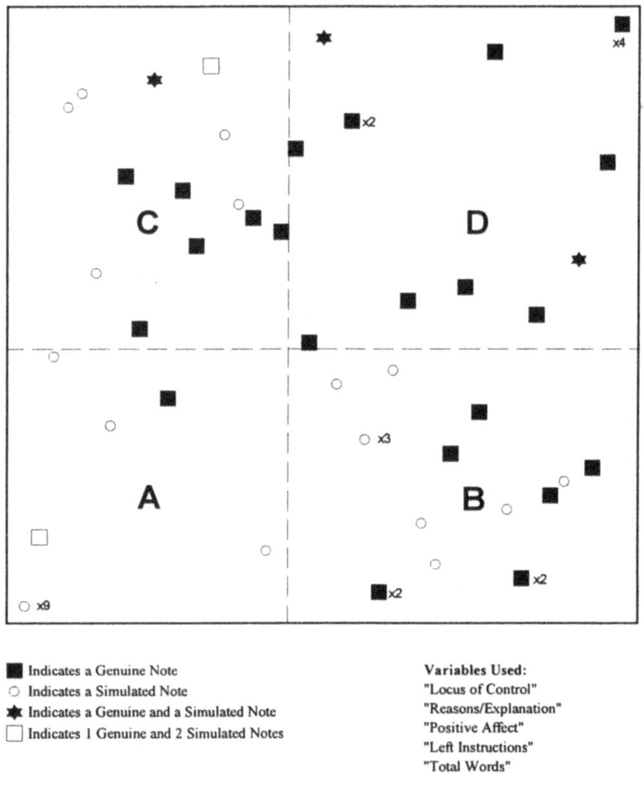

Figure 7.2 POSA of the 66 Suicide Notes Using 5 Content Variables

Since the common order hypothesised that high values will be indicative of genuine notes, it would be expected that the greatest amount of genuine notes would be located in the D region indicating high scores on all variables related to the axes whilst the least amount would be hypothesised to be in the A region where scores are low on these variables, indicative of a simulated note. Regions B and C were therefore hypothesised to contain a mixture (approximately 50:50) of genuine and simulated notes.

Examination of the plot reveals that this is indeed the case, the number of genuine notes compared to the total number of notes in each labelled region is given below.

A = 2 out of 16, (12.5%)
B = 8 out of 17, (47.1%)
C = 8 out of 16, (50.0%)
D = 15 out of 17, (88.2%)

POSA on 4 Structure Variables - A Comparison

A resulting plot from the second POSA, using the 4 variables thought to be measures of the Structure of the suicide notes, is given in Figure 7.3.

In this case, the X axis generally reflects Percentage of Verbs, (coef. = 1.00) whilst the Y axis discriminates largely in terms of Percentage of nouns, (coef = 0.97). There is no clear interpretation to be given for the variables, Sentence Length and Cognitive Process Verbs. Whilst it was possible to identify regions yielding similar expectations to the first POSA in terms of where each note would be plotted, a number of shortcomings can be noted. The most significant of these is that the number of notes in regions B and C is much greater than before (a total of 44, 2/3 of all notes, compared to 33, or 1/2 of all notes previously). Consequently there are fewer notes which fall into the extreme regions of A and D, where discrimination is at its best. Indeed there were only 5 of the 33 genuine notes to be found in region D.

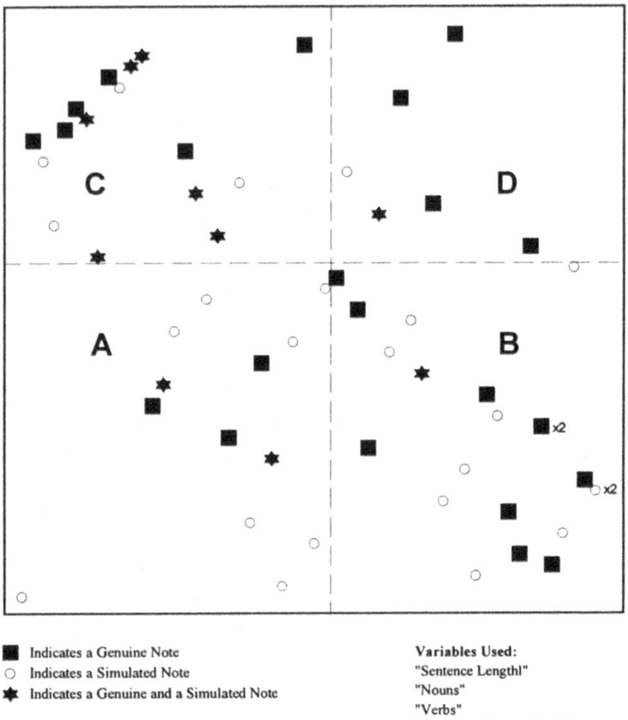

Figure 7.3 POSA of the 66 Suicide Notes Using 4 Structure Variables

Discussion

It is clear that the POSAs of the two independant groups of variables, representing Content and Structure, vary dramatically in their ability to discriminate between genuine and simulated suicide notes. Whilst the interpretation of the Content POSA is clear, utilising all the included variables and providing a high degree of discrimination, the second POSA of the structural variables is largely constructed with reference to only half of the variables used and produces poor discrimination with a large number of the notes present in the mixed regions (B and C) of the plot.

However the observed limitations of this POSA were not entirely unexpected, since in the SSA plot, these four variables were spread out in a broad region of the space, resulting from poor correlations between the variables used. For example the variables largely constituting the X and Y axes, Nouns and Verbs, have a monotonicity coefficient between them of -0.47 which suggests that a sizable portion of the sample with high percentages of Nouns, also have a relatively ***low*** percentage of Verbs, or vice versa. This demonstrates that there is perhaps a lack of structure to the variables in this POSA, which results in there being little similarity in the way that the variables discriminate between the two groups of notes.

A Common Order: The Internalisation of the Decision to Die

The utility of the language Content variables, and the success of the POSA using them, is likely to result from the fact there there exists a strong common order to the measures. It is suggested that this underlying common order is given by the degree to which the author of each note had internalised the decision to die. All five measures of note Content relate to this psychological factor such that as the degree of internalisation increases for any individual, their scores across the five variables are likely to increase acordingly. Therefore, a high degree of internalisation is likely to manifest itself as high values for most or all of the five content measures, an analysis of which will show such a note to be indicative of an individual's genuine intention to take his own life.

However, a closer inspection of how the plot is constructed reveals that a further distinction of this content group may exist, dividing the variables into two sub-groups, thus producing discrimination at two levels. The two axes, X and Y therefore reflect conceptually different types of discrimination. This finding is very important, and has the potential to provide further insight into the processes which underlie the decision to take one's own life, and the way in which different aspects of language come to indicate different aspects of the suicide process.

Firstly it may be suggested that the variables, Reasons/Explanation and Locus of Control are more thematic manifestations of the processes which precede the writing of the note. However, as themes they are still able to reflect the individual's decision to die quite directly. The Locus of Control variable, for a genuine note, tends to be External, indicating that the individual no longer feels that they have ultimate control of their life, but instead that some force in the social world dictates that suicide is the only way out of the situation that they find themselves in. It may further be suggested that this is a situation uncommon to the norms of society and life in general, in as much as people tend to strive for control as being something that they themselves have, at least to some degree. It is perhaps due to this imbalance between what is truly felt and what is socially correct, that results in the trend found in the other variable in this group, Reason/Explanation. The genuine suicide note writer is more likely to not give any reasons or explanation for their action. This could well be due to the individual having no desire to tell survivors of their inability to maintain control of their own existence. Alternatively the genuine note writers who do choose to provide an explanation, do so in very specific terms, giving maximum detail. Perhaps this is done as a way of conveying to the reader of the note, exactly why there really was no alternative, in the hope that they would be convinced. The simulated note writer on the other hand apparently has little trouble providing the reader with a fairly stereotypical (and therefore General) explanation for their decision, in which their locus of control is Internal, such as "I've had enough, can't take any more". This may well be due to the fact that such writers are aware that they are not really going to die, and are therefore less concerned about actually justifying their decision, yet feel that a suicide note should provide the reader with some degree of explanation. However it should also be noted that the lack of specific explanation in the simulated notes could be largely due to the fact that these note writers have no reasons available to them, and instead must draw on their own imagination. The high proportion of general reasons may therefore be a reflection of the inability or unwillingness of subjects to do this.

The second group of variables, consisting of Total Words, Left Instructions, and Positive Affect may be said to more closely represent the content of the notes in terms of the lexical components of which they are composed, since each operates at the word level. Total Words is a measure of cognitive energy and reflects the apparent increase in mental activity of the truly suicidal individual as well as the supposition that they are likely to have more to say. It is only when the individual has accepted that they really will not exist in the time following the writing of their note, that they derive the desire to express their wishes and instructions for survivors, in a full, and highly specific manner. Within this framework of a longer note, is found an increase in the presence of Positive Affect words such as love, and also an increased likelihood of the writer giving explicit instructions of future action to survivors.

With respect to the common order of Internalisation of the decision to die, it is apparent that non-suicidal individuals, tend to be characterised by low scores along this dimension. This manifests itself as their failure to empathise with the true feelings and desires of the suicidal individual. Instead they may assume that anger, revenge, or hatred should feature in their final note, rather than appreciating the need for expressing positive emotion, particularly towards those closest to them as is actually the case. The failure to empathise with these feelings may well be due to them knowing that such emotion can still be expressed in the living world. They also fail to recognise the strong desire to leave instructions to such people. This suggests that the simulated note writer has difficulty in achieving the shift in thoughts away from issues pertinent to the self, towards considerations of the future life of those people who they will be leaving behind, a process indicative of a truly suicidal individual.

It is interesting to note however, that there exist suicide notes which are apparently plotted in incorrect regions of the space. It may be suggested therefore, that some simulated note writers are very good at imagining themselves on the brink of taking their own life, and are therefore able to actually start to think in the appropriate ways. Conversely, some genuine note writers appear to write notes which, within the framework of this study at least, seem more akin to those of a non-suicidal individual. It would be interesting in this later case to know the true intentions of the individuals, the amount of time that the note was written before the suicidal act and also the duration of the time it took for the individual to decide upon suicide, all of which may affect the critical features of their notes, and thus aid explanation of their anomalous placement.

Validation Against a More Diverse Corpus

Since it has been demonstrated that the POSA using the 5 Content variables does indeed discriminate between the original corpus of 66 genuine and simulated suicide notes, its validation against an additional sample is appropriate.

For this reason, a total of 18 more suicide notes were obtained from various sources; mainly from books and papers, all of which were direct and complete replications of notes from genuine suicides. Although details such as precise age, occupational level, country of origin, or date of authorship were not always known, the additional sample was thought to provide a reasonable range or notes, sufficient for a comparison group. The New Genuine notes were scored over the five content variables as before, and their profiles were added to those of the original 66 notes and a POSA was once more performed.

Results and Interpretation

Figure 7.4 shows the plot produced by the POSA of the extended sample of 84 suicide notes. Once more, lines were added dividing the space into four regions, labelled A,B,C and D. These regions were drawn such that they divided the original 66 notes approximately equally in terms of number (A=17, B=16, C=18 and D=15), thus allowing a more accurate examination of where the 18 new genuine letters were placed in relation to the original sample.

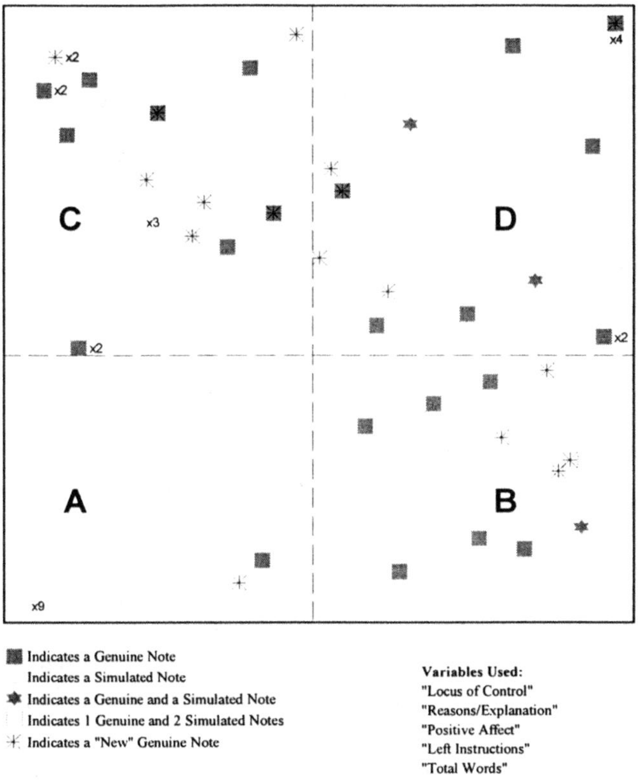

Figure 7.4 POSA of the 84 Suicide Notes Using 5 Content Variables

The structure of the POSA plot was found to be similar to that of the first, although the X and Y axes had switched, such that it was the Y axes which broadly represented Locus of Control, and Reason/Explanation (with correlations of 0.99 and 0.95 respectively) whilst the X axis which correlated highly with Total Words, Positive Affect and Left Instructions (with correlations of 0.84, 0.76 and 0.90 respectively). This switching of axes is not significant since their choice is arbitrary, but it does mean that the properties associated with regions B and C have reversed, if compared to the first POSA (Figure 7.2). Also, it is interesting to note that the monotonicity coefficient of Left Instructions with the appropriate axis, (in this case the X) has increased to 0.90 (from 0.72), which means that it represents this axis more accurately than either of the two variables indicated above. However, the sub-divisions of components and themes identified and discussed previously still appeared to hold.

The distribution of the 18 new genuine notes was found to be broadly in line with the distribution exhibited within the first POSA on the original 66, (Figure 7.2). Their placement according to the four regions indicated was as follows:

C=8	D=5
A=1	B=4

This distribution reflects the increased importance of the Y axis for this corpus, in indicating a genuine note, as 13 of the 18 are categorised as having a high Y value by the regions drawn, whilst only half (9) are labelled high on the X dimension. The key feature however, is that only one note was placed in region A, which is proposed as being the region in which it is most likely to find simulated notes.

The overall distribution of all 84 suicide notes was also similar to that of Figure 7.2, as was hypothesised, suggesting at least some degree of applicability of the original model of discrimination, when applied to notes written more recently, by individuals of a different nationality, and of various age and occupational level. The number of genuine notes located in each region (compared to the total number) is given below:

A = 3 out of 18, (16.7%).
B = 12 out of 20, (60.0%).

C = 18 out of 26, (69.2%).
D = 18 out of 20, (90.0%).

Further Discussion

Since the model generated for the discrimination of suicide notes has been defined, and broadly validated using a separate sample of notes it is worth taking the argument one step further and considering the potential of a model such as this for use as an aid to real life determination of manner of death. Although this may appear to be a natural extension of the principles involved, applying a model based partly upon the language found in Simulated notes, to instances where the note apparently accompanies a death, may in reality be a larger step (or jump) than it seems. Consider the case of a murder, where a note is fabricated in order to make it appear to be a suicide (see Casey 1993). The features of the simulated notes used in this study, and their accompanying explanations, as previously described, can be seen to have only limited applicability in such a case. For example, it could be expected that a suicide note recovered in these circumstances may well offer a specific reason for the alleged action. If murder is being considered, the assailant is likely to require some sort of justification, and is likely therefore to give the explanation much thought. It may also be suggested that the cognitive energy of an individual plotting to kill, would be increased, and therefore closer to that of a suicidal individual, than a normal, well balanced and non-depressed individual (like those in the simulated-note sample in this study). It is apparent therefore, that the model of discrimination used in this study, should not be extended to real life scenarios without first considering the effect of these scenarios on the state of mind of the note writer.

It must be remembered however, that the significance of the note in cases of equivocal death is likely to be very small in comparison with alternative sources of information available to the investigation. Such sources are well documented in the Psychological Autopsy literature, (see Canter and Cremer) reviewed in Volume II of this series and are likely to preclude any analysis of written text and thus the suicide note.

Implications

This study has examined people's written accounts of their decision to take their own lives. An examination of the ways in which they express themselves has lead to a clear, empirical distinction between content and structure.

The fact that two subsequent POSAs revealed that it was the content variables which were the best discriminators of this sample of notes is potentially of great importance. The high utility of variables measuring at a more thematic content level, suggests that content analytical techniques, as typically used for problems such as this, should perhaps move away from the rigid constraints of the more structural computer based analyses (more characteristic of the second POSA, see Figure 7.3), which are becoming increasingly popular, and instead reconsider the more thematic and contextual aspects of language. This study has been successful in demonstrating how such a shift in emphasis, need not mean a loss of objectivity or methodological rigour. As well as having obvious implications for future studies of suicide or suicidal intent, the findings of this study have much broader implications to the analysis of simulation (or deception) in written text generally.

However, it is important to realise that the very nature of the psychological theory underlying this model dictates that its discrimination relates to the circumstances in which each note was written, and the resulting state of mind of that note's author. It is for this reason that further research is recommended before a model such as this can be utilised in the investigation of equivocal death.

References

Arbeit, S.A. and Blatt, S.J. (1973). Differentiation of simulated and genuine suicide notes. *Psychological-Reports*; 33(1), 283-297.

Atkinson, J.M. (1978). *Discovering Suicide: Studies in the Social Organization of Sudden Death.* London: Macmillan Press.

Casey, C. (1993). Making Murder look like Suicide. *Police Review*; Aug, 16-18.

Choron, J. (1972). *Suicide.* New York: Charles Scribner's Sons.

Cummings, H.W. and Renshaw, S.L. (1979). SLCA-III: A metatheoretic approach to the study of language. *Human Communication Research*; 5, 291-300.

Dregne, N. (1982). Psychological Autopsy: A New Tool for Criminal Defense Attorneys? *Arizona Law Review*; 24, 421-439.

Ebert, B.W. (1987). Guide to Conducting a Psychological Autopsy. *Professional Psychology: Research and Practice*; 18(1), 52-56.

Edelman, A.M. and Renshaw, S.L. (1982). Genuine versus simulated suicide notes: An issue revisited through discourse analysis. *Suicide and Life Threatening Behaviour*; 12(2), 103-113.

Gottschalk, L.A. and Glesser, G.C. (1960). An Analysis of the Verbal Content of Suicide Notes. *British Journal of Medical Psychology*; 33, 195-204.

Leenaars, A.A. (1991). Suicide notes and their implications for intervention. *Crisis*; 12(1), 1-20.

Leenaars, A.A. and Lester, D. (1991). Myths about suicide notes. *Death Studies*; 15(3), 303-308.

Lester, D. and Leenaars, A.A. (1988). The moral justification of suicide in suicide notes. *Psychological Reports*; 63(1), 106.

Ogilvie, D.M., Stone, P.J. and Shneidman, E.S. (1966). Some Characteristics of Genuine versus Simulated Suicide Notes. In: P.J. Stone, D.C. Dunphy, M.S. Smith, and D.M. Ogilvie. (eds). *The General Inquirer: A Computer Approach to Content Analysis*. Cambridge, Mass: MIT Press.

Osgood, C.E. and Walker, E.G. (1959). Motivation and Language Behaviour: A Content Analysis of Suicide Notes. *Journal of Abnormal Psychology*; 59, 58-67.

Poythress, N., Otto, R.K., Darkes, J. and Starr, L. (1993). APA's Expert Panel in the Congressional Review of the USS Iowa Incident. *American Psychologist*; Jan, 8-15.

Shneidman, E.S.(ed.). (1976). *Suicidology: Contemporary Developments*. New York: Grune and Stratton.

Shneidman, E.S. and Farberow, L.N.(Eds.). (1957). *Clues to Suicide*. New York: McGraw-Hill Book Company.

Shye, S. (1985). *Multiple Scaling: The Theory and Application of Partial Order Scalogram Analysis*. Amsterdam: Elsevier Science.

Wekstein, L. (1979). *Handbook of Suicidology: Principles, Problems, and Practice*. New York: Brunner/Mazel.

Bibliography

Allport, G.W. (1942). *The Use of Personal Documents in Psychological Science*. New York: Social Science Research Council.

Canter, D. (1983). The Potential of Facet Theory for Applied Social Psychology. *Quality and Quantity*; 17, 35-67.

Douglas, J.D. (1967). *The Social Meaning of Suicide.* Princeton, New Jersey: Princeton University Press.

Dublin, L.I. (1963). *Suicide: A Sociologic and Statistic Study.* New York: Ronald Press Company.

Garman, M. (1990). *Psycholinguistics.* Cambridge: Cambridge University Press.

Jacobs, J. (1967). A Phenomenological Study of Suicide Notes. *Social Problems*; 15, 60-72.

Leenaars, A.A. and Lester, D. (1990). What characteristics of suicide notes are salient for people to allow perception of a suicide note as genuine? *Death Studies*; 14(1), 25-30.

Lester, D. (1991a). Reliability of naive judges of genuine suicide notes. *Perceptual and Motor Skills*; 73(3,Pt1), 942.

Lester, D. (1991b). Accuracy of recognition of genuine versus simulated suicide. *Personality and Individual Differences*; 12(7), 765-766.

Lester, D. and Leenaars, A.A. (1987). Differentiation of genuine suicide notes. *Psychological Reports*; 61(1), 70.

Maris, R.W. (1969). *Social Forces in Urban Suicide.* Illinois: Dorsey Press.

Maris, R.W. (1981). *Pathways to Suicide: A Survey of Self-Destructive Behaviours.* London. John Hopkins University Press.

McLister, B. and Leenaars, A.A. (1988). An empirical investigation of the latent content of suicide notes. *Psychological Reports*; 63(1), 238.

Miller, S. (1984). *Experimental Design and Statistics*, 2nd Ed. London: Methuen.

Osgood, N.J. (1992). *Suicide in Later Life: Recognizing the Warning Signs.* New York: Lexington Books.

Shneidman, E.S. and Farberow, N.L. (1960). A Socio-Psychological Investigation of Suicide. In: D. David and J.C. Brengelmann (eds). *Perspectives in Personality Research.* London: Crosby Lockwood and Sons.

Stengel, E. (1973). *Suicide and Attempted Suicide.* Middlesex, England: Penguin Books.

8 Non Verbal Behaviour and Deception

ROBERT EDELMANN

This chapter examines the extent to which non verbal behaviour can reveal feelings which we are motivated to conceal. Three broad issues are examined. Firstly, the literature concerning non verbal cues, both actual and assumed which accompany deceit, is discussed. Secondly, the question of whether deception can in fact be detected from such non verbal cues is examined and finally, factors influencing both the ability to conceal deception and detect deception accurately are evaluated. The chapter concludes with the assertion that there is little evidence for a link between certain non verbal behaviours and detection of deception. However, much research to date has been conducted with undergraduate students and the next step must be to pursue more ecologically valid research.

Robert Edelmann graduated from Birkbeck College, London, where he obtained his PhD in psychology and trained in clinical psychology at the Institute of Psychiatry, London. He is both a Chartered Clinical and Chartered Forensic Psychologist. He worked as a lecturer in psychology at the University of Sheffield before joining the psychology department at Surrey in 1986 where he was a lecturer, senior lecturer and then reader in clinical psychology. During that time he contributed to clinical psychology training in various ways including acting as course co-director. He was also course director for the M.Sc in Health Psychology and established an M.Sc in Forensic Psychology. He has recently taken up a post as Research Professor in the School of Psychology and Counselling at the Roehampton Institute, London. He has published numerous

*Offender Profiling Series: 1 - **Interviewing and Deception***
Edited by D. Canter and L. Alison. © 1999 Ashgate Publishing, Aldershot. pp 157-182

academic articles, book chapters and books on a variety of topics and is cited in the Law Society Directory of Expert Witnesses.

8 Non Verbal Behaviour and Deception

ROBERT EDELMANN

Introduction

It is frequently assumed that, unlike the spoken word, certain aspects of non verbal behaviour are, at least in part, not under voluntary control. Thus a look, or glance, or tone of voice may be involuntary or unintentional. If this is indeed the case, it could be further assumed that, should we attempt to conceal information, then our involuntary non verbal behaviour may reveal our true feelings. A conflict between the verbal and the non verbal message could then be taken as a sign of attempted deceit. As Freud (1905/1959) comments "if his lips are silent, he chatters with his fingertips: betrayal oozes out of him at every pore" (p.59). The general supposition then is that there are certain non verbal "cues" to deceit. If we suspect someone is lying then displays of nervous movement, together with trembling and blushing are taken as the give away signs of anxiety which we assume to accompany deceit. Detecting deceit is thus a complex two step process necessitating firstly, appropriate attention to relevant cues and secondly, interpretation of those cues as a sign of deceit rather than simply as an emotional state such as anxiety.

Within this context, however, a number of important provisos need to be kept in mind. First, not all channels of non verbal communication are alike, some seem to be more under voluntary control than others. A great deal of research effort has been expended investigating the extent to which one non verbal cue is more or less likely than another to be a source of leakage or deception (e.g. Ekman, 1985; Ekman and Friesen, 1969, 1974). Leakage cues are defined as those non verbal acts which give away information the sender wishes to conceal, while deception cues are those non verbal acts which indicate that deception is occuring without revealing the concealed content of the message. Second, a number of factors influence success in deceiving others. For example, highly motivated deceivers seem, paradoxically, more likely to fail to deceive observers (e.g. DePaulo and Kirkendol, 1988), while experienced and confident liars and those with the opportunity to plan their deceit seem to be more adept at deceiving. Thirdly, situational factors such as the degree of stressfulness of the situation influence detection of deceit. Finally, a range of factors associated with the observer or message recipient influences the extent of detecting deception. For example, degree of suspicion, extent of probing questions asked and experience, although professional 'lie catchers' seem to be no more adept than laypeople at detecting deceit. This chapter thus examines (i) non verbal cues, both actual and assumed, which accompany deceit; (ii) whether deception can in fact be detected from such non verbal cues; and (iii) factors influencing both the ability to conceal deception and detect deception accurately. The extent to which research findings concerning non verbal cues and the detection of deceit can be generalised to the question of criminal detection is discussed.

Explanations for Deceptive Non Verbal Cues

A number of psychological processes have been assumed to underpin deceptive communication (DePaulo, Stone and Lassiter, 1985a; Ekman, 1985, 1987, 1988; Zuckerman and Driver, 1985). Zuckerman and Driver (1985) list these as as control, arousal, felt emotion and cognitive processing; explanations which overlap with DePaulo, Stone and Lassiter's (1985a) hypotheses that lie tellers are insecure, more concerned with the impression they are making, more guilty or anxious, more cognitively challenged, or more aroused than truth tellers.

Because most people tell lies rather less frequently than they tell the truth there may be a general tendency to feel less confident and insecure when trying to deceive. As a result of this insecurity, deceivers may not only attempt to exercise greater control over their behaviour than those telling the truth, but also take more time to plan their performance. As a result, deceptive behaviour may appear to be planned, rehearsed, or lacking in spontaneity. This will inevitably be more apparent for those non verbal behaviours over which some degree of voluntary control can be exerted; for example, taking a longer time to respond before speaking, or speaking more slowly. Inevitably, however, certain situations, such as those which engender uncertainty or where it is important for the speaker to be believed, will result in a similar slowing of speech and a longer delay in responding. Such nonvberbal cues may thus be typical of interrogative interviews even when the person concerned is telling the truth. There is also evidence that some people, such as those who are socially anxious, also exhibit a longer response time and slower speech (Schlenker and Leary, 1982) i.e. they are by nature concerned about making a particular impression but are insecure about doing so; hence their non verbal style is an inherent characteristic rather necessarily being a sign of deceit.

It also seems that deception increases bodily arousal. Behaviours associated with arousal include increased pupil dilation, eye blinks, voice pitch, speech errors and hesitations. Again, however, these cues are not peculiar to deceit and will be present in varying degrees in any situation which increases bodily arousal and may be more evident in some people than others. Given the stressful nature of most interrogative interviews, such signs would be the norm rather than the exception. For example, they would be quite usual when someone is telling the truth but is highly motivated to be believed.

As well as general increases in arousal it is frequently assumed that specific emotions are aroused in relation to deceptive communication. Ekman (1981, 1985, 1987, 1988) suggests that the usual emotion deceivers might feel is guilt about the fact they are trying to hide something, although deceivers may also feel eager to succeed or apprehensive about not succeeding. Some deceivers may also experience "duping delight" at the experience of deceiving others. Emotions result in certain changes in face, body or vocal cues which can be considered to be automatic, from which inferences are made that the person is trying to deceive observers. Thus, indicators of apprehension or anxiety include manipulative hand movements, speech errors and hesitations. Evidence that anxiety plays a role in determining non verbal cues to deceit is provided by the fact that senders state that they feel more nervous when they have been dishonest than when they have been honest (DePaulo, Lanier and Davis, 1983). It also seems plausible to assume that as guilt and anxiety are netagive emotions, then they will be associated with more negative vocal or facial expressions. Indeed, DePaulo, Rosenthal, Green and Rosenkrantz (1982) found that liars sounded more negative than truth tellers to judges who could only hear the tone of voice of the message.

This was the case even when the content of the message was positive. Again, however, such signs are likely to be present in any situation engendering anxiety irrespective of the truthfulness of the message being conveyed; displays of anxiety are no doubt common during interrogative interviews. Such signs are also more likely to be conveyed by inherently anxious people. As Ekman (1987) notes, changes in behaviour associated with fear, guilt or delight only 'betray the lie if they do not fit the liar's line (p.166).

Finally, telling lies is likely to require thought and may well be a more cognitively complex task than telling the truth. A number of non verbal behaviours are associated with cognitive demand including pupil dilation, longer response latency, pausing and decreased number of illustrative hand movements. An opportunity to plan and rehearse may thus be advantageous to some deceivers. Whether planning is also advantageous to some truthtellers is a further issues of importance as noted later in the chapter. It is worth bearing in mind, however, that thought and planning may be required when truthful message senders are highly motivated to convince others they are telling the truth. This is not unusual in many interrogative interviews.

Thus, although it may well be the case that lie tellers, in comparison to truth tellers, are more concerned with the impression they are making, more guilty or anxious, more cognitively challenged, or more aroused there are certain instances when these same motives and feelings may be engendered in truth tellers; for example, during interrogative interviews when it is important that a truthful message is believed. In addition, the motives and feelings assumed to characterise lying are also more likely to be engendered in some people than others irrespective of the truthfulness of their message. As noted above, it is also clear that not all channels of non verbal communication are alike, some seem to be more under control than others. It is thus plausible to assume that certain non verbal cues are more likely to than others to serves as signs of deception.

Are There Specific Non Verbal Cues to Deceit?

The suggestion that some non verbal cues are more difficult to control than others and are more likely to be interpreted as cues to deception derives from Ekman and Friesen's (1969) experimental study. They hypothesised that because facial muscles change rapidly, allowing a variety of expressions to be conveyed, people are more careful to control their facial expressions. Leg and feet movements on the other hand occur much less rapidly and are often screened from view, hence attempts at deception may be more often leaked through movements of the feet and legs. As other channels have also been found to vary in controllability this has led to suggestions of a leakage heirarchy with verbal content and facial expression located at the controllable end of the continuum and body motion and tone of voice at the less controllable and hence leaky end of the continuum (Zuckerman and Driver, 1985). The extent to which certain non verbal cues are more likely to than others to serves as signs of deception is examined below.

Facial Cues

Smiling is one of the most commonly studied facial cues to deceit. A meta-analysis of 19 studies which investigated smiling during deceptive and truthful communications suggested that those trying to deceive did tend to smile slightly less, although there was little actual difference in amount of smiling between liars and truth tellers (Zuckerman, DePaulo and Rosenthal, 1981). It does seem, however, that there are quantifiable differences between smiles during deceptive and smiles during honest communications. Such differences have been noted by Ekman, Friesen and O'Sullivan (1988) who used their Facial Action Coding System (FACS) to measure observable facial movements. When enjoyment was actually experienced, smiles that included the activity of the outer muscle that orbits the eye, in addition to the muscle which pulls the corner of the lips up (referred to as Duchenne's smile; Ekman, 1988), occurred more often than when enjoyment was feigned. When subjects attempted to conceal strong negative emotions with a happy mask, smiles that contained traces of the muscular activity associated with negative emotions such as disgust, anger, fear, sadness or contempt, occurred more often than when no negative emotions were experienced. It seems then that smiles when lying differ from smiles as a consequence of being emotionally upset, the latter being referred to as miserable smiles (Ekman, 1985; 1988). Whether such differences are distinguishable by observers is, however, open to question. As the authors themselves point out, in an earlier study using the same videotape displays as used in their

1988 study, observers did no better than chance in distinguishing honest from deceptive faces (Ekman and Friesen, 1974). It may then require training to discriminate such smiles.

Although smiling may provide actual cues to deception there is some evidence to suggest that laypeople believe that people who are smiling, regardless of the nature of the smile, are less likely to be lying than those who are not smiling (Ruback, 1981; Zuckerman, DePaulo and Rosenthal, 1981). It is worth noting, however, that in one experimental study (Riggio, Tucker and Wideman, 1987) smiling and laughing were negatively related to perceived believability. In general though, the paradoxical situation may exist such that liars may smile less and smiling during deceptive and truthful communications may differ quantifiably, while smiling may actually convince lay observers of one's truthfulness.

Eye Contact

If deception is associated with guilt then one strategy deceivers might use to cover their guilt is to become more distant or withdrawn by, for example, avoiding eye contact. Indeed, there is some evidence to suggest that laypeople assume that anyone lying will tend to avoid eye contact. Yet, in a review of 18 empirical studies, DePaulo, Stone and Lassiter (1985a) found there was an overall tendency for eye contact to increase. It may well be the case that those wishing to deceive also assume they will be caught out if they look away and hence they may compensate for this by actually looking more. There is some evidence, however, that other cues associated with the eyes are more likely to be present during deception. In line with the arousal hypothesis liars blink their eyes more often and have pupils that are more dilated (DePaulo, Lassiter and Stone, 1985a). Yet, these are cues that observers may not even notice.

Body Movement

Given that emotionality is associated with lying, then nervous responses such as fidgeting might be expected to occur which, in certain instances, may be interpreted as clues to deceit (i.e. body movements serve as a source of deception and leakage cues). Some of the first experimental studies conducted in relation to non verbal behaviour and deception investigated this supposition (Ekman and Freisen, 1969, 1974). Student nurses were recorded telling the truth about their feelings while viewing a pleasant film and lying about their feelings while viewing an unpleasant one. Observers subsequently viewed either the faces of the student nurses or their bodies. Observers were significantly more accurate in their judgements when observing the body, but only when they also observed a truthful segment of the deceiver's behaviour. In addition, differences in accuracy of observers of face or body were not particlarly large. Although Ekman and Friesen interpreted their results as supporting the leakage hypothesis they also note the small differences. Subsequent studies have not always supported the notion that body movements serve as cues to deception. For example, liars do not tend to have shifty bodies (although laypeople believe that liars will shift their posture more), but they do tend to exhibit more adaptor movements (self-manipulating gestures such as rubbing or scratching) (DePaulo, Stone and Lassiter, 1985a). However, it seems that not all people engage in such nervous hand movements when lying. Extroverts, who are expressive by nature, tend to engage in fewer nervous movements when lying than when telling the truth (Riggio and Friedman, 1983).

There is also evidence that deception is associated with a decrease in illustrative hand movements (movements which accompany speech and accent, punctuate,modify it etc.) (DePaulo, Stone and Lassiter, 1985a; Ekman, 1988). This may well relate to the possibility that lie telling is cognitively complex and hence attention is focused upon the verbal content rather than the accompanying bodily movement. It may also relate to the possibility that liars over control their actions.

Paralinguistic Cues

Several studies suggest that a range of paralinguistic cues (aspects of voice quality and sounds associated with speech) leak information that is not revealed by the verbal content or facial expression associated with the message (e.g. Bugental, Henker and Whalen, 1976; Zuckerman, Amidon, Bishop and Pomerantz, 1982). It seems that liars give higher pitched and more hesitant answers replete with dysfluencies, such as repetitions and slips of the tongue, show a slower latency in responding, shorter speech duration and slower rate of speech (Depaulo, Stone and Lassiter, 1985a; Zuckerman and Driver, 1985). Thus, some studies suggest that vocal pitch increases when lying (e.g. Ekman, Friesen and Scherer, 1979), although this is not true for all people, some exhibit a decrease in vocal pitch when lying. Findings that speech errors and hesitations increase are consistent with the notion that emotionality is associated with lying. In trying to control the way they present a message, deceivers can appear to be clipped and hesitant, with their language appearing to be overly rehearsed and lacking in spontaneity. Perhaps more than other non verbal cues there seems to be more consistency between actual paralinguistic behaviours during lying and assumed cues to deception. Thus, laypeople assume that lying is associated with utterances which are hesitant, full or errors and highly pitched, this does in fact seem to be the case (DePaulo, Stone and Lassiter, 1985a).

Some non verbal cues do then seem to be associated with deceit. Other non verbal cues are assumed to be indicative of deceit when this is not in fact the case. Is it then possible to judge with any certainty from non verbal cues that a person is lying or telling the truth?

Can Deception be Detected from Non Verbal Cues?

Several reviews of non verbal leakage/deception cues and accuracy of detection have been published (DePaulo, Stone and Lassiter, 1985a; Miller and Burgoon, 1982; Zuckerman, DePaulo and Rosenthal, 1981; Zuckerman and Driver, 1985). Unfortunately, the conclusion from these reviews is that people are generally not very accurate in judging whether or not someone is telling the truth. The usual experimental paradigm in the studies reviewed involves presenting an observer with a series of video- or audiotaped recordings of a person attempting to convey the impression they are experiencing something they are not actually experiencing. For example, can they smell something pleasant and convince the observer that the smell was disgusting; can they talk about someone they dislike and still convey the impression they like that person; can they view an unpleasant film and convey the impression that the film was pleasant? In each instance observers are asked to judge whether or not the person is lying. Average accuracy in detecting deceit from these studies has rarely been above 60% (Ekman and O'Sullivan, 1991), with rates ranging from 40% to 60% and most at or around the 50% or chance level (Miller and Burgoon, 1982; Miller and Stiff, 1992). Based on these figures, a correction for guessing implies that the typical liar foils 86% of would-be detectors (Bond, Kahler and Paolicelli, 1985).

Given that non verbal cues to deceit are actually cues to motives and feelings which *might indicate* deceit it is perhaps not surprising that accuracy in detecting deceit is low. It involves a certain degree of acuity to notice non verbal behaviours, it requires quite a different skill to then accurately infer that these might be indicative of deceit. Even in the former instance there is evidence that some observers/receivers are more sensitive to non verbal cues than others (Rosenthal, 1979). In the latter instance there are further factors which serve to modify the likelihood that an inference of deceit will be accurate. Thus, some people look and sound honest even if they are lying (Bond, Kahler and Paolicelli, 1985; Zuckerman, DeFrank, Hall, Larrance and Rosenthal 1979); others look and sound dishonest even if they are telling the truth (Riggio, Tucker and Throckmorton, 1986); a phenomenon referred to as 'demeanour bias'. People have beliefs about liars' behaviour and attribute deception to those who act in stereotypically deceptive ways, even if they are telling the truth (Bond, Kahler and Paolicelli, 1985). In fact, it seems there is a tendency to infer deceit from non verbal behaviours which simply violate a consistent norm, even if these behaviours are not stereotypic of liars (Bond, Omar, Pitre, Lashley, Skaggs and Kirk, 1992). A number of other reasons for errors in detecting deception have been dicusssed in the literature including individual differences, motivation to deceive and situational factors (Ekman and O'Sullivan, 1989). Indeed, factors which influence the ability to deceive and detect deceit can be usefully summarised under three headings (i) those inherent in the deceiver (motivation, experience, confidence and planning); (ii) those inherent in the situation (degree of stress involved); and (iii) those inherent in the observer (their suspicion, opportunity to ask probing questions and experience). These issues are addressed in the following sections.

Factors Influencing Deception Attempts

Motivation

The research literature suggests that the behaviour of highly motivated deceivers differs from the behaviour of less motivated ones. When people are especially motivated to get away with lying their lies become, paradoxically, more obvious to observers (DePaulo and Kirkendol, 1988). In one of the first empirical investigations of the 'motivational impairment effect', DePaulo, Lanier and Davis (1983) found that judges who could see the the speakers' facial expressions and bodily movements, or hear the tone of voice cues, were more successful at detecting the lies of motivated than unmotivated speakers. In contrast, those judges who only had access to the typed transcript of what had been said were relatively less successful at detecting lies told by motivated speakers.

A similar effect was suggested by DePaulo, Stone and Lassiter (1985b). In this study, undergraduates were urged to make a good impression while telling lies and truths to attractive or unattractive members of the same sex or opposite sex. The authors argued that subjects would be more highly motivated to lie to members of the opposite sex and indeed lies were more readily detected in this instance. In a further study, DePaulo, Kirkendol, Tang and O'Brien (1988) found that subjects who told ingratiating lies under conditions in which they thought that the ability to convey particular impressions was an important skill, were less successful at getting away with those lies when judges could observe their non verbal behaviours.

Reviews of a range of studies suggest that, in comparison to less highly motivated senders, those who are more highly motivated to deceive give slower, shorter, more negative and more highly pitched responses which are accompanied by less eye contact, less blinking, fewer head movements, fewer postural shifts and fewer adaptive gestures (DePaulo, Stone and Lassiter, 1985a; Zuckerman and Driver, 1985). Indeed, in one study, when subjects were specifically instructed to control either facial or vocal cues there was some evidence that their lies were easier to detect from the channels they were trying to control (DePaulo, Kirkendol, Tang and O'Brien, 1988). It seems then that motivated deceivers try harder to either suppress or control their behaviour and, as a result, end up overcontrolling it. Observers notice this and infer that the person might be lying. Attempting to suppress behaviour makes someone look and sound as if they have something to hide (DePaulo, 1992). Attempting to control behaviour may result in less movement and more behavioural rigidity (Zuckerman, DePaulo and Rosenthal, 1981).

As Miller and Stiff (1992) point out, however, such findings are based upon deceptive communication which takes place in laboratory settings.

In these instances motivation to deceive is increased by offering rewards, incentives or instructions, For example, DePaulo, Lanier and Davis (1983) manipulated motivation by emphasising the importance of lying. For one group of subjects their need to deceive was downplayed; they were told that lying was like a game in which some people told lies and truths and others tried to guess when they were lying and telling the truth. Another group of subjects was reminded how important lying can be and their need to deceive observers was emphasised. In addition, they read about research demonstrating that the ability to lie successfully is linked to professional success. Rarely do such studies provide evidence verifying the fact that such manipulations have indeed heighened motivation and subsequent arousal. Even if motivation is varied in such contexts, however, it is hard to imagine that such laboratory effects mirror real-world transactions. For example, the costs involved in interrogative interviews are markedly different from those inherent in the typical experimental setting. One might assume that at extreme levels of motivation even verbal behaviour might be disrupted.

However, highly motivated liars may also be those who are likely to plan their response, be more practiced and more confident in their ability to deceive. As DePaulo and Kirkendol (1988) suggest, not all people are necessarily equally susceptible to the motivational impairment effect. Both experienced and confident liars are likely to be less susceptible. It has also been suggested that the opportunity to plan lies makes them more difficult to detect (Littlepage and Pineault, 1985).

Experienced Deceivers

It seems that the ability to use non verbal behaviour can be improved by practice and experience (DePaulo, 1992). For example, there is some evidence that experienced salespeople are effective liars (DePaulo and DePaulo, 1989). In this study, salespeople were videotaped while making pitches for products they liked and products they disliked but still had to try to sell. With these more experienced liars, observers were unable to detect lies from the truth even when they were directed towards cues which typically help people to detect liars. Indeed, follow-up analysis revealed that the reason for this failure to detect deception was that the relevant cues were simply not present. The salespeople did not engage in key behaviours at different rates during deceptive versus truthful communications. DePaulo and DePaulo suggest four possible explanations for their results: salespeople may be more practiced or experienced at telling similar lies; they may have confidence in their ability to deceive; may have a natural ability to deceive or may lack guilt about lying in relation to selling. Certainly, there is evidence that individual differences in communication skills are closely linked to deception ability and that confidence in ones ability to deceive plays an importance role

Self-confidence

There is some evidence that individuals who are skilled communicators of posed emotions tend to be more successful deceivers (Riggio and Friedman, 1983). Thus, expressive and socially tactful subjects are more successful deceivers, whereas socially anxious subjects are less successful (Riggio, Tucker and Throckmorton, 1987). Indeed, degree of social self-confidence may play an important role in such simulated deception tasks. Socially skilled individuals, in contrast to nonskilled/socially self-conscious people, tend to be more verbally fluent. Verbal fluency is related to believability for both truthful and deceptive communications (Riggio, Tucker and Wideman, 1987). The non verbal behaviours associated with lack of self-confidence thus mirror those associated with deception (i.e. fidgeting, stammering, long silences and longer response latencies). Lies, in comparison to truths, are particularly detectable when it is important for the deception to be successful but the deceiver has a low expectation of their likely success (DePaulo, LeMay and Epstein, 1991). It seems then that certain people under certain circumstances suggest they are lying when this might not be the case while others give little or no indication that they are in fact not telling the truth.

Message Planning

A number of authors have suggested that the opportunity to plan and rehearse deceptive messages makes them more difficult to detect (e.g. Cody, Marston and Foster, 1984; Miller, deTurck and Kalbfleisch, 1983; Littlepage and Pineault, 1985. Thus, Cody, Marston and Foster (1984) found that spontaneous deceptions contained more speech errors and pauses than spontaneous truthful messages. In contrast, there was no difference between liars and truthtellers who were given the opportunity to plan their messages. Similarly, Littlepage and Pineault (1985) found that planned lies were identified less acurately than spontaneous lies, while planning did not consistently affect the accuracy of identification of truthful responses. The authors suggest that planning may increase both the plausibility of the lie and the ability of the deceiver to more effectively mask or inhibit their non verbal deception cues.

However, Miller, deTurck and Kalbfleisch (1983) suggest that message planning may only be advantageous for some people. They found that people who could effectively control their verbal and non verbal behaviour benefitted from the chance to rehearse, while people who lacked such control were more likely to be detected when given the opportunity to plan their deceit. The authors suggest that those lacking ability to control their non verbal behaviour may actually suffer because of the additional focusing of attention on the task of planning a deceptive message.

In summary then experimental studies suggest that it is more likely that a highly experienced, self-confident and socially skilled liar who has taken the opportunity to plan their lies but is not highly motivated to deceive will be erroneously assumed to be telling the truth. Experimental studies typically involve brief snippets of videotaped information of subjects, who are often students, trying to deceive observers, who are also likely to be students, in low demand tasks. It is impossible to say with any certaintly the extent to which such experimental findings can be generalised to more stressful, high demand situations such as interrogative interviews. Certainly, the degree of motivation induced in experimental studies does not match that inherent in real-life situations. Interestingly, truthtellers may be even more highly motivated than deceivers in interrogative situations and yet they are frequently assumed to be lying. It does, however, seem plausible to assume that experienced, confident and skilled liars who plan their response will be more believable, although this may well only apply to a point. Behavioural signs of over confidence could well be interpreted as signs of deceit.

Situational Influences on Deceit Detection

Stressfulness of the Situation

As noted, behavioural cues to deceit are often associated with emotions experienced while lying; when these emotions occur in the absence of lying the same behavioural cues occur. Thus, anxiety, associated with the prospect that a truthful message might not be believed may be mistakenly interpreted as a sign that the person is lying. However, in one study of interest, deTurck and Miller (1985) found that six non verbal behaviours (adaptive and manipulative hand movements, speech errors, pauses, response latency and message duration) reliably distinguished deceivers from unaroused and aroused truthtellers even though the degree of sympathetic activation for deceivers and aroused truthtellers was comparable. The ability to attribute the person's non-verbal cues to deception was though dependent upon the observer also viewing some baseline behaviour.

In other instances, if the situation is regarded as highly anxiety provoking, then the presence of behavioural signs of anxiety may be taken at face value and not interpreted as cues to deceit. Indeed, in a simulated study of juror perception/defendent believability Fedman and Chesley (1984) found that a display of noverbal behaviours associated with deception decreased a defendants' believability if they were suspected of a minor crime but had no effect on believability if they were suspected of a major crime.

As Ekman and O'Sullivan (1989) note, no cue to deceit is foolproof. Given that there are substantial individual differences in non verbal behaviours, someone who habitually engages in clipped and hesitant speech or manuipulative hand movements should not be judged as lying simply because of the occurrence of such behaviours (Riggio, Tucker and Throckmorton, 1987; Rioggio, Tucker and Wideman, 1987). One would need to know the extent to which behaviour exhibited while the person is assumed to be lying or when they are in a stressful context differs from that person's habitual behaviour. Indeed, a number of studies suggest that deception detection is enhanced by futher exposure to the potential liar (O'Sullivan, Ekman and Friesen, 1988). Even in such instances, however, detection is still only slightly better than chance and is only improved if observers see the target person portray honest behaviour prior to deceptive behaviour. In real life deception situations this is an unlikely occurrence except with close friendships or relationships. However, in any real life situation, attempts to detect deception will not involve just a single viewing of an observer portraying a message. Not only are behaviours related to deception likely to change over the course of an interaction (Buller and Aune, 1987) observers/interviewers will have the opportunity to probe for more information to facilitate the task of attempting to detect deception. The extent to which probing influences detection of deceit and whether experienced or suspicious observers are good lie detectors is discussed in the following sections.

Factors Influencing the Detection of Deception

Degree of Suspicion

In most experimental studies it seems that observers tend to give communicators the 'benefit of the doubt' - they rate the videotaped communications as being more honest than they actually are. Indeed, this 'benefit of the doubt bias' is one of the most robust findings in experimental studies of deception (DePaulo, Stone and Lassiter, 1985a). The hallmark of interrogative interviews, however, is a degree of suspicion that the suspect is not necessarily telling the truth. Such wariness could lead to more successful detection of deception. Conversely of course suspicion may simply lead to an overconcentration upon stereotypical deception cues and the misinterpretation of truthfulness as deceit. A study by Toris and DePaulo (1984) evaluated this supposition. They conducted a simulated job interview in which interviewers were or were not warned that the applicants might be providing misleading information (i.e. introverts presented themselves as extroverts and extroverts presented themselves as introverts). The warned (i.e. suspicious) interviewers were no more accurate in detecting deception and were, if anything, slightly worse at detecting the interviewees' true characteristics. Indeed, in comparison to the non suspicious interviewers, the suspicious interviewers were less confident about their judgments and tended to perceive all applicants as more deceptive. In addition, applicants interviewed by suspicious interviewers felt that they were less successful at conveying their intended impression and perceived their interviewers as manipulative. Suspicion seems to decrease confidence and trust while possibly resulting in an increased likelihood that deception will be inferred from those who are telling the truth. Whether such experimental findings can be generalised to real-life situations is inevitably a matter of conjecture. It is worth bearing in mind, however, that suspicion may be associated with the misinterpretation of truthfulness as deceit.

Opportunity to Probe

Despite the rather obvious fact that opportunity to probe for further information might affect ability to detect deception, few studies have investigated this issue (Stiff and Miller, 1986; Buller, Constock, Aune and Strzyzewski, 1989). In Stiff and Miller's (1986) study subjects either attempted to cover up the fact they had cheated at a task, or were truthfully describing their performance, in response to four interview questions. In half the interviews the interviewer acted suspiciously, while for the other half the interviewer acted as if he accepted the subject's response. Probes produced only small differences between the non verbal behaviour of deceivers and truthtellers while neither accepting nor suspicious probes increased overall detection accuracy. Unfortunately, the lack of baseline data meant that changes in behaviour as a result of probing could not be examined. In a further study, Buller, Comstock, Ause and Strzyzewski (1989) examined the effect of probing during an interaction on the non verbal behaviour of deceivers and truthtellers. Probing produced a number of changes in non verbal behaviour. Probing induced truthtellers to make significantly more speech errors and pause more than deceivers and induced deceivers to increase their eye contact although overall they engaged in less eye contact than truthtellers. However, probing did not improve detection of deception while the change in truthtellers' behaviour may have served to enhance suspicion. As Ekman (1985) notes 'it is always a problem (for the observer) to distinguish between the innocent's fear of being disbelieved and the guilty person's deception apprehension' (p.51). It is of course plausible to assume that such distinctions can be made more accurately by those with greater experience of deceit detection.

Experienced Lie Detectors

It is important to bear in mind that the majority of studies investigating accuracy of detecting deceit have been conducted under laboratory conditions and hence may not be a true reflection of the circumstances which prevail in real-life deception contexts. Experimental studies tend to involve brief videotaped displays of senders while interrogative interviews with suspects or witnesses are often repeated, particularly if the credibility of a statement is at question. As noted, there is some evidence that deception detection is enhanced by further exposure to the potential liar, although this is true only if observers see the target person portray honest behaviour prior to deceptive behaviour. Whether deception detection would be enhanced in the context of an interrogative interview is thus largely a matter of conjecture.

In addition, the majority of research studies have involved student populations. One possible explanation for their lack of ability to detect deception is that naive observers have neither the necessary experience nor skill. Perhaps those whose jobs involve the detection of deception have greater success. Unfortunately, the evidence tends not to support this supposition. Kraut and Poe (1980) videotaped mock customs inspections in which U.S. customs officials interrogated airline passengers some of whom had been primed to have smuggled goods in their possession. The videotapes were shown to customs inspectors and laypersons who did not differ in their ability in deciding which travellers should be searched. Regardless of observer status, decisions to search travellers were more likely if they hesitated before answering, gave short answers, shifted their bodies and avoided eye contact i.e stereotypical cues to deception. DePaulo and Pfeiffer (1986) found that from videotapes of undergraduates answering questions either truthfully or deceptively, federal law enforcement officers were no more accurate than college students at detecting deceptiveness. This was true for both inexperienced officers (a group of new recruits) and advanced federal law enforcement officers. Interestingly, the officers were more confident about their judgements than were the students and the advanced officers felt increasingly confident about their performance as the task progressed. Finally, Kohnken (1987) found that police officers did no better than chance when they judged videotapes of college students who had lied or been truthful in an experiment.

There is only one study which has produced evidence to suggest that at least some professional lie detectors are more able to detect deception (Ekman and O'Sullivan, 1991). Over 500 people who were either members of the U.S. secret service, federal polygraphers, judges, police, psychiatrists, working adults or students had to judge whether each of ten persons they saw was lying or telling the truth. Only the secret service performed better than chance and they were significantly more accurate than all the other groups. Those who were more accurate at detecting deception reported using different and more varied behaviours, emphasizing non verbal more than verbal ones. While accuracy was still low, more accurate detectors may possess superior skills in recognising appropriate cues. If this is indeed the case then it should be possible to train observers to detect deceit.

Training Observers to Detect Deceit

Attempts to train observers to detect deceit have produced mixed results. In one of the first such studies Zuckerman, Koestner and Alton (1974) presented subjects with videotaped displays of senders delivering truthful or deceptive messages. Information identifying messages as truthful was given to some subjects but not to others. In general, accuracy of detecting lies was enhanced by the provision of information, but only for judgments made of the person on whom training was given. Increases in accuracy did not generalize to accuracy of detecting lies enacted by other deceivers. In a follow-up study, Zuckerman, Koestner and Colella (1985) investigated whether this result would be modified by the availability of different communication channels. Thus, subjects saw the face only, heard speech only or were shown face plus speech. Feedback improved subjects' ability to detect deception when they had access to the senders speech but not when they only saw the face. In contrast to Zuckerman, Koestner and Alton's findings, improvement in detecting accuracy, although rather small, occurred across senders.

Given the apparent importance of vocal cues suggested by previous research, DePaulo, Lassiter and Stone (1982) instructed observers to pay particular attention to either vocal cues, other non verbal cues or content-related characteristics. A control group were given no special attention related instructions. The results showed that directing perceivers' attention to specific cues, such as tone of voice cues, improved their lie detection success. However, the results were explained more by enhanced accuracy of detecting truthful messages rather than by increasing accuracy for deceptive descriptions. The authors argue that perceivers do not ordinarily take advantage of information inherent in vocal cues without special prompting. In further study (Kohnken, 1987) observers, all of whom were male police officers, were either given no instructions about what to attend to or were directed to attend to certain cues: either paralinguistic, facial or verbal content. Each of the directed groups spent time overviewing the research and cues relevent to their instructions. Those who were not told to pay particular attention to certain cues did as well as the other three groups who also did not differ one from another.

Training in these studies thus involved either the provision of feedback about correct answers or instructions to attend to certain cues. As Ekman and O'Sullivan (1991) note, the training was 'not to provide information about specific behavioural clues, nor to train specific perceptual skills'. They further suggest that if there are certain microexpressions which act as markers to deception (such as the deceptive smiles noted by Ekman, Friesen and O'Sullivan, 1988) then training observers to detect such expressions should also enhance their ability to detect deception.

Overview

The research findings discussed in this chapter are, for the most part, derived from laboratory studies with undergraduate student subjects who are asked to judge the deceptiveness or truthfulness of messages. A range of deception paradigms have been used, such as pretending to like a disliked person, or describing as pleasant something which is unpleasant. From these studies it seems that perceivers generally believe in other peoples' truthfulness, although they tend to perceive deceptive messages as less truthful than truthful messages. In a social context it may actually be socially appropriate to "overlook" instances of deception in order to avoid causing embarrassment by accusing someone of deceit (Ekman, 1985). It also seems that observers often rely on "stereotypical" signs of deceit, such as lack of eye contact and fidgeting when such stereotypical cues may not be very accurate deception cues. The overall conclusion from much of this work is that 'notwithstanding conventional acceptance of the link between certain non verbal behaviors and subsequent detection of deception, precious little evidence supports it' (Miller and Stiff, 1992 p.218). Indeed, although such findings of surprisingly low accuracy of detecting deceit are largely based upon the performance of undergraduate student subjects, there is little evidence to suggest that the performance of professional lie catchers is much better. Training also does not seem to enhance peoples' ability to detect deception. Whether this position will change if future research can pinpoint specific microexpressions associated with deceit and observers can be trained to detect such expressions remains to be seen.

The need to bear in mind the fact that the studies on which these findings are based show little approximation to real-life deception situations cannot be overstated. There is, for example, little relationship between experimental studies and the circumstances associated with interrogative interviews. As Miller and Stiff (1992) further note "Police investigative interviews... involve victims, witnesses and supects who are motivated to communicate honestly or deceptively and investigators who are motivated to make accurate veracity judgments" (p.234). Although research suggests that motivated liars are easier to detect, the level of motivation involved in experimental studies is unlikely to resemble that inherent in investigative interviews. It also seems that not all people are equally susceptible to the 'motivational impairment effect'. Experienced liars are likely to be more adept at deceiving (DePaulo and DePaulo, 1989). This is likely to be a particularly important factor inherent in many investigative interviews. In addition, few studies have investigated the efficacy of probing upon accuracy of deception detection and this is an essential ingredient of investigative interviews. In order to investigate such parameters, future research could usefully be directed towards evaluating deception detection in real-life situations, taking into account the effect of moderating variables such as degree of suspicion and experience. While the results of experimental studies provide essential background information, as Miller and Stiff (1992) point out, the next step must be to pursue more ecologically valid research.

References

Bond, C.F. Jr., Kahler, K.N. and Paolicelli, L.M. (1985). The miscommunication of deception: An adaptive perspective. *Journal of Experimental Social Psychology*, 21, 331-345.

Bond, C.F. Jr., Omar, A., Pitre, U., Lashley, B. R., Skaggs, L. M. and Kirk, C. T. (1992). Fishy-looking liars: Deception judgment from expectancy violation. *Journal of Personality and Social Psychology*, 63, 969-977.

Bugental, D. B., Henker, B. and Whalen, C. K. (1976). Attributional antecedents of verbal and vocal assertiveness. *Journal of Personality and Social Psychology,* 34, 405-411.

Buller, D. B. and Aune, R. K. (1987). Non verbal cues to deception among intimates, friends, and strangers. *Journal of Non verbal Behaviour*, 11, 269-290.

Buller, D. B., Comstock, J., Aune, R. K. and Strzyzewski, K. D. (1989). The effect of probing on deceivers and truthtellers. *Journal of Non verbal Behavior*, 13, 155-170.

Cody, M. J., Marston, P. J. and Foster, M. (1984). Deception: Paralinguistic and verbal leakage. In R. N. Bostrom (ed.), *Communication Yearbook 8.* Newbury Park, CA: Sage.

DePaulo, B. M. (1992). Non verbal behaviour and self-presentation. *Psychological Bulletin,* 111, 203-243.

DePaulo, B. M. and Kirkendol, S. E. (1988). The motivational impairment effect in the communication of deception. In J. Yuille (ed.), *Credibility Assessment.* Norwell, MA: Kluwer Academic.

DePaulo, B. M. and Pfeiffer, R. L. (1986). On-the-job experience and skill at detecting deception. *Journal of Applied Social Psychology*, 16, 249-267.

DePaulo, B. M., Lanier, K. and Davis, T. (1983). Detecting the deceit of the motivated liar. *Journal of Personality and Social Psychology,* 45, 1096-1103.

DePaulo, B. M., Lassiter, G. D. and Stone J. I. (1982). Attentional determinants of success at detecting deception or truth. *Personality and Social Psychology Bulletin,* 8, 273-279.

DePaulo, B. M., LeMay, C. S. and Epstein, J. A. (1991). Effects of importance of success and expectations for success on effectiveness at deceiving. *Personality and Social Psychology Bulletin*, 17, 14-24.

DePaulo, B. M., Stone, J. I. and Lassiter, G. D. (1985a). Deceiving and detecting deceit. In B. R. Schlenker (Ed.), *The Self and Social Life.* New York: McGraw-Hill.

DePaulo, B.M., Stone, J. I. and Lassiter, G. D. (1985b). Telling ingratiating lies: Effects of target sex and target attractiveness on verbal and non verbal deceptive success. *Journal of Personality and Social Psychology*, 48, 1191-1203.

DePaulo, B. M., Kirkendol, S. E., Tang, J. and O' Brien, T. (1988). The motivational impairment effect in the communication of deception: Replications and extensions. *Journal of Non verbal Behavior,* 12, 177-202.

DePaulo, B. M., Rosenthal, R., Green, C. R. and Rosenkrantz, J. (1982). Diagnosing deceptive and mixed messages from verbal and non verbal cues. *Journal of Experimental Social Psychology*, 18, 433-446.

DePaulo, P. J. and DePaulo, B. M. (1989). Can attempted deception by salespersons and customers be detected through non verbal behavioral cues. *Journal of Applied Social Psychology*, 19, 1552-1557.

DeTurck, M. A. and Miller, G. R. (1985). Deception and arousal. Isolating the behavioral correlates of deception. *Human Communication Research*, 12, 181-201.

Ekman, P. (1981). Mistakes when deceiving. *Annals of the New York Academy of Sciences*, 364, 269-278.

Ekman, P. (1985). *Telling lies: Clues to deceit in the marketplace, politics and marriage.* New York: W. W. Norton.

Ekman, P. (1987). Lying and non verbal behavior: Theoretical issues and new findings. *Journal of Non verbal Behavior*, 12, 163-176.

Ekman, P, (1988). Why lies fail and what behaviors betray a lie. In J. Yuille (ed.), *Credibility Assessment.* Dordrecht, The Netherlands: Kluwer Academic Publishing.

Ekman, P. and Friesen, W. V. (1969). Non verbal leakage and clues to deception. *Psychiatry,* 32, 88-106.

Ekman, P. and Friesen, W. V. (1974). Detecting deception from the body or face. *Journal of Personality and Social Psychology*, 29, 288-298.

Ekman, P. and O'Sullivan, M. (1989). Hazards in detecting deceit. In D.C. Raskin (ed.), *Psychological Methods in Criminal Investigation.* New York: Springer Publishing Co.

Ekman, P. and O'Sullivan, M. (1991). Who can catch a liar? *American Psychologist,* 46, 913-920.

Ekman, P. Friesen, W. V. and O'Sullivan, M. (1988). Smiling when lying. *Journal of Personality and Social Psychology*, 54, 414-420.

Ekman, P., Friesen, W. V. and Scherer, K. (1979). Body movement and voice pitch in deceptive interaction. *Semiotica,* 16, 23-27.

Feldman, R. S. and Chesley, R. B. (1984). Who is lying, who is not: An attributional analysis of the effects of non verbal behavior on judgements of defendant believability. *Behavioral Sciences and the Law*, 2, 451-461.

Freud, S. (1959). Fragments of an analysis of a case of hysteria. *Collected papers* (vol 3). New York: Basic Books. (Original work published 1905).

Kohnken, G. (1987). Training police officers to detect deceptive eye-witness statements: Does it work? *Social Behavior*, 2, 1-17.

Kraut, R. E. and Poe, D. (1980). Behavioral roots of person perception: The deception judgments of customs inspectors and laymen. *Journal of Personality and Social Psychology*, 39, 784-798.

Littlepage, G. E. and Pineault, M. A. (1985). Detection of deception of planned and spontaneous communications. *Journal of Social Psychology*, 125, 195-201.

Miller, G. R. and Burgoon, J. K. (1982). Factors affecting assessments of witness credibility. In N. L. Kerr and R. M. Bray (eds.), *The Psychology of the Courtroom*. New York: Academic Press.

Miller, G. R. and Stiff, J. B. (1992). Applied issues in studying deceptive communication. In R. S. Feldman (ed.), *Applications of Non verbal Behavioral Theories and Research.* Hillsdale, NJ.: Erlbaum.

Miller, G. R., deTurck, M. A. and Kalbfleisch, P. J. (1983). Self-monitoring, rehearsal, and deceptive communication. *Human Communication Research*, 10, 97-117.

O'Sullivan, M., Ekman, P. and Freisen, W. V. (1988). The effect of behavioral comparison in detecting deception. *Journal of Non verbal Behavior*, 12, 203-215.

Riggio, R. E. and Friedman, H. S. (1983). Individual differences and cues to deception. *Journal of Personality and Social Psychology*, 45, 899-915.

Riggio, R. E., Tucker, J. and Throckmorton, B. (1987). Social skills and deception ability. *Personality and Social Psychology Bulletin*, 13, 568-577.

Riggio, R. E., Tucker, J. and Wideman, K. F. (1998). Verbal and non verbal cues as mediators of deception ability. *Journal of Non verbal Behavior*, 11, 126-145.

Rosenthal, R. (ed.) (1979). *Skill in Non verbal Communication: Individual Differences.* Cambridge, MA.: Oelgeschlager.

Ruback, R. B. (1981). Perceived honesty in the parole interview. *Personality and Social Psychology Bulletin,* 7, 677-681.

Schlenker, B. and Leary, M. R. (1982). Social anxiety and self-presentation: A conceptualization and model. *Psychological Bulletin*, 92, 641-669.

Stiff, J. B. and Miller, G. R. (1986). "Come to think of it...." Interrogative probes, deceptive communication, and deception detection. *Human Communication Research*, 12, 339-357.

Toris, C. and DePaulo, B. M. (1984). Effects of actual deception and suspiciousness of deception on interpersonal perceptions. *Journal of Personality and Social Psychology*, 47, 1063-1073.

Zuckerman, M. and Driver, R. E. (1985). Telling lies: Verbal and non verbal correlates of deception. In A. W. Siegman and S. Feldstein (eds.), *Multichannel Integration of Non verbal Behavior*. Hillsdale, NJ.: Erlbaum.

Zuckerman, M., DePaulo, B. M. and Rosenthal, R. (1981). Verbal and non verbal communication of deception. In L. Berkowitz (ed.), *Advances in Experimental Social Psychology*. Vol 14. San Diego, CA: Academic Press.

Zuckerman, M., Koestner, R. and Alton, A. O. (1984). Learning to detect deception. *Journal of Personality and Social Psychology,* 46, 519-528.

Zuckerman, M., Koestner, R. W. and Colella, M. J. (1985). Learning to detect deception from three communication channels. *Journal of Non verbal Behavior*, 9, 188-194.

Zuckerman, M. Amidon, M. D., Bishop, S. E. and Pomerantz, S. D. (1982). Face and tone of voice in the communication of deception. *Journal of Personality and Social Psychology*, 43, 347-357.

Zuckerman, M., DeFrank, R. S., Hall, J. A., Larrance, D. T. and Rosenthal, R. (1979). Facial and vocal cues of deception and honesty. *Journal of Experimental Social Psychology,* 15, 378-396.

9 The Psychophysiology of Deception and the Orienting Response

MURRAY KLEINER

The use of the polygraph or 'lie detector', for purposes of detecting deception has been the subject of social and academic controversy. Acceptance of the accuracy of the basis polygraph paradigms has been conditional upon agreement with the psychological theories underlying the test procedures. In this chapter a theoretical standpoint is proposed to reconcile and encompass both the accepted Guilty Knowledge Test and the contested Control Question Test, in one general theory. The Guilty Knowledge Test is considered in terms of Sokolov's (1963) orienting response theory and Tversky's (1977) contrast model of similarity. The 'diagnosticity principle' of Tversky's model serves as a bridge to the Control Question test, acting in concert with evaluative self-concepts, to explicate the resulting psychophysiological processes in this test paradigm. The cognitive and emotional processes included in the notion of self-concepts are relevant in considering the relationship between the significant cognitive constructs of offenders and the way in which they commit their offences.

Chief Superintendent Murray Kleiner (BA Psychology and Biology M.Sc Neurobiology) has been a polygraph examiner for twenty years and is the director of the Jerusalem Polygraph Laboratory, in the Behaviour Section of the Division of Identification and Forensic Sciences in the Investigative Branch of the Israel National Police.

*Offender Profiling Series: I - **Interviewing and Deception***
Edited by D. Canter and L. Alison. © 1999 Ashgate Publishing, Aldershot. pp 183-208

9 The Psychophysiology of Deception and the Orienting Response

MURRAY KLEINER

Introduction

Polygraph testing has been used extensively by law enforcement and private agencies over the last thirty years to determine if suspects are telling the truth. Yet it has not received scientific or legal acceptibility. This technique has been criticized on the basis of nonstandard physiological measurement, inadequate instrumentation, lack of specific deception response, contamination via interpersonal interaction, flawed methodology and insufficient validity (Ben-Shakhar and Furedy, 1990).

However, the objection to polygraph use has not been total. Use of the Guilty Knowledge Technique of polygraph testing (GKT; Lykken, 1959) has been academically accepted and recommended as being theoretically and empirically valid, deriving from orienting response theory and research, whereas the Control Question Technique (CQT; Reid and Inbau, 1977), the most widely used polygraph procedure, has been emphatically rejected as being devoid of any theoretical and empirical foundation (Ben-Shakhar and Furedy, 1990; Lykken, 1974, 1981). Indeed, the continuing controversy surrounding CQT polygraph practice has been irreconcilable and heated (Lykken, 1974, 1981; Raskin and Podlesny, 1978; also see Furedy and Heslegrave, 1989; and comments by Raskin, Kircher, Honts and Horowitz, 1988; culminating in a US Federal law which, in effect, limits polygraph testing to law enforcement and Federal agencies from 1990.

Outwardly, the GKT and CQT test procedures are quite different in form and content. In the Guilty Knowledge Technique of polygraph testing, the examinee is a suspect who denies commission of the crime and knowledge of crime-relevant details which only the perpetrator could possess. For each item of crime-related information in his possession, the polygraph examiner composes a series of several alternative items, only one of which originates in the actual case at hand. The series is composed so that the crime-related alternative may be easily distinguished by the perpetrator of the crime, and by him only. The items in the series are presented to the examinee in the form of questions regarding his knowledge of the crime-related alternative, for example, "Do you know that the amount of money stolen from Jones' office was $100, $200,...,$900?".

The examinee, whose physiological activity is continuously monitored on the polygraph, replies "no" to each alternative, and the series is repeated several times. If the examinee's physiological response to the crime-related alternative is consistently greater than those to the other alternatives, he is considered to possess guilty knowledge. The GKT has been proved effective in many laboratory studies (see Lykken, 1981), and to a lesser extent in the field (Elaad, Ginton and Jungman, 1988; Elaad, 1990). The main reason for the scientific acceptance of the GKT as a potentially accurate procedure for the detection of deception (Ben-Shakhar and Furedy, 1990) is the manifest internal logic and consistency of its basic underlying premises with Orienting Response (OR) theory, which is based upon an extensive body of empirical research.

In the Control Question Technique, the examination begins with a pretest interview, during which the test questions are formulated together with the examinee, typically a suspect who denies commission of the crime. Following the interview, the question series is presented a minimum of three times to the examinee, whose physiological and verbal responses are continuously recorded on the polygraph. The question series in the CQT is comprised of relevant questions, such as "Did you take the $700 from Jones' office?", directly related to the focus of a crime, and control questions, such as "Before 1989, did you ever steal anything of value?", which are used for purposes of comparison. Control questions are designed to provoke greater responses in truthful examinees, so as to cause them to be doubtful and concerned about the truthfulness of their answer to an issue similar in type to that of the relevant issue (Raskin, 1979). The test criterion utilized in the CQT assumes that the responses of deceptive examinees to relevant questions will be greater than those to control questions (Rrq>Rcq), AND the responses of truthful examinees to control questions will be greater than those to relevant questions (Rcq>Rrq).

The main objection concerns the test criterion of the CQT, which determines the whole procedure. Specifically, people find it difficult to conceive that an innocent person, suspected of a serious crime, is capable of producing greater responses to control questions - apparently concerned with minor misbehaviours which have little to do with the criminal suspicion - than to relevant questions in the polygraph setting. Lykken (1974) directly challenged the basis of the Control Question Technique polygraph examination: "As a general rule, one would expect most subjects to be more concerned about the relevant questions than about the controls, whether they answer (the former) deceptively or truthfully, because it is the relevant questions that refer directly to the source of their immediate jeopardy". Ben-Shakhar (1992), in his opinion to the parliamentary committee inquiring polygraph accuracy and practice, has stated about this counterintuitive criterion, "Unfortunately, aside from the strong belief of polygraphists in this assumption, it has no foundation in psychological or psychophysiological research, and is not convincing in its internal logic".

While CQT procedure and decision criteria have been consistently rejected by scientists because of the counterintuitive prediction regarding innocent examinees, polygraph data presents a different picture. The Israel National Police, which conducts over a thousand CQT examinations on criminal issues yearly, finds that for the majority of examinees, a consistent 70% per year, exhibit greater responses to control questions than to relevant questions, resulting in a truthful evaluation. The technical memorandum of the Office of Technological Assessment of the United States Congress (Saxe, 1983) reviewed and evaluated available research on the validity of CQT polygraph testing in the field and analogue laboratory situations. The data from the response distribution in the studies selected by the OTA are presented in Table 9.1.

Table 9.1 Response Distribution to cq and rq

	(Detection Rates) "Ground truth" In Field Studies n=624		In Analogue Studies n=1009	
Diagnosis	Guilty	Innocent	Guilty	Innocent
Deceptive (Rrq>Rcq)	86.3 +	19.1 x	63.7 +	14.1x
Nondeceptive (Rcq>Rrq)	10.2 x	76.0 +	10.4x	57.9+
Inconclusive (Rcq=Rrq)	3.5	4.9	25.9	28.0
Total	100.0	100.0	100.0	100.0

+ = correct decisions, x = incorrect decisions.
Rrq = evaluated magnitude of recorded physiological responses to relevant questions.
Rcq = evaluated magnitude of recorded physiological responses to control questions.

The observations of the response distribution in Table 9.1 demonstrate that the response magnitudes to relevant and control question actually do discriminate between guilty and innocent examinees in the CQT setting, despite Lykken's 'rational' prediction to the contrary. Saxe (1983) found that, relative to base rates, the results of CQT polygraph examinations conducted in respective field and analogue CQT laboratory studies improved the prediction of deception and nondeception by 65%, and 43% above chance, and does in fact exhibit counterintuitive psychophysiological phenomena in innocent examinees, especially in field conditions. Similar response distributions have been observed in more recent field studies (Raskin et al., 1988), and analogue studies (Kircher et al., 1988; Patrick and Iacono, 1989) utilizing relatively severe rules of physiological evaluation. Critics of the CQT fail to explain, or even to address, this phenomenon.

As Saxe (1983) concluded, "The controversy surrounding the CQT calls for a serious attempt to understand the processes involved within existing psychological theory".

The following paper presents a theoretical basis capable of reconciling both CQT and GKT procedures with accepted theory and research. Since the GKT is well understood in terms of Orienting Response theory, this will serve as the starting point of the discussion. The theoretical implications for Investigative Psychology which evolve from the model, and models of this type, will be considered.

Orienting Response

Pavlov (1927) found that stimuli chosen for use as conditioned stimuli evoked a response of directing attention towards the stimulus, or orienting response (OR), before the initiation of the conditioning process, and that only stimuli evoking this response were effective as conditioned stimuli. Pavlov originally described OR as the investigatory, or "What-is-it?" reflex. The orienting response has motor components, such as changes of posture directing receptor organs towards the stimulus; physiological components, such as the phasic changes in skin resistance and heart rate; and cognitive components (Maltzman and Raskin, 1965), the focus of attention towards the stimulus. While these, especially the electrodermal response, have been the object of empirical study over the years (Raskin, 1973), a consensus has yet to be achieved regarding the underlying basis responsible for the phenomena observed (O'Gorman, 1979; Bernstein, 1979; Maltzman, 1979).

Two stimulus characteristics are each recognized as sufficient conditions in order to observe the physiological components of the orienting response: **novelty and signal value** (Lynn, 1966).

Ben Shakhar and Gati (1990) postulated a mechanism analogous to that of Sokolov (1963, 1966), capable of detecting environmental novelty, as well a distinguishing signal stimuli from non-signal stimuli. In this mechanism sensory input from the environment is compared to two cognitive models. One model contains a temporary representation of the preceding stimuli, and is therefore a model of the current environment. The other model contains an enduring representation of the learned signal stimulus, whose accumulated information constitutes past environmental contexts. Ben Shakhar and Gati used Tversky's (1977) contrast model of similarity to accomplish the comparison. In Tversky's model, descriptive object features are compared to target features, producing a continuous value which is the degree of similarity.

Ben-Shakhar and Gati (1990) defined novelty as the degree of **dissimilarity** between a stimulus and the stimuli preceding it (in accordance with Sokolov), and significance (signal value) as the degree of **similarity** between a stimulus and the signal. They found that the electrodemal OR magnitude corresponded to these definitions of novelty and significance.

The model proposed by Ben-Shakhar and Gati (1990) advances OR theory considerably, demonstrating how the **similarity relation**, operating between stimulus input and two models, can determine the magnitude of the evoked OR, by novelty and signal value. The comparison essentially classifies stimulus input, with reference to the appropriate model, as novelty, by temporal discrimination, and/or as a previously learned signal, significant, by a combination of generalization and discrimination.

Motivational factors also influence the orienting response. Maltzman (1979a) has pointed out that any reinforcer - positive or negative - is a signal, because it evokes approach or avoidance behaviour. Lykken (1974) also postulated **motivation** as a factor of signal value. Elaad and Ben-Shakhar (1989) observed greater OR differentiation between signal and neutral stimuli in conditions of high motivation than in low motivation conditions, despite the identical classificatory information of the relevant stimuli for all examinees.

These approaches enable the consideration of the OR from another, more real-life perspective, from which novelty and significance are not intrinsic properties of the stimulus, rather **they reflect the similarity of the representations in the cognitive models**, established by events antecedent to the stimulus, **to the stimulus**. The comparison process determines the similarity relations between sensory input and models of antecedent events, enabling **attributions** of relative degrees of novelty or significance to the stimulus, where the magnitude of the motivational features contribute to the determination of the magnitude of significance. This is a pedantic way of saying "Beauty is in the eye of the beholder". Actually, we all know this.

The degree of similarity between compared events is a function of the features describing the properties of each. The features involved in the matching function are diagnostic features, because the similarity dimension enables classification (identification, generalization and discrimination) of a target with respect to a reference. Features which also describe positive or negative reinforcing properties are of a special type and are motivational features. Motivational features are diagnostic features which represent properties such as pain, sweetness, praise, disapproval, etc. Following this reasoning, a stimulus attributed with significance - becomes a signal - when, having been detected, it is classified as motivating, in correspondence to the degree of motivation. The ability to be aware of the consequences of events - to avoid the sting of the wasp, or to seek the honey trove of the bee - without the neccessity to physically experience the contiguous reinforcing properties, is a handy evolutionary endowment.

The Orienting Response model, only partially elaborated here, is capable of detecting environmental events, classifying and differentiating them with reference to past experience and assessing their subjective significance. Learning, memory, vigilance and the development of goal oriented behaviour may also be described in terms of this model. This model of cognition is not animated exclusively by external environmental events. Associational thinking and problem solving, may be accomplished by updating the model of the current events with events, accessed from the model of past events, and subsequent comparison: access: updating between the two internal models.

The Orienting Response model is compatible with, and similar to, Ohman's (1979) model of attention. Recurrent combinations of externally and internally animated routes to significance can achieve the highly complex information processing, concept formation, and managment of attention needed by organisms in a dynamic environment. The model is a sufficient vehicle for the establishment, maintenance and operation of human behaviour as delineated in Kreitlers' theory of Cognitive Orientation (CO; Kreitler and Kreitler, 1976, 1982). In the CO theory, the first stage deals with conventional orientation to novelty and significance - "What is it?" - whereas the latter three stages include combinations of meanings which share self-reference as the basic characteristic: "How am I involved?", "What will I do?", and "How will I do it?". With very little stretch of the imagination, Freudian and Proustian dynamics and phenomena may be expressed in terms of this model of Orienting Response.

The Guilty Knowledge Technique of polygraph testing has been described in reference to orienting response theory (Lykken, 1974; Ben-Shakhar and Furedy, 1990), however this has not been attempted for the Control Question Technique. Expressing both in terms of the Orienting Response is intended to provide a theoretical framework in which both GKT and CQT may be addressed objectively and precisely.

Orienting Response Mechanisms in the Guilty Knowledge Test

In the Guilty Knowledge Technique, all tested examinees deny commission of the crime and knowledge of crime-relevant details (diagnostic features) which only the perpetrator could possess. The test criterion is essentially the examinee's ability to distinguish crime-relevant details from crime-irrelevant ones, by the assessment of significance, as reflected by the OR.

During the pretest interview the examiner explains to the examinee the general classification, but not the specific identity, of a diagnostic feature of the crime to be tested (e.g., the amount of money stolen from Jones' office last week, or, in other cases, something that the burglar dropped at the scene of the crime, the weapon used, the color of the victim's shirt, the street where the getaway car was abandoned, etc.). This information defines a general, superordinate, category which includes the significant event, as well as nonsignificant events, which may be chosen for the alternative items of the series.

Since all examinees, guilty or innocent, are suspects, the crime is a significant event whose motivational features are fear of prosecution and conviction, and the category is significant. The examinee automatically and involuntarily processes these diagnostic features (i.e., theft, Jones' office, last week, amount of money) comparing them to events stored in the model of past events.

For the examinee who is the culprit, commission of the crime is a significant event whose motivational features were monetary gain (positive) and fear of punishment (negative), and whose diagnostic features describe the circumstances of the event: date time, place; Jones' office, desk, right middle drawer, blue plastic envelope, money; $700; three $100 bills and eight $50 bills. These and other features were stored in past cognitive model when the crime was committed, and are retrieved to the model of the current environment, remembered.

For the examinee who is innocent of the crime, some features of the criminal act have not been stored in a previous model. Since the examinee is a suspect, the crime is a significant event whose motivational features may be fear of prosecution and conviction, and contextual diagnostic features which may be: Jones' office, money, last week.

Again, this constellation of features has been stored in the past model and retrieved to the current model, but lacks the $700 diagnostic feature.

Thus, for all examinees, information retrieved from the past model is the significant event contained in the current model, tested in the next stage of the GKT.

The items in the series are presented to the examinee in the form of questions regarding his knowledge of the crime-relevant alternative, for example, "Do you know that the amount of money stolen from Jones' office was $100, $200,...,$900?". The examinee, replies "no" to each alternative, while his physiological activity is continuously monitored on the polygraph, and the series is repeated several times, in different order.

The motivational features of the significant event in the current model is a "momentary motive" (fear, punishment) whose diagnostic features define a source of threat, a significant event for the examinee. These diagnostic features are the "momentary set" (amount of money stolen from Jones' office last week) used in the matching function, to detect the specific stimulus in the environment, predetermining the significance of each of the stimuli in the series.

For the examinee who is the culprit, the momentary set includes the feature "$700". As the stimuli are presented, those which are dissimilar to the set are thus identified as nonsignificant. When the relevant stimulus appears, the feature "$700" produces a result of similarity to the set, and the stimulus is identified as significant.

The strength of the orienting response evoked by each stimulus corresponds to the degree of motivation of the significant event in the current model (which is relatively constant over the series), and the degree of similarity resulting from the feature matching function, which is greater for the crime-relevant event than for the crime-irrelevant alternatives. Inspection of the physiological record of the corresponding ORs indicates consistent discrimination of significant and nonsignificant events.

For the examinee who is innocent of the crime, the momentary set of diagnostic features in the current model does not include "$700", and discrimination between the significant crime-relevant stimulus and the nonsignificant alternatives is not possible. As the stimuli are presented, attentional processes towards them persist, maintained by momentary motives, and the degree of similarity of each stimulus to the set is essentially the same. The magnitude of the OR evoked by each stimulus comparison is not differentiated by similarity, and reflects the constant motivation, and therefore the physiological record of ORs does not indicate discrimination of significant and nonsignificant events.

The above discussion of the GKT has considered the "classical" general situation where the guilty examinee is capable of classifying the alternative stimulus items according to crime-relevant significance, while the innocent examinee cannot.

Field polygraph testing of criminal acts reveals that actual life situations are occasionally more varied and complex. For example, an innocent examinee, naive with regard to the details of the crime investigated, may have experienced a significant event in a different context, which shares diagnostic features with the crime-relevant feature being tested. If the examinee had recently received a hard-earned amount of money, or paid a long-overdue debt, the presentation of the question series, "Do you know that the amount of money stolen from Jones' office was $100, $200,...,$900?", may inadvertently confound the general classification of the crime-relevant feature and a crime-irrelevant feature. In most instances of this type the diagnostic crime-relevant and crime-irrelevant features do not coincide. If, for instance, the examinee received $500, or any sum other than $700, that stimulus elicits an OR by the stimulus-to significance route. A maximal response to a stimulus which is crime-irrelevant indicates the innocence of the examinee.

In cases where the examiner knows in advance that the crime-relevant stimulus in a GKT series has crime-irrelevant significance for the examinee, that series is not presented for testing, because of the inability to determine if the response to that alternative is based upon reference to the crime-related features or crime-irrelevant features. The probability of the crime-relevant stimulus to evoke an OR because of coincidentally diagnostic crime-irrelevant features is a function of the number of stimuli in the series. In the example above, the probability that a maximal response to the crime-relevant stimulus is due to the chance correspondence of an identical crime-irrelevant feature, rather than the crime-relevant feature, is at most one to nine, or 11%. The probability of this type of false-positive error decreases with the number of GKT tests for additional crime-relevant details. For example, in the case of a bank robbery, two suspects were examined in the Guilty Knowledge Technique regarding: the amount of money taken, the type and color of mask used by the robbers, a code-name used by the robbers while in the bank, the model of the getaway vehicle the colour of the vehicle, the town where the vehicle was stolen and the location where the vehicle was abandoned. Altogether, seven question series, each of which containied seven items - one crime relevant item and six crime irrelevant alternatives. Both suspects exhibited a greater orienting response to the crime relevant item than to the crime irrelevant items in each of the series, for which the the likelihood of responding to all by chance or coincidence is 12 in *ten million.*

In a properly conducted GKT examination the examiner does not inadvertantly communicate the identity of the relevant item to the examinee. On the contrary, recent research (Elaad, 1997) indicates that guilty subjects yielded weaker responses to relevant items when the examiner was aware of them than when he did not have the knowledge.

Innocent examinees may, for various reasons, deny knowledge of crime-relevant information which they have acquired. The GKT enables detection of crime-relevant information possessed by examinees, but not the manner in which the information was acquired, or the degree of involvement in the crime. For this reason polygraph examiners do not use information which has been available to the examinee from legitimate sources (from the media, interrogation, the victim) as a basis for GKT tests, but rather limit the test issue to crime-relevant details which are not available from legitimate sources (commission of the crime, communication from the culprit, or as a witness to the crime). This limitation occasionally results in the use of crime-relevant information which the guilty examinee does not possess, because the detail was not perceived or attended at the time of the crime, or forgotten afterwards. In such a case the information is not stored in cognitive model of the past environment. For an extreme, but true, example, two examinees were tested regarding two crime-relevant details: which floor of a six story building was the site of the robbery, and how many shots were fired. Both examinees participated in the same robbery, but responded only to one of the crime-relevant details, reflecting the involvement of a culprit who led his accomplice to the crime scene, and the involvement of the other, armed, culprit who fired the weapon. The probability of this type of false-negative error decreases with the number of GKT tests for additional crime-relevant details, and when those details are most salient - essential to the perpetrator for commission of the crime. In Japan, where the GKT is the sole polygraph technique used by the police, the examiner visits the crime scene to collect 10 - 15 crime related details, whose particulars are concealed from the media and eventual suspects. The most salient are used to prepare at least five GKT series of questions for testing. The Japanese policy reduces the likelihood of coincidental false positive outcomes, while maximizing the guilty suspect's ability to identify and respond to the crime related items.

To summarise, in the Guilty Knowledge Technique the question series is assessed by the subject for significance to identify the relevant stimulus among irrelevant stimuli as his ORs are monitored. The act of lying, per se, is **incidental** to the process.

Orienting Response Mechanisms in the Control Question Technique

In both, the GKT and the CQT, 'crime-related' issues are highly significant for the examinee, whether innocent or guilty, due to their motivational concomitants and consequences. The CQT criterion requires a process capable of influencing the attribution of significance to relevant and control questions, differentially, for guilty and innocent examinees. In the GKT, this is accomplished by diagnostic processes, in which the examinee is tested for possession of the features necessary to classify the alternative items as 'crime-relevant' and 'crime-irrelevant'. This diagnostic criterion cannot be utilized in the CQT, since all examinees can identify the relevant questions as 'crime-relevant', and the control questions as 'crime-irrelevant'. Instead, the examinee's differential attribution of significance to the test questions is established by referring the criminal act and the criminal attributes to himself.

Before considering the CQT, two cognitive processes must be reviewed in terms of the OR model presented above.

The 'Self' as a Category

Data from cognitive research indicates that the self acts as a cognitive schema (Markus, 1977) or prototype (Kihlstrom and Cantor, 1984). Information processed with reference to the self (i.e. whether or not it 'describes you') is more easily recalled than when processed in reference to other schema (Bower and Gilligan, 1979; Rogers, Kuiper, and Kirker, 1977). Information which matches, or does not match, a self-prototype is processed more rapidly than information of intermediate degree of matching (Kuiper, 1981). Information is more likely to be falsely reported as having been previously presented, when consistent with a self-prototype (Rogers, Rogers and Kuiper, 1979). Thus, the self may be considered a diagnostically robust category, and motivationally of paramount importance.

Context Changes

According to Tversky's (1977) contrast model of similarity, the diagnostic value of a feature is determined by the importance or prevalence of the classifications that are based on it, which change with the context. While it is generally assumed that classifications are determined by similarities among the objects, the effects of context support the converse hypothesis: similarity of objects is modified by the manner in which they are classified. Thus, similarity has two faces: causal and derivative. It serves as a basis for the classification of objects but is also influenced by the adopted classification. Tversky termed this the diagnosticity principle.

In the Control Question Technique, all tested examinees deny commission of the crime and the possession of negative behavioural attributes connotated by the crime. The procedure and processes involved in the CQT are analogous to those of the GKT.

The CQT begins with a pretest interview in which the examiner develops the relevant and control issues, in a procedure directed at **modifying the diagnostic context** of significance. At the outset of the pretest interview the examinee gives his version of the suspicion against him, the crime, and its circumstances. At this stage the crime issue is the source of motivation.

As the crime issue is discussed, the examiner communicates information to the examinee regarding the general characterization of both the culprit and his criminal act as the criterion for evaluation of the examinee. This is usually implicit in the discussion (e.g., "Are you like the person who did this? Have you ever done something like this? What sort of person could do such a thing? Are you capable of this kind crime?"), but may also be explicit (e.g., "Experience has shown us that the person we're looking for - who stole $700 from Jones's office - is basically dishonest, and is consistently predictable: unreliable, unfair, deceitful, self-centered, betrays, misleads, takes advantage of others, etc."). This information defines a superordinate category: "the person who committed this crime", which fulfills certain requirements:

1 The diagnostic features of the category are behavioural traits which describe the crime as well as the culprit.

2 The diagnostic features of the category are continuous traits, rather than discrete ones, which include the crime (relevant issues) at the high end of the scale, but are not specific only to the crime. At the low end of the scale, the same traits characterize universal misbehaviour of all persons (i.e., a white lie), not related to the crime (control issues).

3 The relevant and the control issues of the category are discussed with reference to the examinee, establishing self-reference as a diagnostic feature, i.e., "Are you capable of ... (relevant/control)?, Did you do ...? Does this describe you ...? Have you ever ...? etc".

The information establishes an implied examination criterion, by which the category 'the person who committed this crime' or 'the culprit', describes the examinee if he possesses **any** of the criterion behaviours and attributes, producing a negative evaluation for the examinee if he identifies himself in any of the test questions, relevant or control. At this stage the superordinate category 'the culprit' is the source of motivation.

In essence, this procedure performs a **context shift**, enabling the examinee to conduct a self-referent comparison with respect to a 'culprit' criterion, rather than a 'crime-related' criterion.

The use of the Self as a feature of the category 'culprit' is especially effective in accomplishing the context shift. Any negative evaluative self-referent characteristic is highly motivating and therefore significant

(Cantor and Kihlstrom, 1986). Evaluation apprehension (Rosenberg, 1980), is an anxiety - toned concern that reflects the subjects desire to win a positive evaluation from the experimenter, or at least that he provide no grounds for a negative one, occurring spontaneously when a negative evaluation by another person is possible. This phenomenon is expected to be stronger and more specific when the evaluation is explicit, and the judged characteristic is overtly indicated. Self-Discrepancy Theory postulates that we are motivated to reach a condition where our self-concept matches our personally relevant self-guides (Higgins, 1987). In the CQT the examiner serves as a salient 'significant other', conveying to the subject the relevant self-guide - not to possess the negative attributes characterizing the culprit.

The importance of self-reference makes that feature of the test questions highly diagnostic, and tends to act as the basis for the classification of the subject with regard to the test questions; the combination of motivational and diagnostic factors enables the similarity outcome of the subject to the test questions to reflect the features of the subjects' behaviours that he remembers - retrieves from the past cognitive model.

During the pretest interview, the examinee himself often initiates the culprit category by spontaneously claiming "I've never done such a thing in my life. I'm an honest person". For the examiner, expressions of this type verify the establishment of a self-referent superordinate category. In any case, examinees deny possessing the category attributes.

The examiner ends the pretest interview by formulating the test questions, together with the examinee, regarding the diagnostic features of the criterion category - the attributes of the person who committed this crime. The questions are structured to fulfil certain requirements:

1 All the questions are phrased to be self-referent for the examinee.

2 The diagnostic features of Relevant Questions (i.e., Did you take the money from Jones' office last Tuesday?), are crime-specific, restricting the matching function to only one event in the past cognitive model because of their distinctiveness (the money, Jones' office, last Tuesday),

3 The diagnostic features of Control Questions (e.g., Did you ever do something dishonest to acquire something of value before 1990?),

a are categories of behavioural traits which describe the crime and as well as the culprit.
b enable similarity to, and retrieval of, a wide range of significant events because of their indistinctiveness (something of value, dishonestly, before 1990), and
c are crime-distinct, exclusive of the investigated crime, through the use of a time bar (e.g. Before 1990, before age 24, etc) or location bar (e.g. in other places of work).

The examinee automatically and involuntarily processes the features of the category: "the person who committed this crime" for significance. Essentially, the examinee asks himself "Am I like the culprit?" , and finds himself in a lose/lose situation if either, the relevant or the control questions, describe him.

All examinees remember behaviours which are similar to the culprit category features of the control questions. Moreover, these memories are accessed according to their importance, ensuring that the most significant instances of the category that match the control question category are retrieved, consisting of crime-distinct instances of past misbehaviour, not related to the crime.

Although this description of the cognitive process stresses its automatic, mechanistic character, the examinee subjectively experiences and exhibits a high degree of distress. During the pretest interview the examiner may ask the examinee a question such as "What kind of person committed this crime?", the reply to which often is an intense explanation regarding the despicable character and background of "the dishonest person". This transaction may be continued with the question "Before this incident, did you ever get money or something of value dishonestly?". Inevitably, the examinee will exhibit a startle reaction, often followed by some hesitation, and adjustments in verbal tone, volume, rate of speech, body posture, position of limbs, eye contact, and facial expression - fleeting indications of surprise, fear, sadness, agitation or some combination of these. The reply will usually be a short "no" , and may be accompanied by claim of honesty, good family background, position and responsibility, or good name. Some examinees may qualify their answer, referring to their childhood, finding something, not remembering any such act, or point out that everyone has done some insignificant act of that nature - taking a pen from work, etc. It is not uncommon for the examinee to make admissions of a relatively minor nature at this point. Sometimes an attempt is made to change the subject by returning to the crime issue. The actual route of transactions vary according to the responses of the examinee, but the dynamic leads to the same outcome.

Behaviours such as these serve the examiner by verifying that the examinee has adopted the 'culprit characterisitics' as the test criterion, and that the the examinee actually regards the content of the control question as relevant for himself. The verbal and non-verbal behaviour of the examiner, indicating a position of disapproval towards the 'culprit characterisitics' - raising an eyebrow is quite effective - discourages admissions of misbehaviours by the examinee, reinforcing 'evaluation apprehension' and 'self-discrepancy' dynamics, while preventing the venting and depletion of examinee control features.

Only guilty examinees can retrieve self-referent events which match the relevant question category consisting of crime-specific features - recognize themselves as actually having committed the crime at issue.

All examinees, innocent or guilty, experience the motivational features (fear of exposure, censure, punishment) of the category, whose self-referent diagnostic features (crime-specific and/or crime-distinct features), retrieved from the past cognitive model to the current model, define his "momentary set" of significant events.

The test questions are presented in sequence. The examinee, denying the characteristics of the culprit category, replies "no" to each question, while his physiological activity is continuously monitored on the polygraph. The series is repeated several times.

As the test questions are presented, their significance is differentially assessed. The examinee automatically and involuntarily conducts the comparison between the features of the relevant and control questions and the momentary set, determining the similarity between himself and the features of each question. Therefore, for deceptive and truthful examinees, the identical context of relevant and control questions will result in different degrees of subject: question similarity and attribution of significance, and corresponding differences in the OR evoked by each.

For the examinee who is the culprit, the momentary set includes the crime-specific diagnostic features of his criminal act (date, time, place, $700, etc), as well as crime-distinct diagnostic features of instances of his past misbehaviour, not related to the crime. The correspondence of features between the relevant question and the criminal act in the current cognitive model produces a greater similarity result than the match between the control question and instances of past misbehaviour in the current model. Essentially, the guilty examinee identifies himself in the relevant question to a greater degree than in the control question. These similarity relations attribute a greater degree of significance to the relevant question than to the control question, distributing OR responsivity accordingly so that **Rrq > Rcq**. This is to be expected, due to the convergence of all the apparent factors - the greater severity and specificity of threat eminating from the relevant questions acts in consort with the self referent concern of the examinee.

For the examinee who is innocent of the crime, the momentary set includes crime-distinct diagnostic features of his past misbehaviour, but not crime-specific diagnostic features of a criminal act. The correspondence of features between the control question and instances of past misbehaviour retrieved to the current cognitive model produces a greater result of similarity than does the match between the relevant question and the criminal act in the current cognitive model, so that the innocent examinee identifies himself in the control questions to a greater degree than in the relevant questions. This similarity relation attributes a greater degree of significance to the control question than to the relevant question, and produces an opposite distribution of OR responsivity, **Rcq > Rrq**. As in the GKT, for both guilty and innocent examinees the act of lying, per se, is **incidental** to this process.

This result is the basis of the controversy surrounding the CQT. For most of the critics of the technique the relative specificity, severity and relevance of the relevant questions, as compared to the control questions, is the sole apparent factor. This assumption is contradicted by results from laboratory and field studies, which indicate that additional factors are active in the CQT context, and indeed, outweigh and govern the expression of the salient factor. The model discussed above shows how the relevant, crime related issue converges with, and is captured, encapsulated, within an evaluative, self referent category (the identity of the culprit) comprised of both the relevant and the control issues. The robustness, spontaneity, and fundamentality of the self referent prototype, descriptive and evaluative, takes precedence as the context in which the innocent examinee recognizes himself, identifies himself, in those elements of 'the culprit' embodied in the control questions to a greater degree than in the relevant questions. This dynamic can account for the redistribution of attention, concern and responses observed in truthful examinees in the CQT, **Response [control question] > Response [relevant question]**.

The model of orienting response has apparent descriptive value with respect to the Control Question Technique criterion of physiological detection of deception. Additionally, it enables the demonstration of the underlying cognitive processes common to both GKT and CQT.

Reconsidering the GKT in light of the processes involved in the CQT, the contribution of self-referent factors to the cognitive processes involved, enabling differential physiological response, are clearly recognizable. The judgemental features arising from Evaluation Apprehension and Self-Discrepancy, implicit in the test situation, are diagnostically specific features of the relevant alternative item for deceptive, but not for truthful, examinees. The actions and emotions experienced by the culprit during the crime - breaking and entering, violence, evasion, danger, gain - are also features of the event specific to the relevant alternative item for deceptive, but not for truthful, examinees.

Polygraph testing is an instance of a basically reliable and robust procedure that was developed in the field by it's practitioners, lacking the theoretical and empirical benefits of the scientific method. The model offered here is simply a reorganization of what many polygraph examiners and psychologists know already, with reference to this particular context. Remarkably, the cognitive and physiological dynamics do not deal with lying *per se*, but rather with the examinee's ability to process the significance of the information about himself, in the test contexts. Similarly, Ekman (1985) was able to infer deceptive communication by detecting microexpressions, fleeting facial and body gestures of subjects, indicating emotions (fear, disdain, sadness, glee) inconsistent with the verbal content expressed. The contradictory emotional leakage was observed, indicating lying - not the lie itself.

This model of orienting response is offered as a conceptual framework within which polygraph issues may be redefined theoretically and operationally, and examined empirically. Once based on a theoretical framework, research observations may amend, elaborate and refine the processes involved, with consequent improvements in cognitive management and physiological assessment procedures in the GKT and CQT. This approach is open to refutation, or to substitution by a more appropriate and valid system of concepts, and frees the CQT, to a certain extent, from overall validity as the sole instrument of evaluation. The theoretical approach encourages clear and consistent communication among polygraph examiners, trainers and trainees, as well as meaningful scientific dialogue in the academy and legislature.

The above model is a partial explication of a general model of cognition. As such it has relevance to other applications of psychology in the field of criminal investigation. The hypothesis central to offender profiling is based upon the assumption that the way an offender carries out a crime on one occasion will have some characteristic similarities to the way he carries out crimes on other occasions, and that these consistencies emanate from characteristics typical of the offender, not of the crime situation (Canter, 1994a). Whatever theoretical approach is applied to the offender consistency hypothesis - psychodynamic, personality, criminological, sociological, interpersonal transaction, or preferably, an integration of such approaches - the model of cognition can serve as a medium to describe and explore the relations between the crime and the culprit.

If the crime actions, recorded by the police in the course of an investigation, are regarded as embodying diagnostic and motivational features which participate in the significant cognitive constructs of the culprit, they may be used as a bridge to his characteristics and identity. The crime actions may contain expressions of the motivation and/or goal of the criminal action, the attitude towards the victim or the significance of the selected target, the degree of familiarity/security within the surroundings, skills and/or training possessed by the perpetrator, personal knowledge concerning information of limited access, verbal and non-verbal indices of background and character - in short, a multitude of features emanating from the specific and private 'terms of reference' of the culprit. Obviously, the presence of a specialty knot commonly used in stables at the crime scene would indicate a different search for a culprit than would a knot used in the navy.

For instance, some of these features, when correctly parsed at the appropriate categorical level, may embody characteristics of the culprit which may be useful for establishing a set of priorities (e.g., marital status, type of occupation, location) for screening crime suspects (Canter, 1994b). Systematic evaluation of the relations among features of crimes and aspects of the culprits' backgrounds has revealed that a given type of crime may be structured - carried out in identifiably different ways

(Canter and Heritage, 1990), by culprits possessing correspondingly different, identifiable characteristic complements. Furthermore, common features of crime actions are likely to be found in other instances of crimes by the same culprit, enabling accurate linking of seemingly isolated events to the same perpetrator (Canter, 1994b).

The exploration of repertoires of crime action and culprit features, and their interrelations, currently under way (see Canter and Alison, Offender Profiling Series: Volumes 3, 4 and 5) presents a fascinating promise of productiveness in the investigation of crime.

References

Ben-Shakar, G. (1992). *Expert Opinion to the Parliamentary Committee inquiring polygraph accuracy and practice.* Written as Expert Opinion from Moshe Musak, LLB, March 1987, page 3, (Hebrew).

Ben-Shakhar, G. and Furedy, J. J. (1990). *Theories and Applications in the Detection of Deception.* New York: Springer-Verlag.

Ben-Shakhar, G. and Gati, I. (1987). Common and Distinctive Features of Pictorial Stimuli as Determinants of Psychophysiological Responsivity. *Journal of Experimental Psychology*, 116, 2, 91-105.

Ben-Shakhar, G. and Gati, I. (1990). Novelty and Significance in Orientation and Habituation: A Feature-Matching Approach. *Journal of Experimental Psychology*, 119, 3, 252-263.

Ben-Shakhar, G., and Lieblich, I. (1982). Similarity of auditory stimuli and generalization of skin conductance response (SCR) habituation. *Physiological Psychology*, 10, 331-335.

Berlyne, D.E. (1961). Conflict and the orientation response. *Journal of Experimental Psychology*, 26, 476-483.

Bernstein, A.S. (1969). To what does the orienting response respond? *Psychophysiology*, 6, 338-351.

Bernstein, A.S. (1979). The orienting response and novelty and significance detector: reply to O'Gorman. *Psychophysiology*, 16, 263-273.

Bower, G.H., and Gilligan, S.G. (1979). Remembering information related to one's self. *Journal of Research in Personality*, 13, 420-432.

Canter, D. (1994) "Psychology of Offender Profiling" in R. Bull and D. Carson (eds) *Hand book of Psychology in Legal Contexts.* Chichester: Wiley.

Canter, D. (1994b) *Criminal Shadows* London: Harper Collins.

Canter, D. and Heritage, R. (1990). A multivariate model of sexual offence behaviour: developments in 'offender profiling'. I. *Journal of Forensic Psychiatry*, Vol. 1, No. 2.

Cantor, N. and Kihlstrom, J.F. (1986) *Personality and social intelligence.* Englewood Cliffs, NJ: Prentice-Hall.

Connoly, J.G. and Frith, C.D. (1978a). Effects of stimulus variability on the amplitude and habituation of the electrodermal orienting response. *Psychophysiology,* 15, 550-555.

Connoly, J.G. and Frith, C.D. (1978b). Effects of varying stimulus context on habituation and sensitization of the OR. *Physiology and Behavior*, 21, 511-514.

Ekman, P. (1985). *Telling Lies*. New York: W.W. Norton and Co.

Elaad, E. (1990). Detection of guilty knowledge in real life criminal investigations. *Journal of Applied Psychology*, 75, 521-529.

Elaad, E. (1997). Polygraph Examiner Awareness of Crime-Relevant Information and the Guilty Knowledge Test. *Law and Human Behavior*, 21, 1, 107-120.

Elaad, E. and Ben-Shakhar, G. (1989a). Effects of motivation and verbal response type on psychophysiological detection of information. *Psychophysiology*, 26, 442-451.

Elaad, E., Ginton, A. and Jungman, N. (1988). Respiration line length and GSR amplitude as detection measures in criminal guilty knowledge tests. Paper presented at the NATO ASI conference on credibility assessment. Maratea, Italy.

Furedy, J.L. and Heslegrave, R.J. (1988). Validity of the lie detector: A psychophysiological persepctive. *Criminal Justice and Behaviour* 15(2), 219-246

Gati, I., Ben-Shakhar, G. and Oren, C. (1986). The Relationship Between Similarity Judgments and Psychophysiological Responsivity. *Acta Psychologia*, 62, 123-139.

Higgins, E.T. (1987). Self-discrepancy: A theory relating self and affect. *Psychological Review*, 94,319-340.

Houck, R.L. and Mefferd, R.B. (1969). Generalization of GSR habituation to mild intramodal stimuli. *Psychophysiology*, 6, 202-206.

Hull, J. G., Van Treuren, R. R., Ashford, S. J., Propsom, P. and Andrus, B. W. (1988). Self-Consciousness and the Processing of Self-Relevant Information. *Journal of Personality and Social Psychology*, 54, 3, 452-465.

Kihlstrom, J.F. and Cantor, N. (1984). Mental representations of the self. In L. Berkowitz (ed.), *Advances in experimental and social psychology* (Vol.17, pp.1-47). New York: Academic Press.

Kircher, J.C., Horowitz, S.W. and Raskin, D.C. (1988). Meta-analysis of mock-crime studies of the control question polygraph technique. *Law and Human Behavior*, 12, 79-90.

Kreitler, Hans and Kreitler, Shulamith. *Cognitive Orientation and Behavior.* New York: Springer Pub. Co. 1976.

Kuiper, N.A. (1981). Convergent evidence for the self as a prototype: The "inverted-U RT effect" for self and other judgments. *Personality and Social Psychology Bulletin*, 7, 438-443.

Lykken, D.T. (1959). The GSR in the detection of guilt. *Journal of Applied Psychology*, 45, 6, pp. 385-388.

Lykken, D.T. (1974). Psychology and the lie detector industry. *American Psychologist* ,October, 725-739.

Lykken, D.T. (1981). *A Tremor in the Blood: Uses and abuses of the lie detector.* New York: McGraw-Hill.

Lynn, R. (1966). *Attention, Arousal and the Orientation Reaction.* Oxford: Pergamon.

Maltzman, I. (1979a). Orienting reflexes and significance: A reply to O'Gorman. *Psychophysiology*, 16, 274-282.

Maltzman, I. and Langdon, B. (1982). Novelty and significance as determiners of the GSR index of the orienting reflex. *Physiological Psychology*, 10, 229-234.

Maltzman, I. and Raskin, D.C. (1965). Effects of individual differences in the orienting response on conditioning and complex processes. *Journal of Experimental Research in Personality.* 1, 1-16.

Markus, H. (1977). Self-schemata and processing information about the self. *Journal of Personality and Social Psychology*, 35, 63-78.

O'Gorman, J.G. (1979). The orienting reflex: novelty or significance detector? *Psychophysiology*, 16, 253-262.

Ohman, A. (1979). The orienting response, attention and learning: An information processing perspective. In: H.D. Kimmel, E.H. Van Olst, and J.F. Orlebeke (eds.), *The Orienting Reflex in Humans.* Lawrence Erlbaum Associates: Hillsdale, N.J. pp. 443-471.

Ohman, A. (1986). Face the Beast and Fear the Face: Animal and Social Fears as Prototypes for Evolutionary Analyses of Emotion. *Psychophysiology,* 23, 123-145.

Patrick,C.J. and Iacono, W.G. 1989. Psychopathy, threat and polygraph test accuracy. *Journal of Applied Psychology*, 74, 347-355.

Pavlov, I.P. (1927). *Conditional Reflex.* Oxford: Charmadon Press.

Pudlesney, J.A. and Raskin, D.C. (1978) Effectiveness of technqiues and physiological measures in the detection of deception. Psychophysiology July 15(4), 344-359.

Raskin, D.C. (1973). Attention and arousal. In: W.F. Prokasy and D.C. Raskin (eds.), *Electrodermal Activity in Psychological Research.* London: Academic Press.

Raskin, D.C. (1979). Orienting and Defensive Reflexes in the Detection of Deception. in: H.D. Kimmel, E.H. Van Olst, and J.F. Orlebeke (eds) *The*

Orienting Response in Humans. Hillsdale, New Jersey: Lawrence Erlbaum Associates, Publishers.

Raskin, D.C., Kircher, J.C., Honts, C.R. and Horowitz, S.W. (1988). *A study of the validity of polygraph examinations in criminal investigation* (Grant No. 85-IJ-CX-0040). Salt Lake City: University of Utah, Department of Psychology.

Reid, J.E. and Inbau, F.E. (1977). *Truth and Deception - The Polygraph Technique*, 3rd, ed., Baltimore: The Williams and Wilkins Co.

Rogers, T.B., Kuiper, N.A. and Kirker, W.S. (1977). Self-reference and the encoding of personal information. *Journal of Personality and Social Psychology*, 35, 677-688.

Rogers, T.B., Rogers, P.J. and Kuiper, N.A. (1979). Evidence for the self as a cognitive prototype: The "false alarms effect". *Personality and Social Psychology Bulletin*, 5, 53-56.

Rosenberg, M.J. (1965). When dissonance fails: on eliminating evaluation apprehension from attitude measurement. *Journal of Personality and Social Psychology*. 1, 28-42.

Rosenberg, M.J. (1980). Experimenter expectancy, evaluation apprehension and the diffusion of methodological angst. *The Behavioral and Brain Sciences*, 3, 472-474.

Saxe, L. (1983). *Scientific Validity of Polygraph Testing: A Research Review and Evaluation - A Technical Memorandum* (Wash., D.C.: U.S. Congress, Office of Technology Assessment, OTA-TM-H-15, Nov. 1983)

Sokolov, E.N. (1963). *Perception and the conditioned reflex.* New York: McMillan.

Sokolov, E.N. (1966). Orienting reflex as information regulator. In: E. Rosch and B. Lloyds (eds.), *Cognition and Categorization* (pp 79-98). Hillsdale, NJ: Erlbaum.

Stern, J.A. (1972). Physiological response measures during classical conditioning. In: N.S. Greenfield and R.A. Sternbach (eds.), *Handbook of Psychophysiology*. NY: Holt, Rinehart and Winston, Inc.

Tversky, A. (1977). Features of Similarity. *Psychological Review*, 44, 4, 327-352.

Tversky, A. and Hutchinson, J.W. (1986). Nearest Neighbor Analysis of Psychological Spaces. Psychological Review, 93, 3-22.

10 A Comparative Study of Polygraph Tests and Other Forensic Methods

EITAN ELAAD

An attempt was made to compare the accuracy of two major polygraph methods, used in criminal investigations by the Israeli police, with other common criminal identification methods such as: fingerprint identification; voice identification; handwriting identification and eyewitness identification. Results indicated that three methods were free of false positive errors; fingerprint identification, the guilty knowledge polygraph test (GKT) and natural handwriting identification. While the more subjective handwriting identification task seemed to be rather easy, fingerprint identification and the GKT are standard and relatively objective procedures that require more expertise. Furthermore, they differ from the handwriting identification procedure by providing control over the probability of false positive errors.

Eitan Elaad has been with the National Police of Israel since 1976. He received his Ph.D. in psychology from the Hebrew University of Jerusalem in 1988. He is a member of the Society for Psychophysiological Research (SPR) and for many years lectured in the Department of Criminology at Bar-Llan University. His research has focused on psychophsiological detection of deception and concealed knowledge. He also studied social factors which have influence on deception and its detection, forensic methods and decision making processes.

Offender Profiling Series: I - ***Interviewing and Deception***
Edited by D. Canter and L. Alison. pp 209-231

10 A Comparative Study of Polygraph Tests and Other Forensic Methods

EITAN ELAAD

Criminal investigations conducted by the Israeli Police often use the polygraph as an aid for pointing at the guilty suspect or eliminating innocent suspects, thus directing the investigation. The polygraph itself is no more than a device to record physiological changes. Each polygraph records changes in respiration, electro dermal responses and cardiovascular activity. Respiration is recorded by two pneumatic rubber tubes positioned around the thoracic area and abdomen. The electro dermal recording is made with stainless steel electrodes attached to the volar side of the index and fourth fingers of the examinee's left hand. Cardiovascular activity is recorded with a pneumatic pressure cuff positioned around the upper portion of the examinees right arm. The polygraph examination is conducted in a quiet, plainly furnished, soundproof comfortable room where the examiner is alone with the examinee. While operating the instrument, questions are presented to the examinees to which they are instructed to answer yes or no. According to the recorded physiological responses the assessment of truthfulness is made.

Several methods of psychophysiological detection have been developed and used in field practice (see, Lykken, 1981; Raskin, 1989; Reid and Inbau, 1977; Saxe, Dougherty and Cross, 1985). These methods are based on a comparison between physiological responses to relevant questions (i.e., questions that focus on the issue under investigation) and some form of control questions. Two common methods are the focus of the present study: one, which is called the Control Question Technique (CQT), should have been called the comparison question technique. The other, which is known as the Guilty Knowledge Test (GKT) should have been referred to as the concealed knowledge test (Honts, Devitt, Winbush and Kircher, 1996).

The Control Question Technique

The CQT is the most commonly used method in field practice. It emphasizes the interaction between the polygraph examiner and the examinee as the basis for the elicitation of appropriate physiological recordings (Raskin, 1982). For this purpose the examiners consent has to follow knowledge of the suspicion against him or her, and the examinee must be of sound mental and physical health.

Briefly, the CQT consists of several stages. First the examiner becomes familiar with the facts of the crime by reading the case file and by speaking directly to the investigating officer. Information such as previous criminal records, the basis for suspicion, motives, the desired questions to be asked, etc. are useful to confirm that the examinee understand the charges, to resolve any discrepancies, and construct the appropriate questions.

During the next stage the examiner conducts an extensive pre-test interview. The pre-test interview may last up to one hour, during which the examiner establishes a degree of rapport with the examinee. The examinee is given the opportunity to present his or her version of the crime and the examiner makes sure that the facts reported by the examinee correspond to those presented by the investigator. Then, the questions are formulated so that the examinee can give a direct "yes" or "no" answer to each question. If there is a need for clarification, the examiner does so and, if necessary, questions may be reformulated. Finally, the examiner explains the testing procedure and ensures that the examinee understands all the questions.

The next stage is the actual examination stage during which the examinee is attached to the polygraph and asked the questions. Essentially, the questions are of the following three types: (a) relevant questions which bear on the issue under investigation in the "Did you do it?" form (e.g., "Did you take $100 from the drawer last Monday?"). Relevant questions are specific with regard to time and place and are typically answered "no". This indicates that the examinee denies involvement with the crime; (b) control questions which deal with undesirable acts committed by the suspect in the past which are of the same kind as those covered by the relevant questions (e.g., "Before 1995, did you ever take something that didn't belong to you without permission?").

Control questions focus on general, non-specific misconducts and are expected to be answered "no". In other words, the examinee denies any involvement with the indicated act; (c) irrelevant questions which correspond to a neutral issue to which the affirmative answer is a known truth (e.g., "Are you sitting on a chair?"). The irrelevant questions are intended to absorb the initial orienting response evoked by any opening question and to enable rest periods between the more loaded questions. Typically, the whole question series consist of 10-12 questions which are repeated three or four times.

It is assumed that the relevant questions will generate more concern and arousal in the guilty examinee while an innocent examinee will attend and respond more to the control questions. The pre-test interview is used to produce concern about the control questions. The innocent examinee who is truthful with regard to the relevant questions and either deceptive, or at least unsure of being truthful in answering the control questions, is expected to react with greater strength to the control questions. The guilty examinee, who is more concerned about the relevant issue, will not be able to divert attention from the relevant questions, and therefore is expected to react more to these questions.

Finally, the examinee is released from the transducers and is accompanied to a waiting room. The examiner analyzes the records and reaches a decision by comparing the physiological responses given to the relevant questions with those given to the adjacent control questions. Each chart is quantitatively scored.

In cases where a deceptive outcome is reached the examiner may return for a post-test interrogation. An attempt to elicit an admission is made. Here the examiner may use the rapport he has developed during the examination which may help him get a confession. Confessions, either by the polygraph examiner or later on by the interrogator are achieved in about 5% of the cases of the Israeli police.

The assumptions underlying the CQT and its inference rule have been criticized as implausible (e.g., Ben-Shakhar and Furedy, 1990; Furedy and Heslegrave, 1991; Lykken, 1974, 1981). It was argued that in terms of eliciting arousal, the specific relevant question is not equivalent to the more general control question from the point of view of either innocent or guilty examinee. Therefore, the CQT should yield a very high false positive error rate. According to Podlesny and Raskin (1977), the control question technique attempts to set up a situation in which the innocent examinee will be more concerned about the control questions despite the knowledge that the relevant questions pertain to the crime under investigation and therefore have substantial arousal value. This can be done by a proper pretest interview. The debate continues but ultimately, the effectiveness of the CQT is an empirical question.

Ben-Shakhar and Furedy (1990), argued that the CQT is not a psychological test in its normal sense because it does not provide an objective and standardized procedure. The CQT is highly dependent on the operator in the formulation of the control questions and in how these questions are presented to the examinees. It is also likely that information other than that which emerges in the polygraph charts may influence the examiner's decisions. Podlesny and Raskin (1977) argued, that it is important that field polygraph examiners be well trained and base their decisions on the physiological recordings in order to avoid as much as possible the danger that in arriving at a decision the examiner would subtly affect the outcome or be influenced by factors other than the physiological recordings.

The Guilty Knowledge Test

Lykken (1959,1960), the most determined opponent of the CQT, suggested another method, developed earlier, which he called the Guilty Knowledge Test (GKT). The GKT is less controversial than the CQT and is considered to be objective and scientific. The GKT is used in applied settings to detect information that an individual cannot or does not wish to reveal. The GKT is based on a series of multiple-choice questions (items), each having one relevant alternative (e.g., a feature of the crime that would be known to the perpetrator but not to innocent suspects) and several control alternatives. For example, the suspect might be asked, "Do you know that the color of the stolen car was?" (1) grey, (2) white, (3) yellow, (4) blue, or (5) red. It is assumed that only a guilty suspect will be able to single out and respond differentially to the true color of the stolen car, while innocent examinees, who have no guilty knowledge, are unable to distinguish crime-related information from other alternatives.

Inferences are made on the basis of the GKT by comparing the responses elicited by the relevant item with the responses to irrelevant items. Only if the responses to the relevant item are consistently larger, guilty knowledge is inferred. This provides a proper control against false positive outcomes, inasmuch as the likelihood that an innocent examinee might show consistently greater responsiveness to the correct alternative just by chance can be reduced to a low level by using many irrelevant items, by utilizing several GKT questions and by repeating each series of questions.

The rate of correct detection of guilty and innocent examinees reported in simulated experiments is quite impressive. Lykken (1959) and Davidson (1968) used a mock-crime procedure in which participants simulating the guilty condition tried to prevent six crime-related details from being detected by the polygraph. Lykken (1959) used a global score for each examinee, computed over the six GKT questions, and decided, according to a pre-defined decision rule, whether the examinee possessed the guilty knowledge or not. Lykken found that 44 of the 50 interrogations of perpetrators yielded correct detections, and that the classification of innocent examinees was perfect. Davidson (1968) replicated this study and reported a detection rate of 92% for guilty examinees and 100% for innocent participants. It seems, therefore, that the GKT is potentially a highly accurate method of detecting guilty knowledge.

Ben-Shakhar and Furedy (1990), selected ten GKT laboratory studies and summarized their results. All ten studies used the electrodermal measure, most of them as the sole measure. Results indicated a range of correct detections among the guilty examinees from 61% to 100%, but in only two out of the ten studies was the rate less than 85%. In the innocent condition the correct detection rate ranged between 81% and 100%.

It should be noted that seven of the ten studies indicated perfect detection. Ben-Shakhar and Furedy (1990), concluded that the GKT assumptions are compatible with psychological theory and are supported by extensive research. Furthermore, the GKT can be designed very much like a standardized and objective test.

However, recent field studies (Elaad, 1990; Elaad, Ginton and Jungman 1992) revealed that detection rates of guilty examinees in true examination conditions are much smaller.

To assess the applied value of the polygraph tests, a comparative approach, which compares the accuracy of the polygraph techniques with other commonly used forensic methods, under similar conditions, may be useful.

The Widacki and Horvath Study

The first attempt to compare the validity and utility of the CQT with three other methods of criminal identification, was made by Widacki and Horvath (1978). In this study, the participating students were assigned to 20 groups of four students each. Within each group one student was randomly selected to perform the role of the perpetrator and the remaining three students were assigned to the role of the innocent suspects. The task of the perpetrator was to collect a parcel from a doorkeeper in return for an envelope and the instruction sheet. The perpetrator was asked by the doorkeeper to complete a receipt form by signing "I acknowledge the receipt" and a signature of a fictitious name. The perpetrator was advised to try to deform the handwriting which was to be used as a means of identification. All the participating students underwent a CQT polygraph examination. Perpetrators were promised a reward of small value if found innocent in the polygraph test. Innocent examinees received no reward. In addition, Widacki and Horvath (1978) employed three other criminal identification methods (a). Fingerprints were lifted from the envelope and instruction sheet using ninhydrin. The fingerprint expert was aware of the four students assigned to each perpetrated event, and his task was to decide which of the four prints matched those on the evidence. (b). The handwriting expert matched the handwriting on the receipt with the proper exemplar in each case. He was also aware of the four students assigned to each case. (c). Two doorkeepers served as eyewitnesses. Two days after the perpetrated crime the appropriate eyewitness was shown photographs of the four suspects in each case, and was asked to identify the perpetrator.

Results indicated that with the polygraph 18 cases were correctly resolved (correctly resolved cases are events in which the perpetrator and the three innocent suspects were correctly identified). The handwriting expert was successful in resolving 17 cases, the eyewitness succeeded in 7, and the fingerprint identification expert in only 4. However, when incorrect decisions were considered, the polygraph examiner yielded 1 incorrect decision, the handwriting expert 1, and the eyewitnesses 4. The fingerprint expert could not make any decision in 16 cases.

The shortcomings of the Widacki and Horvath (1978) study are considerable. The comparison between the forensic methods was flawed by the disadvantageous nature of the setting. Hence, identifiable fingerprints were found only in four cases. The CQT polygraph technique suffered from the low motivation of the students to yield truthful outcomes and from the fact that the polygraph examination was administered immediately after the completion of the assigned task. The analysis of the handwriting evidence was flawed by the short sentence of only four words and by the advice to the perpetrators to try and deform their handwriting.

On the other hand, the fact that the polygraph examiner and the handwriting expert were aware of the prior probabilities of guilt and innocence, may have lead to an overestimation of the polygraph and handwriting identification rate.

The results of Widacki and Horvath cannot be generalized to the real life situation because of the laboratory-based character of the study (the use of students with no incentive to produce truthful outcomes, the location in the university campus), and because of the closed trial method which indicated that one of every four suspects must be the perpetrator.

Therefore, a constructive replication of the Widacki and Horvath study is necessary. The replication must take into account the many flaws of the study in order to be more informative about the proper place of the polygraph tests among other common forensic methods.

The Purpose of the Present Study

The purpose of the present study is threefold: first, to assess the accuracy of the CQT and GKT polygraph tests in comparison to other common conditions for identification. To this end, the identification experts were asked to define their demands and the experiment tried to meet them under the limitations of a mock-crime experiment.

Second, the present study was designed to resemble field conditions more than the study of Widacki and Horvath. Thus an open trial method was employed, the number of suspects in each case changed from 2 to 6 and the number of perpetrators were either none, one or two. This prevented the experts from estimating the prior probabilities of guilt and innocence. In addition, standard field equipment and measurement procedures were utilized. The promised reward for guilty examinees, in the case of truthful outcomes, was high and innocent examinees were punished if found deceptive. The setting was designed to impress the participants and to make them believe that their task is to cope with highly professional forensic experts. The participants were recruited from outside the Israel Police Headquarters, but the test was conducted in the headquarters building where many policemen in uniform were present. The participants enacted the crime several days before they were assigned to the polygraph tests as is usual in actual interrogations. Finally, they went through a standard procedure of interrogation, gave their fingerprints, were photographed, and were submitted to other forensic examinations such as handwriting analysis and voice identification.

Finally, the present study considers additional criminal identification tests such as the GKT and voice identification, which makes the comparison more informative.

Method

Participants

The participants were 81 males, with an age range from 19 to 51 years (M=25.0, SD=5.34). All participants reported good health. Participants were recruited either from the local community by the local employment services, or by the student employment agency of the Hebrew University of Jerusalem. Participants were offered 100 NIS (about $40) for participation in a forensic science experiment. It was noted that there might be a possible bonus for successful performance. Participants responded by telephone and were given general information about the experiment. They were told that the experiment was a two-session project. Those who agreed to participate were assigned an appointment for the first session.

The Mock Crime Procedure

Participants arrived at the forensic laboratories individually at a predetermined time. On arriving for the first session they met the experimenter who informed them of the nature of the experiment and requested their cooperation. Participants were then asked to complete a form requesting background information and signed a consent agreement to be interrogated with forensic tests about a mock crime in which they might be involved. Twenty five participants were assigned to the role of the perpetrator in 20 perpetrated events. They received written instructions that informed them to enact a mock crime which consisted of entering a closed room, opening a box located on a desk and stealing money from an envelope which was placed inside that box. While entering the room they were observed by either one or two eyewitnesses recruited beforehand from the staff of the Israeli police. Perpetrators were instructed to take the money and put it in their pocket. To avoid disclosure, they were asked to falsify a receipt indicating that a certain person, whose name was indicated in the instructions, received the money in return for delivering equipment to the Israeli police. Of the 25 perpetrators, 13 were advised to try and change their handwriting. In one case the perpetrator was asked to leave two receipts, one with his natural handwriting and one in which he deliberately deformed his handwriting.

Guilty participants were further instructed to make a phone call to a certain number, notifying a partner that the theft was accomplished and that they should meet at a certain street, indicated in the instructions, where they would deliver the money to the accomplice. The phone call was recorded. Thirteen perpetrators were instructed to try to disguise their voices whereas the other 12 did not receive such instructions.

After enacting the crime, 13 of the guilty participants were instructed to go to a nearby room, take a parcel addressed to a certain person and bring it to the experimenter who waited downstairs. The other 12 guilty participants were instructed to take another envelope with a different amount of money in it and deliver it to the experimenter. Four guilty knowledge items were produced, the stolen sum of money, the color of the envelope, the street in which the suspect would meet his partner, and the falsified name on the receipt. Finally, to ensure that participants were aware of the four GKT items, the experimenter asked the perpetrator to repeat them.

56 innocent participants received instructions that informed them to enter the nearby room, take the parcel (or envelope), and bring it to the experimenter. After receiving the parcel (or envelope), the experimenter informed all participants that they would receive 100 NIS (about $40) for participating in the experiment. Guilty participants were further informed that in addition to the 100 NIS, they were entitled to the money they stole, if found innocent. The stolen sum ranged from 40 to 480 NIS (from about $16 to $190). If found deceptive, guilty participants would not get their stolen money and would be punished with a reduction of 25 NIS of their

participation fee. To enhance the motivation of the innocent participants they were told that if they would yield deceptive outcomes, they would also be punished with a reduction of 25 NIS of their participation fee.

The experimenter informed the participants that they were under suspicion of stealing the money and therefore, they were to be interrogated. He cautioned the suspects not to confess the mock crime to the interrogator or to anyone else. In the case of confession, the suspect could expect to lose all the money. Suspects were then individually interrogated by a police interrogator as to their involvement in the crime. They were told that they would have the opportunity to clear themselves from suspicion through forensic examinations. They gave their written consent for the polygraph examination which was scheduled to take place several days later, and signed their testimony. Next, suspects were asked to give their fingerprints and were photographed in three positions. All participants were then assigned an appointment for the continuation of the examinations.

Several days (range from 1 to 7) after executing the mock crime, each suspect returned for additional identification tests. Upon arrival, the experimenter reminded the suspect about the suspicion against him. The suspect was further reminded of the incentive conditions and of the importance of yielding an innocent outcome. Guilty suspects were not, however, reminded of the relevant GKT items. Participants were then sent to give handwriting specimens in the Israel Police Document and Handwriting Identification Laboratory, and voice samples in the Israel Police Voice Identification Laboratory. Finally, they were polygraphed. Following field practice, the CQT preceded the GKT. The GKT was conducted by a different examiner who was unaware of the previous CQT result.

Data Acquisition and Analysis

The Control Question Test

The polygraph tests were conducted by eight polygraphers of the Israel police, all experienced in operating the polygraph. All examiners were uninformed of the base rates of guilt and innocence. The CQT examiner scored the polygraph records according to the numerical scoring procedure which was proposed originally by Backster (1963). According to this scoring procedure, two or three pairs of relevant control questions are identified in each polygraph chart, and numbers (-3,-2,-1, 0, 1, 2, 3) are assigned to each pair for each physiological measure. The absolute value of the assigned number reflects the magnitude of the difference between the responses evoked by the two questions within the pair (e.g., -3 or +3 reflect a very large difference, -1 or +1 reflect a small difference and 0 reflects no difference), and the sign of the assigned number reflects the direction of the difference, such that positive numbers are associated with a pattern of larger physiological reactivity to the control question, and negative numbers reflect the opposite pattern. These numbers are then summed up across question pairs, across physiological measures and across polygraph charts to yield a total score.

Using this scoring procedure, each examiner scored his own records. In addition, the records were given to another experienced examiner for a blind scoring. The blind scorers were unaware of the outcome of the test and of the content of the questions presented to the examinee. They identified the relevant and control questions according to their corresponding number. The correlation coefficient between the total scores assigned by the original examiners and those of the blind examiners was .88.

The two total scores were averaged. If the averaged score exceeded +5 the examinee was classified as truthful; if the score was less than -5, the examinee was classified deceptive; and if the averaged total score ranged between -5 and +5, inclusive, the record was classified as inconclusive. The relative frequencies of the three decisions made for innocent and guilty examinees are presented in Table 1. Note that two innocent examinees were examined only with the GKT. This reduced the total number of CQT examinees to 79.

Table 10.1 Decision Frequencies made for Perpetrators and Innocent Participants according to the Various Forensic Methods

	Perpetrators			Innocent Participants		
Decisions	**ID Guilty**	**Inconclusive**	**ID Innocent**	**ID Guilty**	**Inconclusive**	**ID Innocent**
Polygraph						
CQT	10	7	8	2	13	39
GKT	19	3	3	0	9	46
Fingerprints						
	19	6 **	- *	0	56**	- *
Voice						
Natural	11	0	1	1	0	39
Deformed	10	2	1	1	8	33
Handwriting						
Natural	13	0	0	0	0	40
Deformed	9	3	1	2	6	35
Eyewitness						
Lineup	17	0	8	2	0	59
Photo Archive	6	0	8	1	0	40

* **The absence of fingerprints do not imply innocence**
** **Including two cases in which fingerprints were not developed**

The Guilty Knowledge Test

Examinees were presented with four series of GKT questions: the stolen sum of money, the color of the envelope from which the money was taken, the name of the street in which the culprit was going to meet his partner, and the name the culprit falsified on the receipt. The four GKT series were constructed by the experimenter. To each relevant item the experimenter added six neutral items, one of which was introduced at the beginning of each series to serve as a buffer. In two GKT series a target item, which the examinee could discriminate from the other items, was included instead of one neutral item, and in two GKT series the polygraph examiner was informed about the relevant item - the knowledge and target effects are discussed in Elaad, (in press). The order of questions was counterbalanced across cases. Each series was repeated three times. The position of the relevant items were randomly determined in each repetition. The seven GKT items in each series were presented with a 15-20 second inter-stimulus interval between them.

Skin resistance response amplitude (SRR) was used to measure the responses to each item in the GKT. This indice is considered a highly reliable and accurate measure for detecting concealed knowledge in laboratory settings (Balloun and Holmes, 1979; Thackray and Orne, 1968). Cardiovascular and respiration tracings were monitored but not scored.

Acquisition of the SRR responses was carried out by measuring the maximal difference between SRR onset and peak (SRR amplitude) within ten seconds starting immediately after the presentation of the item. The response to the first item in each set of items was excluded from measurement because it served as a buffer to dissipate the examinee's tendency to react strongly to the initial item. In cases where some kind of external disturbance (movements, deep breath, noise, etc.) occurred, the item was excluded from the analysis. The whole set was excluded when the disturbance occurred during presentation of the relevant item.

Excluding the buffer, the SRR amplitudes in each repetition were ranked from 1 (the largest) to 6 (the smallest). The mean ranking across the three repetitions was computed for each alternative item. If the mean rank of the relevant alternative was the smallest, the question was assigned the score of 2. If the mean rank of the relevant alternative was the second smallest, the question was scored 1. For any larger mean rank of the relevant alternative the question was scored 0. The question scores were summed up for each examinee. The following decision rule was employed to classify examinees: the examinee was classified as guilty if $S > Q$, where S stands for the computed sum and Q stands for the number of questions presented to the examinee. Thus, a score of at least 5 is needed to classify an examinee presented with four questions as guilty. An inconclusive decision was reached if S=Q, and an innocent decision was made whenever the score computed for the examinee was less than the number of questions presented.

The correct detection rates computed for guilty and innocent examinees are displayed in Table 10.1. In one case an innocent examinee was examined only with the CQT. Thus, the total number of GKT examinees is 80.

Fingerprint Identification

The fingerprint pattern is unique and individual for a given finger. It is unique because of ridge characteristics such as ridge ending, bifurcation or a dot which are known as "points of identification". Given that the frequency of each type of ridge characteristic in large populations is known, it is possible to compute the probability of obtaining a certain combination of identification points in two fingers. The "12 point" rule has been adopted for identification in many countries because for any combination of 12 points the probability is low enough to confirm identification. However, in reality, circumstances such as time and locality may limit the potential suspects to a small group. Identity can therefore be confirmed with only 8 points. The USA and Canada do not require a minimum number of identification points and leave the decision to the expert but it is rare that identification is made with less than 7 or 8 points (Margot and Lennard, 1994).

Three types of fingerprints may be found: a. Indented fingerprints which are caused by the contact of the finger with a malleable substance which retains a three dimensional image of the print. b. Visible fingerprints which may be found on dust, blood or paint. c. Latent fingerprints which are invisible. To make the fingerprint visible the print must be treated physically (powdering) or chemically (ninhydrin). Such fingerprint development requires detailed knowledge about where the prints have been stored and what are the optimum techniques for development.

In the present study the fingerprints were all latent and were developed from hard surfaces such as the desk surface and the box. For this, black powder, aluminum powder and magnetic flake powder were used. The prints were lifted using lifting tape which was pressed evenly and smoothly over the powdered image and a near perfect powder reproduction of the ridges was obtained. The prints on the receipt were developed using ninhydrin. The lifts were then transferred to the identification experts for identification. In two perpetrated events the experts failed to develop prints. The results of the fingerprint identification are presented in Table 10.1.

Voice Identification

Participants were sent to give voice samples in the Israeli Police Voice Identification Laboratory. The expert who recorded the voices used established procedures that ensured the obtained speech samples were reasonably representative of the perpetrator's voice. She attempted to duplicate the wordings of the original text verbatim and maintain the same physical and acoustic conditions associated with the original recording (e.g., using the telephone, eliminating noises, etc.).

Three experienced voice identification experts compared the voice of the perpetrator ("unknown voice") with the voices of the suspects using auditory recognition and visual spectrographic examination of the data. Features that could be unique, variations within the voice of the same speaker and similarities and differences between the unknown voice and the suspects' voices, were considered when the expert reached a decision. The results appear in Table 10.1.

Handwriting Identification

Participants were also sent to give handwriting specimens in the Israeli Police Document and Handwriting Identification Laboratory. Similar to the voice identification, the handwriting expert attempted to duplicate the wordings of the original text and ensure that the writing specimens were representative of the perpetrator's writing.

Three experienced handwriting identification experts compared the questioned writing on the falsified receipt and the specimens written by the suspects. The similarities between the two samples of writings need not be identical in the sense that the two sets can be matched bit by bit. However, the differences between the disputed writing and the handwriting specimens should not exceed the variations usually found in such writings. Furthermore, individual features should appear in both, to establish a decision that the two sets of writing must have been the work of the same person. Table 10.1 presents the decisions reached by the handwriting experts for guilty and innocent participants.

Eyewitness Identification

Descriptions of a person can be elicited in a number of ways. First, a free description invites the witness to provide a description of the person. Then, the witness is required to respond to a series of specific questions such as, "how old was the person". Finally, the witness is offered a range of alternatives from which he is asked to choose the most appropriate one. This can be done by a police artist or by a composite system. The latter is a kit of facial components such as the American Identikit or the British photo-fit. The witness describes the person he saw and accordingly the appropriate components of the face are selected. The face is shown to the witness for comments and amendments can then be made. The aim is to produce a schematic drawing of the culprit's type. Guilty participants in the present study were observed by either one or two eyewitnesses while they entered the office in which the mock crime took place. Each eyewitness made a composite picture of the person they saw.

After the composite has been compiled, the witness was presented with several lineups of pictures according to the number of suspects in the perpetrated event. Each lineup contained the picture of one suspect (either guilty or innocent) and 7 pictures of other people. The correct identification frequencies of the lineups are displayed in Table 10.1.

In cases where two witnesses watched the culprit, the second witness was asked to search a crime archive of photos. The picture of the culprit and of all innocent suspects of the relevant event were put in that archive. Identification frequencies are presented in Table 10.1.

A legal system that is designed to protect the innocent should base its decisions on methods that are relatively free of false positive errors (e.g., classifying an innocent suspect as guilty). The results point at three methods that comply with this demand, fingerprint identification, the GKT and the identification of natural handwriting. The natural handwriting yielded perfect classification of perpetrators and innocent participants. It seems, however, that this was an easy task. To examine this further, the questioned writing and the specimens written by the suspects were handed to 10 students, without any training in handwriting identification, for identification. The students classified correctly 9 (69%) perpetrators and all innocent participants.

In contrast to the natural handwriting identification, fingerprint identification and the GKT require some expertise. Both employ standard and objective procedures and may not be contaminated by examiner or examinee factors. Furthermore, both enable control over the probability of false positive errors. However, effort invested to minimize false positive errors may elicit an increase of false negative error rate (e.g., a failure to detect guilty suspects). The desired exchange rate between the two types of errors can be determined according to the purpose of the test and the social context.

It should be noted that the two methods differ in the identification of innocent people. Fingerprint identification is not designed to identify innocents and the fact that prints were not detected does not imply that a person is innocent. The GKT detects innocent as well as guilty examinees. This has its advantages but the GKT is also susceptible to errors of classifying a guilty examinee as innocent.

The CQT results showed a considerable false negative error rate (32%), and a much smaller false positive error rate (3.7%). This contradicts claims made by many critics of CQT polygraphy (e.g., Ben-Shakhar, Lieblich and Bar-Hillel, 1982; Lykken, 1974, 1978) according to which the CQT is biased against the innocent, because the obvious differences between the control and the relevant questions should produce a pattern of relatively larger responses to relevant questions in both guilty and innocent examinees.

On the other hand, the participants in the present experiment knew perfectly well that they are participating in an experiment, and that no harm would be inflicted upon them as a consequence of the forensic tests results. Hence, they were not exposed to the real threats confronting suspects undergoing real CQT examinations. This may lead to the neglect of relevant questions which are related to unreal crimes and to increased concern about control questions which deal with real problems of the examinee. However, many other CQT mock-crime studies produced relatively accurate detection rates for both guilty and innocent examinees (e.g. Dawson, 1980; Honts, Raskin and Kircher, 1987; Kircher and Raskin, 1988; Raskin and Hare, 1978).

The explanation lies in the training of the polygraphers. These polygraphers, with psychological background and with knowledge of the bias against the innocent in the CQT, were trained to emphasize the control questions in the pretest interview and in the test itself. In actual CQT examinations this approach seems to be beneficial since it balances the relevant questions that may introduce the biggest threat.

The examiners in this study knew that their ability as professional polygraphers was being tested. Thus, they adopted the approach they usually employ in typical CQT examinations. The combination of enhanced emphasis on control questions and the fact that these questions deal with actual problems of the examinee whereas the relevant questions deal with a mock-crime, paved the way to the high false positive error rate. Hence, the present CQT is not typically analogous to the real-life situation and its results should not be generalized.

The CQT joins the spectrographic voice identification, the handwriting identification and the eyewitness identification in the sense that all these methods were influenced by the expert's or eyewitness' subjective impressions and, excluding the natural handwriting identification, yielded false positive errors. A variety of studies reviewed by Dawes (1979) demonstrated that experts in a field are good at selecting the right predictor variables and at coding them in such a way that they have a monotonic relationship with the criterion, but that these experts fail to integrate information from diverse sources.

Einhorn (1972), for example, asked expert physicians to examine biopsies of patients with Hodgkin's disease and make an overall rating of the severity of the process. The correlations of the experts' rating and actual survival time of the patients were all virtually zero. When the variables on which the physicians based their decisions were used in a multiple regression model, they predicted survival time with relative accuracy. This leads to the conclusion that standard methods should be preferred to methods based on experts' opinion.

The present study intended to provide a look at the efficiency of criminal identification methods operating under conditions that were nearly perfect for identification. Hence, spoken and written sentences were long and detailed. The area where fingerprints may have been stored was restricted and defined. Eyewitnesses were advised beforehand that they will have to identify the person they are going to see. Perpetrators were provided with the four relevant GKT items and the experimenter ensured that they were aware of them. Finally, the experimental setting was designed to resemble actual CQT procedures more than many other laboratory studies. This was expected to increase the concern of perpetrators about the test outcomes which is essential for the application of the CQT.

However, optimal conditions were only partly accomplished. The recordings of the unknown voices were in some cases not as clear as desired. The receipt the perpetrators left behind was sometimes not detailed enough. The removal of fingerprints from the boxes was not as easy as was planned. In some cases the two eyewitnesses talked while waiting for the culprit to appear and missed his arrival. Thus, they saw only the perpetrator's profile. Finally, on the second session five guilty participants forgot one GKT item, each. The affect on the identification rate is not known. However, this limits an effective comparison between the method's theoretical accuracy under optimal conditions.

Beside the recommendation that criminal identification methods should employ standard and objective procedures, no other applied conclusions should be drawn from this study. Future research should examine the actual utility of the various methods instead of their theoretical accuracy. This can be accomplished by using a random sample of criminal files and determine which of the various criminal identification methods could have been applied in each case

References

Backster, C. (1963). Polygraph professionalization through technique standardization. *Law and Order*, 11, 63-64.

Balloun, K.D. and Holmes, D.S. (1979). Effects of repeated examinations on the ability to detect guilt with a polygraphic examination: laboratory experiment with a real crime. *Journal of Applied Psychology*, 64, 316-322.

Ben-Shakhar, G. and Furedy J.J. (1990). *Theories and application in detection of deception.* New York: Springer-Verlag.

Ben-Shakhar, G., Lieblich, I. and Bar-Hillel, M. (1982). An evaluation of polygrapher's judgments: A review from a decision theoretic perspective. *Journal of Applied Psychology*, 67, 701-713.

Davidson, P.O. (1968). Validity of the guilty knowledge technique: The effects of motivation. *Journal of Applied Psychology*, 52, 62,65.

Dawes, R.M. (1979). The robust beauty of improper linear models in decision making. *American Psychologist*, 34, 571, 582.

Dawson, M.E. (1980). Physiological detection of deception: Measurement of responses to questions and answers during countermeasure manoeuvers. *Psychophysiology*,17, 8-17.

Einhorn, H.J. (1972). Expert measurement and mechanical combination. *Organizational Behavior and Human Performance*, 13, 171-192.

Elaad, E. (1990). Detection of guilty knowledge in real-life criminal investigations. *Journal of Applied Psychology*, 75, 521-529.

Elaad, E. (in press). Polygraph examiner awareness of crime-relevant information and the guilty knowledge test. *Law and Human Behavior*.

Elaad, E., Ginton, A. and Jungman, N. (1992). Detection measures in real-life criminal guilty knowledge tests. *Journal of Applied Psychology*, 75, 521-529.

Furedy, J.J. and Heslegrave, R.J. (1991). The forensic use of the polygraph: A psychophysiological analysis of current trends and future prospects. In: J.R. Jennings, P.K. Ackles and M.G.H. Coles (eds.), *Advances in Psychophysiolgy, 4*, Greenwich, CT: JAI Press.

Honts, C.R., Raskin, D.C. and Kircher, J.C. (1987). Effects of physical countermeasures and their electromyographic detection during polygraph tests for deception. *Journal of Psychophysiology*, 1, 241-247.

Honts, C.R., Devitt, M.K., Winbush, M. and Kircher, J.C. (1996). Mental and physical countermeasures reduce the accuracy of the concealed knowledge test. *Psychophysiology*, 33, 84-92

Kircher, J.C. and Raskin, D.C. (1988). Human versus computerized evaluation of polygraph data in laboratory setting. *Journal of Applied Psychology*, 43, 385, 388.

Lykken, D.T. (1959). The GSR in the detection of guilt. *Journal of Applied Psychology*, 43, 385, 388.

Lykken, D.T. (1960). The validity of the guilty knowledge technique: The effects of faking. *Journal of Applied Psychology*, 44, 258-262.

Lykken, D.T. (1974). Psychology and the lie detector industry. *American Psychologist*, 29, 725-739

Lykken, D.T. (1978). Uses and abuses of the polygraph. In: H.L. Pick (ed.) *Psychology: From Research to Practice*. New York: Plenum Press.

Lykken, D.T. (1981). *A tremor in the blood*. New York: McGraw-Hill.

Margot, P. and Lennard, C. (1994). *Fingerprint detection techniques* (Lausanne, 6th ed.).

Podlesny, J.A. and Raskin, D.C. (1977). Physiological measures and the detection of deception. *Psychological Bulletin*, 84, 782-799.

Raskin, D.C. (1982). The Scientific basis of polygraph technique and their uses in the judicial process. In A. Trankell (Ed.), *Reconstructing the Past: The Role of Psychologists in the Criminal Trial*. Stockholm, Sweden: Norsted and Soners.

Raskin, D.C. (1989). Polygraph techniques for the detection of deception. In D.C. Raskin (ed.), *Psychological methods in criminal investigation and evidence* (pp. 247-296). New York: Springer.

Raskin, D.C. and Hare, R. (1978). Psychopathy and detection of deception in a prison population. *Psychophysiology*, 15, 126-136.

Reid, J.E. and Inbau, F.E. (1977). *Truth and deception: The polygraph ("lie detection") technique*. Baltimore: Williams and Wilkins.

Saxe, L., Dougherty, D. and Cross, T.P. (1985). The validity of polygraph testing: Scientific analysis and public controversy. *American Psychologist*, 40, 355-366

Thackray, R.I. and Orne, M.T. (1968). A comparison of physiological indices in detection of deception. *Psychophysiology*, 4, 329-339.

Widacki, J. and Horvarth, F. (1978). An experimental investigation of the relative validity and utility of the polygraph technique and three other common methods of criminal identification. *Journal of Forensic Sciences*, 23(3), 596-601

For Product Safety Concerns and Information please contact our EU representative GPSR@taylorandfrancis.com Taylor & Francis Verlag GmbH, Kaufingerstraße 24, 80331 München, Germany

Batch number: 10725923

Printed by Printforce, the Netherlands